"This book is both stimulatingly provocative and deeply questioning of much of the literature on the bureaucratic phenomenon. Tom Vine advances a Deleuzian perspective on bureaucracy as an 'emergent and immanent force' in late modernism. Repetitive and recurrent 'differences' within and across its operational planes require life-skills in their positive resolution. In presenting his arguments he draws from a wide range of alternative perspectives."

*Ray Loveridge, Professor Emeritus, Aston University, UK; Visiting Professor, University of Suffolk, UK; Visiting Associate, University of Cambridge, UK*

"Tom Vine's erudite and engagingly personal reexamination of bureaucracy offers compelling alternatives to the familiar debate on 'post-bureaucracy' and the pejorative caricatures of bureaucracy in popular management literature. Rather than arguing for or against bureaucracy, Dr Vine's unique approach is to ask how people in organisations experience, navigate and make sense of this phenomenon. He combines autoethnography, literary criticism and expansive scholarship to develop a phenomenology of bureaucracy. Written with refreshing style and a colourful wit, his book offers invaluable insights for the critical study of contemporary organisations."

*Samuel Mansell, Lecturer in Business Ethics, University of St Andrews, UK*

# BUREAUCRACY

Bureaucracy is a curse—it seems we can't live with it, we can't live without it. It is without doubt one of the fundamental ideas which underpin the business world and society at large. In this book, Tom Vine observes, analyses, and critiques the concept, placing it at the heart of our understanding of organization.

The author unveils bureaucracy as an endlessly emergent phenomenon which defies binary debate—in analysing organization, we are all bureaucrats. In building an experiential perspective, the book develops ways to interact with bureaucracy that are more effective in theory and practice. Empirical material takes centre stage, whilst the book employs ethnographic and autoethnographic methods to illuminate the existential function of bureaucracy.

Taking examples from art, history, and culture, this book provides an entertaining alternative academic analysis of bureaucracy as a key idea in business and society which will be essential reading for students and scholars of work and organization.

**Tom Vine** completed his first two degrees at Warwick Business School before moving to Essex Business School for his doctorate. He is currently Associate Professor at Suffolk Business School, where he leads the PhD programme. An ethnographer and organization theorist, Tom's research explores agency, belief, complexity, and paradox. When he's not grappling with Nietzsche, Tom enjoys charity-shop crawls and restoring old boats.

# KEY IDEAS IN BUSINESS AND MANAGEMENT

Edited by Stewart Clegg

Understanding how business affects and is affected by the wider world is a challenge made more difficult by the disaggregation between various disciplines, from operations research to corporate governance. This series features concise books that break out from disciplinary silos to facilitate understanding by analysing key ideas that shape and influence business, organizations and management.

Each book focuses on a key idea, locating it in relation to other fields, facilitating deeper understanding of its applications and meanings, and providing critical discussion of the contribution of relevant authors and thinkers. The books provide students and scholars with thought-provoking insights that aid the study and research of business and management.

Titles in this series include:

**Global Oligopoly**
A Key Idea for Business and Society
*Chris Carr*

**Luck**
A Key Idea for Business and Society
*Chengwei Liu*

**Feminism**
A Key Idea for Business and Society
*Celia V. Harquail*

**Hierarchy**
A Key Idea for Business and Society
*John Child*

**Bureaucracy**
A Key Idea for Business and Society
*Tom Vine*

For more information about this series, please visit: www.routledge.com/Key-Ideas-in-Business-and-Management/book-series/KEYBUS

# BUREAUCRACY

## A Key Idea for Business and Society

*Tom Vine*

LONDON AND NEW YORK

First published 2021
by Routledge
2 Park Square, Milton Park, Abingdon, Oxon OX14 4RN

and by Routledge
52 Vanderbilt Avenue, New York, NY 10017

*Routledge is an imprint of the Taylor & Francis Group, an informa business*

© 2021 Tom Vine

The right of Tom Vine to be identified as author of this work has been asserted by him in accordance with sections 77 and 78 of the Copyright, Designs and Patents Act 1988.

All rights reserved. No part of this book may be reprinted or reproduced or utilised in any form or by any electronic, mechanical, or other means, now known or hereafter invented, including photocopying and recording, or in any information storage or retrieval system, without permission in writing from the publishers.

Trademark notice: Product or corporate names may be trademarks or registered trademarks, and are used only for identification and explanation without intent to infringe.

*British Library Cataloguing in Publication Data*
A catalogue record for this book is available from the British Library

*Library of Congress Cataloging-in-Publication Data*
A catalog record has been requested for this book

ISBN: 978-1-138-48330-9 (hbk)
ISBN: 978-1-138-48331-6 (pbk)
ISBN: 978-1-351-05526-0 (ebk)

Typeset in Bembo
by Taylor & Francis Books

# CONTENTS

*List of figures* ix

1  (Re-)introducing bureaucracy  1

**PART I**
**Bureaucracy: Rave, Rant, Repeat**  23

2  Bureaucracy, post-bureaucracy and identity crisis  25

3  Beyond post-bureaucracy: A brave new organizational geography?  41

**PART II**
**Understanding Bureau-phobia**  65

4  Understanding Bureau-phobia part I: Pathological bureaucracy  67

5  Understanding Bureau-phobia part II: Dystopian bureaucracy  83

**PART III**
**Towards a New Education in Bureaucracy**  97

6  A bureaucratic biography  99

| 7 | Working *with* bureaucracy | 116 |
| 8 | Concluding thoughts | 133 |

*References* 159
*Index* 167

# FIGURES

2.1 Attitudes towards bureaucracy: a cyclical pattern     26
2.2 Bureaucracy: you're damned if you do and damned if you don't     29
3.1 Pan-organizational association     60
4.1 The neutralisation of moral responsibility towards Jews in Nazi Germany     77
5.1 The representation of bureaucracy in academic literature and fiction     92
8.1 The paradox of bureaucracy     144

# 1

# (RE-)INTRODUCING BUREAUCRACY

Bureaucracy is generally considered undesirable. This view pervades party politics, civic governance, commercial organization, and—more generally—the public psyche. This book represents an attempt not so much to defend bureaucracy but to facilitate an understanding of the concept through fresh eyes. Despite reams of scholarly coverage, there remain important under-addressed questions: Does it make any sense to speak of organization *without* bureaucracy? To what degree is bureaucracy—like organization more generally—an emergent logic that 'patterns' our institutional existence irrespective of whether or not it is willed? Is bureaucracy self-replicating? Is bureaucracy self-sustaining? What exactly constructs our fear of bureaucracy and to what extent is it warranted? Is bureaucracy a *proto* management methodology and, if so, what marks it out as distinct from the plethora of commercially-available methodologies that are deployed—at great effort and expense—throughout organizations today? And what can be said of the relationship between bureaucracy and institutionalisation? Is institutionalisation necessarily undesirable? To what extent is the proverbial 'jobsworth' a ramification of bureaucracy and why has the jobsworth been all but ignored by the academy? There are broader macrosociological questions too: Has the rhetoric of post-bureaucracy (I'm thinking here of concepts such as 'adhocracy' and 'projectification') had its time? Will bureaucracy now experience a resurgence in reputation? Is there any sense in distinguishing 'good' bureaucracy from 'bad,' or should we seek out completely new ways to engage with the concept?

## Who is this book aimed at?

Historically, commentary on bureaucracy has either been directed at practitioners (and tends to be damning in its assessment of the topic), or at scholars (where its assessment is more variable). While the materials trained at practitioners typically fails to acknowledge the nuance and social context of the concept, those trained at scholars have lacked traction. This book therefore deliberately sets in its sights a broad church: it has practitioners, scholars, and students in mind. But this represents a formidable challenge: the argumentation presented must reflect the complexity of the topic, while at the same time remain accessible and (relatively!) free of jargon. I am an organization theorist and so inevitably my approach to bureaucracy prioritises its manifestation in respect of work, organization, business and management. But this should not deter scholars, students, and practitioners of other disciplines from reading it. Indeed, my analysis of bureaucracy is considerably wider in scope than my native disciplinary credentials should suggest. To this end, I very much hope that the book will also appeal to those from cultural anthropology, economics, government studies, philosophy, political sciences, social psychology, and sociology.

## What's the problem?

Most people berate bureaucracy. I believe they are misguided. Indeed, the empirics suggest that efforts to ameliorate bureaucracy have failed to improve organizational life or performance; on the contrary, it seems that the only empirically-validated outcome of these efforts is greater job insecurity (as chapters 2 and 3 go on to explore). Furthermore, these efforts have rarely—if at all—displaced bureaucratic measures, but rather created new forms of the same. There is, however, a small cohort of researchers determined to defend bureaucracy. Regrettably, though typically erudite, their work has failed to make waves beyond the proverbial hallowed halls of academia. Moreover, these scholars often overlook the fact that there is only so much to be gained from distinguishing rhetoric (the 'bullshit') from the empirical (the 'reality'). The point here is that it is often the bullshit that matters most. We'll come back to this.

On to Wagner. Who? The composer. For Wagner, as Magee (2000: 181) notes, 'words fail.' Contrary to what you might imagine, words rarely do a good job of conveying complex ideas. Where for Wagner music—specifically opera – did the talking, in this book ethnography, autoethnography, and storytelling takes on this mantle. Of course, all three methods involve words but as I go on to demonstrate there is much more to these methods than the more conventional—and abstract—argumentation scholars are noted for. Perceptions, as I have argued elsewhere (see Vine, 2020a: 480) are paradoxically more important than reality. (I told you we'd come back to it.) Conscious of this, I urge the curious reader to endeavour to understand why *perceptions* of bureaucracy remain so negative; and to determine to what degree and how exactly these negative perceptions can be addressed.

## Bureaucracy: a working definition

In some respects there is limited value to defining bureaucracy. Every word uttered—scholarly or otherwise—'both enhances our understanding of a phenomenon *and* creates further bias.' (Vine, 2018b: 289; original emphasis). Nonetheless, definitions are customary and help marshal the reader. The *Oxford English Dictionary* (*OED*) imparts two brief definitions of bureaucracy: (a) 'government by bureaux; usually officialism'; and (b) 'government officials collectively.' Regrettably, neither provides much assistance in pursuit of the more nuanced approach to the concept for which I am championing in this book. Etymologically, it is generally accepted that the word originated in the French language combining the French word *bureau*—desk or office—with the Greek word κράτος (*kratos*)— rule or political power. The economist Jacques Claude Marie Vincent de Gournay is normally credited with coining the term in the mid-18th century (Riggs, 1979), but clearly bureaucracy long predated the word's creation and formal adoption into the linguistic canon.

Now, while I have no desire to instil a rigid definition of bureaucracy in my readership, I do wish to promote a more sophisticated understanding of the concept. To this end, an interpretive epistemology is invoked; one which regards the world as co-constructed through social interaction, rather than existing 'out there.' This approach reveals interesting tensions. So, for example, while Deutscher (1969: 12) suggests that 'the roots of bureaucracy are indeed as old as our civilization,' for Kallinikos (2006: 612) 'there have never been Chinese or Egyptian bureaucracies as is sometimes claimed.' Neither position is correct. Neither is incorrect. What *is* clear, and as Willmott (2011: 257) has noted: 'there is uncertainty and disagreement about what "bureaucracy" is, and what it is becoming.' Ultimately, as with so many complex concepts, answers to questions such as these are contingent on our specific designation of bureaucracy. I thus develop a working definition of bureaucracy here not to impose a sense of order to the field (social concepts should, I my mind, remain contested), but to provide readers with a frame of reference.

How might we go about developing such a definition? I deliberately avoid overly exclusive or restrictive designations. Of these, there are many. Garston (1993b: 5), for example, suggests that '[a] bureaucracy is a particular form of organization comprised of bureaus or agencies, such that the overall bureaucracy is a system of consciously coordinated activities which has been explicitly created to achieve specific ends.'

I take issue with this definition for several reasons: First, *all* organizations are bureaucracies, as I go on to argue in this book; second, I do not share the ontological conviction that bureaucracies are 'consciously coordinated'; and finally, contrary to received wisdom, I'm not convinced that all bureaucracies are geared towards specific ends. So where do we go from here? I present an expansive definition of bureaucracy in its place, one that is sensitive to its historical precedent, mindful of its institutional logic and appreciative of the fact that it 'patterns' (as a verb) social and organizational configuration. To this end, bureaucracy is here presented as *immanent* and *emergent*.

I also stress at this early stage that this book focuses less on bureaucracy as a legal-administrative concern and more on the concept as *existential* and *anthropological*.

Bureaucracy is thus regarded as acutely relevant in respect of organizational participation and realising a sense of organizational belonging. We coalesce around organizational units. Moreover, bureaucracy facilitates what has become known as 'reflexive practice,' something I go on to explore in respect of pro formas and paperwork more generally later in the book. As such, I understand bureaucracy as *socially-embedded*. Following Casey (2004: 59), I wish to prioritise an 'analytic, interpretive exploration [which] draws bureaucratic organization back into society and social analysis.' I am also conscious of the fact that bureaucracy has long been considered a *Schimpfort* (term of abuse). Merton observed this as long as 1940, and it is implicit in political science dating back to at least to future US President Woodrow Wilson's academic work in the late 1800s (Merton, 1940). Since this time the evolving semantics associated with bureaucracy, at least in the English language, have perpetually reinforced this negative appraisal: red tape, sterility, inflexibility, and so on. It will henceforth take a Herculean effort to address this, including as I later argue, measures to counteract the predominant 'bureaucracy-as-dystopia' attitude found in both literature and cinema.

Beyond this, and echoing what noted scholar of bureaucracy Paul du Gay (2004: 37) has already stressed, bureaucracy is *used imprecisely*. It is. No question. It has become the whipping boy for most—perhaps all—things undesirable in organizations. You can pretty much justify any criticism of anything in the world of work, provided it evokes the damning of bureaucracy. But really what we're doing when we damn bureaucracy is identifying areas of the organization or its processes or its people that we dislike.

I also wish to stress bureaucracy's mystifying *complexity*. For Wilson (2000: 10), bureaucracy is both varied and complex; it is much more than a simple social category or political epithet. Of this complexity, Styhre (2007: ix) has argued, that it is bureaucracy's content rather than its form that determines its outcome and effects. The question is: when we criticise bureaucracy, are we criticising its form or its particular content? My suspicion is that we are almost always doing the latter. Bureaucracy's inherent complexity is noted by others, too. For Albrow (1970: 14, cited in Styhre, 2007: 11–12), for example:

> The student coming to the field can be excused bewilderment. Sometimes bureaucracy seems to mean administrative efficiency, at other times the opposite. It may appear as simply as a synonym for civil service, or it may be as complex as an idea summing up the specific features of modern organizational structure. It may refer to a body of officials, or to the routines of office administration.

Finally—and invariably—definitions are as much about what they are not. To this end, recent decades have seen a veritable explosion of scholarly coverage in respect of bureaucracy vis-à-vis post-bureaucracy. And this deserves serious comment. Clegg (2011: 223), for example, notes that '[b]ureaucracy is both being superseded by post-bureaucracy and not being superseded by post-bureaucracy.' Willmott

(2011: 257) makes a similar observation. By this, of course, it is meant that bureaucracy is protean. I'll resist invoking Heraclitus; suffice it to say, change is an existential inevitability. The point is, I think, that bureaucracy is characterised—defined even—by an extraordinary *resilience to change*. This is what makes it so remarkable.

In sum, bureaucracy is here defined as *immanent, emergent, existential, anthropological*, and *socially-embedded*. We also have noted that it is *used imprecisely* and frequently as *term of abuse*. Finally we have acknowledged that it is characterised by a bewildering *complexity* and *resilience to change*.

Having presented this multifaceted definition of bureaucracy, we could do likewise in respect of bureaucrats. However, I remain to be convinced that there is much to be gained from such an endeavour. Perhaps even more so than bureaucracy the word bureaucrat is loaded with negative connotations. Once again, Gartson (1993b: 18–19) presents a restrictive definition:

> [A] bureaucrat [is] identified as someone who refers any decision either to an interpretation of a rule (policy determination) or a precedent—a past decision/interpretation accepted by policymakers and, therefore, carrying their authority. This aspect is one of the things which helps distinguish between a bureaucrat and one who may function within an organization, but who should not be classified in that fashion.

This sort of definition is overly functionalist. It ignores the cultural essence of bureaucracy. More pertinently, it is problematic to distinguish 'bureaucrat' from 'non bureaucrat' in industrial society. Whether we are prepared to admit it or not, this is because we *all* 'do bureaucracy.' We all invoke bureaucratic rules when they suit us, and discredit them when they do not. Earlier in his book Garston (ibid. 3) poses the following: If you ask the public what their opinion of bureaucracy is, they are likely to put it high on the list of what is wrong with the world, so much is the fault of the 'damn bureaucrats.' Most academic studies of bureaucracy endeavour to 'rise above' the populist damnation of bureaucracy. But does this miss a trick? Are we perhaps better off asking what is it that the public dislikes about bureaucracy and why it is that this dislike is so pervasive? Is there something more fundamental going on here—a sort of masochistic self-hatred? After all, and as this book goes on to demonstrate, the vast majority of us seek out existential refuge in bureaucracies of one type or another. *We are all bureaucrats.*

## Why have I written a book on bureaucracy?

As should be clear by now, I am intrigued by the inordinate amount of time we collectively spend berating bureaucracy. We are haters. In fact, we seem to garner a perverse pleasure from hating. Bureaucracy is somehow representative of an institutional *Other*. Bureaucracy-bashing represents easy points in both political and organizational arenas. Consider current affairs. As we inch forward into a world of uncertainty plagued by the Covid-19 pandemic, anti-bureaucratic sentiment is churned out on a daily basis by journalists charged with evaluating official responses: 'Britain's coronavirus testing is bogged down by bureaucracy' declares *The Spectator*'s Matt Ridley (2020), while *City Journal*'s John Tierney (2020) voices comparable frustrations in respect of the United States: 'Absurd bureaucratic strictures are hindering efforts to fight Covid-19'. And things were no different in the pre-pandemic world. Take the UK's referendum in 2016 on European Union membership. A key aspect of the controversial Leave Campaign was focussed on absolving the nation of *Brussel's Bureaucrats*, a convenient alliterative device deployed by the British conservative media for years. Trump, too. As part of his campaign for the presidential election that would take place the following year, in 2015 he tweeted that 'Bureaucratic red tape and overregulation are discouraging the American dream. It's time for a bold new direction!'

A comparable sense of bureaucracy-bashing is routinely touted in the world of business and management. In December 2018, *Harvard Business Review* led with the following cover story: 'The End of Bureaucracy: How to Free Your Company to Innovate.' This, I think, illustrates more so than anything else why it is that I wrote this book. Despite reams of coverage over the past century or so, we are still churning out the same sort of sensationalised garbage. The message lacks nuance. It lacks sophistication. The narrative the authors present in the *Harvard Business Review* article is an all-too-familiar one (although presented as if it were groundbreaking): 'from monolithic businesses to microenterprises' (p53); 'from incremental goals to leading targets' (ibid.); 'from internal monopolies to internal contracting' (p54); 'from top-down coordination to voluntary collaboration' (p55); 'from rigid boundaries to open innovation' (p56); 'from innovation phobia to entrepreneurship at scale' (p57)... You get the idea.

As an undergraduate management student, we were cautioned about populist coverage of management, such as that presented in *Harvard Business Review*. One of my professors described it as 'Heathrow Airport Management Theory'; the sort of crap you'd find for sale in an airport bookstore. The point he was making was that if it sounds sensationalist it is most probably codswallop. What astounds me most about this—and, frankly, much of the research published in *Harvard Business Review*—is that it blissfully ignores a generation of research to the contrary.

At this point, I should stress that I am not writing this book to defend bureaucracy *per se*, as some other scholars have done. Candidly, I regard both the critique and defence of bureaucracy as fruitless enterprises. As I will argue in this book, bureaucracy *just is*. Instead, we need to develop an understanding of how and why bureaucracy has developed such a negative press, and then figure out how best to work *with* bureaucracy.

Bureaucracy is a peculiar beast. And this is another reason I wanted to write a book about it. I have a long held a scholarly interest in contradiction and paradox and, to some degree, bureaucracy embodies both. Everyone loves to hate bureaucracy and yet—concurrently—bureaucracy *contains us*, psychologically and existentially. Moreover, bureaucracy appears to transcend Left and Right political ideologies (historically, it is the Left that has been criticised for bureaucratic expansion; and yet at the same time bureaucracy is, by definition, a fiercely conservative phenomenon).

Finally, I saw this book as an opportunity to share and reflect on my own experiences of bureaucracy, and encourage others to do likewise. Each of us has our own experiences of how bureaucracy is susceptible to being run over by ideological traffic travelling in both directions. This is of course part of the reason that bureaucracy-bashing remains a perennially popular soundbite; its appeal is transcendent. For me—I have early memories of my mum reading *The Daily Mail* (a right-wing British tabloid newspaper) and echoing the sentiment contained therein; 'Bloody bureaucrats!,' she'd roar, in reference to north London's Haringey Council who she felt (or at least *The Daily Mail* felt) were a bunch of feather-bedders. Dad, too. A lifelong entrepreneur (and in his prime in the 1980s; Car-phone, check; Filofax, check; dodgy oversized suit, check...), he moved to Belgium in the late 1990s to bring up his second family. 'You wouldn't believe the amount of red tape in Belgium; it's no wonder nobody wants to start a business—they throw every possible obstacle in your path.' These were my early recollections of adults talking about bureaucracy; I don't suppose they are much different to anybody else growing up in post-industrial society. And even today, I periodically find myself counselling my wife (a Left-winger) as she weathers the various bureaucratic challenges her employer, the National Health Service, present. She's a clinical psychologist. 'I've had enough,' she said recently, 'nothing *ever* changes; nothing *will* ever change. Our clients are in desperate need of help and the ways things are set up prevent us from providing that help. It's soul-destroying.' The Trust for which she works been in special measures for several years. Is inadequate administrative conduct at least partially to blame? And even me, an organization theorist who (perhaps) ought to know better, find myself day-dreaming about evermore elaborate tortuous ends to some of the University's administrators. 'How on earth do they add value?,' I think to myself. 'All they seem to do is get in the way. On the one hand we want the University to grow and be financially successful; on the other, each time we think of a new and exciting initiative, we are met with a barrage of paperwork and demands for information which somebody, somewhere will feed into a spreadsheet of no consequence. What the fuck?'

## Re-introducing bureaucracy

What makes this book different? To mobilise a fresh approach to the study and interpretation of bureaucracy, I pose several guiding principles, each of which is outlined below. These principles build upon the definition of bureaucracy developed earlier in this chapter.

  **I argue that bureaucracy is an emergent logic:** Others have noted that bureaucracy is *resilient*. du Gay (2005: 1), for example, begins his influential text by noting the following:

The demise of bureaucracy has been anticipated, and demanded, many times throughout the history of management thought, as well as in modern social and political theory. However, despite the scorn regularly heaped upon it, bureaucracy both as an organizational ideal and as a diversely formatted organizational device, have proven remarkably resilient. Reports of its death have turned out to be somewhat premature.

Kallinikos (2004: 13), too, has highlighted the 'historically unique adaptive capacity of bureaucracy.' However—and what strikes me as surprising is that these same scholars have felt compelled to *defend* bureaucracy. So, for example, and in a later publication, Kallinikos (2006: 623) says: 'the defining characteristic of non-inclusive human involvement in organizations is currently endangered by developments that take place beyond the state organization.' Similarly, Willmott (2011: 264) asks: 'What, then, is it about modern bureaucratic organization that merits preservation?'

In my mind, such questions miss the point. Bureaucracy doesn't need preserving; *it preserves itself.* Any attempt to eliminate it paradoxically results in more of the same, just in a different guise. Its resilience aside, I also argue that bureaucracy is both immanent and emergent. This is a position that has yet to be systematically explored and it is something this book is dedicated to. In some respects this oversight in the literature is strange since none less than Weber noted that 'rationally regulated association within a structure of domination finds its typical expression in bureaucracy' (Weber, 1978: 954, as cited in Willmott, 2011: 262). Furthermore: 'The bureaucratic structure is everywhere a late product of historical development. The further back we trace our steps, the more typical the absence of bureaucracy and of officialdom in general' (Weber, 1968: 1002). Weber was, I believe, presenting bureaucracy as a logic or inevitability. More recently, Kohli (2007: 254) notes that our behaviour and the behaviour of organizations more generally presupposes 'an institutional pattern that shapes lives both in terms of movement through positions and of biographical perspectives and plans,' but does not explore the analytical potential of pattern, or indeed the argument that to some degree we can effectively conflate organization and bureaucracy. This is another oversight this book seeks to address. Anxieties in respect of preservation aside, Kallinikos reminds us of the intimate relationship between bureaucracy and the division of labour:

> The emergence of the bureaucratic form of organization was predicated on a major anthropological innovation (that is, a new way of conceiving humanity and institutionally embedding it) that we have tended to take for granted these days, namely, the clear and instrumentally supported separation of work from the rest of people's lives. The conception of work as a distinct sphere of social life, sufficiently demarcated vis-à-vis other social spheres, has had a decisive significance for constitution of the modern workplace.
>
> *(Kallinikos 2003: 216)*

For Kallinikos, the modern workplace owes its very existence to the division of labour. Regrettably, and to the best of my knowledge, this idea has yet to be explored further, and certainly not methodically. To do such analysis justice would, I suspect, require collaborative research efforts involving not just organization theorists, but historians and anthropologists, too. I am inevitably limited in terms of scope, but present several arguments later in this book which help redress this omission. The most accessible of these argument relates to putative cultural universals such as technology, consideration of which enables us to present a convincing argument that bureaucracy is an organizational universal. By way of simplified summary, and notwithstanding Braverman's (1974: 11) 'societas ex machina' musings, consider the following rationale: *Technology is a cultural universal. The nature of technology is such that it necessarily implies a desire to advance that technology (with certain exceptions; for example,* The Amish, *who lay claim to a specific identity premised on the rejection of technological advance beyond a sanctioned level). To advance technology we will—eventually—necessitate organization involving a division of labour or area of expertise. The division of labour manifests itself through bureaucracy. Bureaucracy thus becomes an organizational universal.*

**I argue that bureaucracy *is* organization:** Some theorists have casually conflated organization and bureaucracy. For example, DeGregori and Thompson (1993: 86) note that 'complex organizations or bureaucracies have played a key role throughout history in this technological process.' However, this conflation is left unpacked and, notably, conflicts with sentiment presented earlier in the book in which their chapter appeared, where the editor—Garston—was clear to stress that bureaucracy is a *particular* form of organization. Contrariwise, a clear rationale is presented in this book that although we can hypothesise organization without bureaucracy, its empirical existence is highly improbable. Weber (1947 [1915]: 339) puts it best: '[In the field of administration] the choice is only between bureaucracy and dilettantism.' To demonstrate any semblance of organization is to bureaucratise. Or put yet another way, if we are to take organization and administration seriously—and hence seek to move beyond the realm of the amateur—we are, by implication, bureaucrats.

**I move away from binary debates about bureaucracy:** There are countless critics of bureaucracy and, in recent years, increasing numbers of scholars determined to defend the concept too (du Gay, 2000, 2005; Goodsell, 2004; and Kallinikos, 2004, 2006, for example). My own research reveals a slightly different picture. I note that attitudes to bureaucracy—like so much else—appear to be cyclical. However, since current coverage inevitably focuses on the recent shift from pro-bureaucratic to anti-bureaucratic attitudes, the cyclical nature of the broader macrosociological attitudes is obscured. I hope to make things clearer. More pertinently my thesis rejects binary debates regarding bureaucracy and post-bureaucracy. Instead I argue that bureaucracy and its counterpoint represent parameters *between which organizational life unfolds.* Too great an emphasis on bureaucracy renders life dysfunctional; too great an emphasis on adhocracy does likewise. To this end, this book is not intended to damn bureaucracy or to lend support to post-bureaucratic alternatives (of which there are many, dating back at least to the work of Warren Bennis in the early 1970s). Nor is it intended to defend bureaucracy. Instead, I explore bureaucracy from an experiential perspective. In so doing, I hope to develop more effective ways to *interact with* bureaucracy.

To some degree at least, this approach echoes claims made by Styhre (2007: 5):

> Rather than subscribing to the binary machine of bureaucracy/post-bureaucracy, the dichotomous thinking assuming a series of dualities in opposition to one another, [I] explore how bureaucracy can operate efficiently in an age favouring fluidity and change rather than past virtues and predictability.

However, while I certainly agree with Styhre that the binary machine of bureaucracy/post-bureaucracy must be rejected, my analytical approach is different. I am interested less in how 'bureaucracy can operate efficiently,' not least because I accept bureaucracy as an immanent aspect of organizational life. Furthermore, my ontological position is such that I must reject the conceptualisation of bureaucracy being 'operated.' I am also apprehensive about the use of the term efficiency. Efficient in what sense and from whose perspective? No—my analytical approach is experiential; I am interested in how each of us—as employee, consumer, civic creature, and/or institutional subject—engages with bureaucracy.

Finally, it is worth noting that extant discussions of bureaucracy vis-à-vis post bureaucracy are characterised by confusion. There are at least two disagreements: one is *descriptive* i.e. whether or not our society is bureaucratic or post-bureaucratic. Another is *normative*, i.e. empirics aside, is bureaucracy desirable? Frankly, neither question gets us very far. In my mind, the first is largely about how we choose to define bureaucracy. For those who choose to define it narrowly, there is credence to the argument that we can distinguish between bureaucracy and post-bureaucracy. For those who authorise a broader definition (Casey, 2004, or Rhodes and Price, 2011, for example), the evidence for the shift is less compelling. It comes down to semantics. And, philosophical musing aside, the second question is redundant. This is because bureaucracy is emergent; it is an existential inevitability.

**I explore the manner in which bureaucracy is represented in the arts:** One of this book's objectives is to develop a more comprehensive understanding of why it is that bureaucracy has become so maligned in the public consciousness. Bureaucracy has inspired (consciously or otherwise) legions of novelists and filmmakers, especially those interested in existential and dystopian themes. There is of course something discernibly labyrinthine and Kafkaesque about bureaucracy; a peculiar sense of the hermetic and impenetrable. I explore the manner in which bureaucracy is represented in the arts not just by way of indulgent curios; in ascribing significant cultural agency to the arts, the negative portrayals of bureaucracy in fiction and films in effect moulds our real world attitudes. Notably, however, it is clear the casting of bureaucracy in the arts has rarely—if ever—ventured beyond cliché. In effect, this hackneyed representation has both constructed and continually reinforces its negative reputation.

**I prioritise analysis of our lived experiences of bureaucracy:** Rather than add to the already substantial abstract literature on bureaucracy, I instead focus on our lived experience of bureaucracy. On the one hand, this enables me to explore the minutiae of bureaucracy. Others, including Kallinikos (2004), have argued that a fixation on the more prosaic aspects of bureaucracy such as routine has both contributed to its bad press and propagated a misunderstanding of the concept. These are compelling arguments. However, I'm not convinced that these aspects of bureaucracy are without value. On the contrary, I confess to feeling rather fond of menial tasks when tired. Filing and record-keeping, for example, hold a peculiar sense of satisfaction. When tired but with time on my hands, with a relatively little effort a sense of accomplishment can be achieved by engaging in the practice of filing. Here I am inspired, in part, by du Gay (2000). His book 'aims to recover a certain ethical dignity for the mundane routines of bureaucratic administration in the face of these persistent populist, philosophical, and entrepreneurial critiques' (du Gay, 2000: 9) There is indeed something to be said for repetitive tasks. It is, perhaps, part of the reason I also enjoy splitting logs for firewood in the autumn. I rather like the mechanomorphic implications; of being 'machine-like'.

Furthermore, and in reflecting intellectually on our experiences of bureaucracy—particularly, but by no means exclusively, in respect of public governance—I argue that *bureaucracy is knowledge*. Initially, this may appear to be a rather peculiar ontological position on which to rest my broader thesis. However, through its mediating influence bureaucracy is presented as the epistemological apparatus which brings 'legitimate' knowledge into being; it constructs, officiates, and validates the status quo. To this end, bureaucracy is a leveller. And this appears to hold both at the level of the organization and at the mesolevel of the bodypolitik.

Finally, we bring into relief the distinction between theory and art by recourse to an explication of experience, in this case contrasting Weber to Kafka: 'While Weber wrote about the impersonality of bureaucracy, Kafka vividly evoked the lived experience of its supplicants being constantly confounded by its imaginations' (Clegg et al., 2016: 157, 158). The issue, as I see it, is that while Weber was an *intentional* scholar of bureaucracy, Kafka was *unintentional*. His meandering thoughts represent an extremely evocative account of bureaucracy but it was, ultimately, a medium for entertainment. This is not to devalue it (on the contrary, and as I point out in chapter 5, fiction constructs our attitudes towards bureaucracy). However, my broader point is we are poorly resourced in respect of scholarly first-hand experiential accounts of bureaucratic life.

**I place the empirical materials centre-stage:** In an epistemological tradition that dates back at least to Erving Goffman, I prioritise *working through the empirical materials* rather than relying on abstracted analytic models. Indeed, many of the most notable scholars, irrespective of field, do precisely this; they focus on the data—which is frequently generated through first-hand experience, rather than existing frameworks. Had Michel Foucault, for example, obsessed over existing analytic models he may have spent his entire career regurgitating Marxist theory. Thankfully, he didn't. And the same, I hope, is true for me in respect of Weber. I have written this book in Mill's (1959) spirit of sociological imagination, and as such it is sensitive to the importance of recognising how each of our biographies unfolds within a particular historical—and historiographic—context. I thus mobilise the methods of ethnography and autoethnography (see below) to help leverage the underreported but strange compulsions many of us feel. As Graeber (2016: 149, emphasis added) notes: 'the *experience* of operating within a system of formalised rules and regulations, under hierarchies of impersonal officials, actually does hold—for many of us much of the time, for all of us at least some of the time—a kind of covert appeal.'

**I use ethnographic methods:** This book engages with less conventional approaches to scholarship in a bid to improve our understanding of bureaucracy. These include those gleaned through literary analysis (as previously noted), ethnography, and autoethnography. Some readers may be wary of techniques repurposed from the humanities or anthropology; however, it is hoped that their inclusion not only contributes to an engaging narrative throughout, but enhances the scholarship on which the broader thesis rests as well as adding to the ethnographic record.

In a line of reasoning that extends from Schwartzmann (1993) who describes ethnography as a method 'for exploring culture from the inside-out,' to Bryman and Bell (2007: 441) who argue that ethnography is the 'obvious method for understanding work organizations as cultural entities,' the ethnographic approach is teeming with potential in our broader field. Furthermore, if we accept the proposition that bureaucracy *is* organization, and reflect on Thompson's (1993: 191), observation that 'bureaucracy is undoubtedly affected by culture and cannot be understood without placing it in its broad cultural context,' then ethnography represents an unparalleled methodological point of departure for studying bureaucracy in particular.

I am also compelled to invoke the epistemological wisdom of Louis Wirth. Wirth translated and supplied the superb preface to the 1955 edition of Mannheim's *Ideology and Utopia: An Introduction to the Sociology of Knowledge*. He makes the following observation:

> [A] dispute ... has raged for many years between the behaviourists ... who would have dealt with social life as exclusively as the natural scientist deals with the physical world, and those who took the position of sympathetic introspectionism and understanding along the lines indicated by such a writer as Max Weber.
>
> *(Wirth, 1955: xxi)*

It seems Weber himself was disposed to ethnographic methods, but—perhaps constrained by the epistemological conventions of his day—did not venture into the introspective depths I present in this book.

Finally, this book is also an opportunity to add to the ethnographic record and hence enable scholars of the future to get a feel for what bureaucracy was like in the early 21st century. With the notable exception of Gouldner's 1954 case study of bureaucracy within a gypsum plant, it is one of my frustrations that despite the reams of historical coverage in respect of bureaucracy, at no point do we get a flavour of what bureaucracy was *actually like* for these writers and their subjects. Ultimately, I feel confident that the ethnographic flavours presented in this book yield some pertinent developments in our understanding of bureaucracy; advances that would not have been possible had a more conventional approach been embraced.

**I use autoethnographic methods:** I make no claims to be the first to pair autoethnography with bureaucracy. Graeber (2015), for example, punctuates his prose with autoethnographic vignettes. However, I do believe this book is the first to do so systematically and, notably, to reflect on the pertinence and underuse of the method in the field. I have provided rigorous defences of both ethnographic and autoethnographic methods elsewhere (see, for example, Vine, 2018a) and do not plan to rehearse these here. However, it is hoped that these three words—self-as-datum—will help those suspicious of autoethnography recognise its potential; it is about reflecting on—and making scholarly sense of—our own experiences, typically presented as reportage, story or narrative. Now, as Law (1994: 9) cautions, 'to tell a story about anything is already to simplify it.' However, and as he goes on to stress, storytellers 'are less prone to heroic reductionisms than some, for they assume, that [their stories] are incomplete' (ibid.). I take heed of this advice when I tell my autoethnographic stories. I recognise that they are incomplete and can never lay claim to being representative of comparable encounters, but this does not invalidate them as important pedagogical devices. It is here that I invoke Nietzsche: 'What men [sic] have found it so difficult to understand from the most ancient times down to the present day is their ignorance in regard to themselves' (Nietzsche, 2007 [1881]: 120).

**I argue that bureaucracy has an important and oft-overlooked existential function:** Both in respect of its social function and architectonic ramifications, bureaucracy influences us in ways we are rarely conscious of. Are bureaucracies existentially desirable? To a large extent they are. Think about hospital emergency rooms. Some time ago, healthcare administrators realised that people begin to relax once they are triaged at hospitals. This means that the experience becomes more agreeable with a triage system in place, even if ultimately the period lapsed between arrival at hospital and treatment is no different. There is clearly something reassuring about being admitted to the machinations of the hospital; the clinical attention is only part of the equation (and, arguably, in some cases perhaps not even the most important; see, for example, Vine, forthcoming). While du Gay (2000, 2005) has noted the significance of bureaucracy in terms of both efficiency and representation; I stress its significance from an existential perspective. Bureaucracy is the outcome when we inject science and order into the collective. Looked at slightly differently, perhaps bureaucracy is a substitute for religion. As part of a recent documentary for BBC4 ("Indian Hill Railways"), Himalaya Railway ticket inspect, Neema, makes a revealing observation: public service is the greatest religion' (BBC FOUR, 2019), So *does* bureaucracy represent a sort of organizational spirit? Questions such as this have the potential to take me well beyond the remit of this book. Nonetheless, I am committed to exploring the existential characteristics of bureaucracy. On a more prosaic level, bureaucracy enables organizations to outlive human beings. As Weigert and Hastings (1977: 1175–6) have noted, '[B]ureaucracies perdure beyond the time measured by a member's biography …. [B]usiness corporations, sports teams, symphony orchestras, armies, even entire societies survive members' biographies and remain somehow the same.' This helps explain why retiring entrepreneurs struggle to relinquish their businesses; without a nuanced understanding of bureaucracy, they are unable to envisage their creation surviving without them. Bureaucracy, I go on to argue, is the fabric that helps meld our disparate *umwelts* together in the form of shared institutional experience.

**I explore the pervasiveness of bureaucracy as life pattern:** Willmott (2011: 262), has noted there is pervasiveness to the principle of modern bureaucracy. For him, this comes in the form of the separation of the tasks comprising office or work role from the personal allegiances and moral enthusiasms of the office-holder. In my mind, however, there is more to this pervasiveness than task separation. Our world propagates bureaucracies and it does so without much in the way of engineered direction. This appears to be immanent: bureaucracy is *patterned* into the very fabric of our emergent civilisations. Another—perhaps more accessible—way to think about 'bureaucracy as pattern' is the extent to which bureaucracy transcends disparate organizational forms. The British National Health Service (NHS); yes, of course. But what about the Mafia? For Graeber (2016: 216), the mafia *is* a bureaucracy: '[A]ny criminal organization does, inevitably, begin developing its own—often quite elaborate—set of internal rules and regulations. They have to, as a way of controlling what would otherwise be completely random violence.' And beyond the rather peculiar pairing of the NHS and the mafia, bureaucracy is found in even more bizarre circumstances. In the 2000s and 2010s, I was an independent adjudicator on the once popular television show, *Big Brother*. On one particular eviction night, I overheard one of the producers on the phone: 'All early cunts need to be signed off by Aaron,' she said. I was curious and pushed for clarification. Although the programme was broadcast post-watershed, it turns out that expletives aired shortly after this watershed time of 9pm were considered to be quite risky and the word cunt was deemed one of the most offensive. Over a period of time, Channel 5 had developed a policy whereby the broadcast of this term needed to be formally signed off. In some respects, the biggest contribution this book makes is the realisation that bureaucracy is found in the most unlikely of places. In chapter 6, for example, I document its emergence at a commune and, paradoxically, note how it constitutes a principal part of its appeal.

**I argue that bureaucracy is characterised by a pervasive form of paradox:** Forget questions of efficiency; perhaps more so than anything else bureaucracy represents a clear manifestation of the agency–structure duality. It both enables and constrains; empowers and emasculates. This paradox is perhaps illustrated most readily by recourse to *Parkinson's Law*; that is, the maxim that work expands so as to fill the time available for its completion. Notably, Parkinson (1958) developed this theory from his experience working in the British Civil

Service. It is often seen as a light-hearted evaluation of organizational life but my own feeling is that there is something more pertinent here. Many of us have, I suspect, observed among our own family and friends the behaviour he identifies. Those who are retired or out of work dedicate a large amount of time to selecting, buying and posting a birthday card, for example. They exercise extraordinary care in doing so. And this is interesting. The flip side to all this, of course, is the adage: if you want something done, ask a busy person. So how might we respond to *Parkinson's Law*? One response—and implicitly, this has been the professional response in recent decades—has been to try to weed out this 'inconvenient' human frailty in organizational life. Another response, and the one I'm cheerleading, is to explore bureaucracy as something with significant existential purpose. If we admit even some validity to this latter position, then perhaps we need to refine our approach to working with bureaucracy. The field of business, management, and organization has begun to engage seriously with the study of paradox (see for example, Smith et al., 2017; Vine, 2018b); it is therefore timely that our understanding of bureaucracy is subject to this analytical lens.

**I explore bureaucracy as a receptacle for organizational knowledge:** Bureaucracy (or at least paperwork and record-keeping) captures an organization's historical knowledge. It is thus through bureaucracy that the organization becomes a container of knowledge. And the word container is apt as it hints at the fact that some people consider paperwork 'containing' (see chapter 6); it also hints at the existential qualities of bureaucratic life. When people formally leave an organization, their experience and wisdom—in short, their legacy—is not lost if they have contributed to the written records of that organization (typically, in the shape of various *pro formas*). Think about the role of a university lecturer or instructor. More often than not a newly-appointed lecturer inherits written artefacts from a previous lecturer. These artefacts include module guides, lecture plans, slide decks, assessment briefs, and grading rubrics. The appointee will then modify this documentation to suit both the evolving expectations of the module and, of course, their own teaching style and research interests. When the time comes for them to formally leave their post, and somebody else takes over, he or she will inherit that paperwork and the cycle continues. For, Phillips and Hardy (2002: 3) 'social reality is produced and made real through discourses, and social interactions cannot be fully understood without references to the discourses that give them meaning.' Bureaucratic artefacts—by which we mean primarily *paperwork*—carve out the organization's very essence as a form of discourse; the organizational reality is produced and made real through paperwork.

**I emphasise bureaucracy's historical-mnemonic function:** Nietzsche (1968 [1889]: 93) notes that the institution—or organization—is a vital conduit that binds together 'centuries-long ... solidarity between succeeding generations backwards and forwards *in infinitum.*' Turning our back on bureaucracy therefore has serious consequences. Standing (2016: 14, emphasis added), for example, notes the following in respect of what he refers to as the precariously employed. They are in 'career-less jobs, without traditions of *social memory,* a feeling they belong to an occupational community steeped in stable practices, codes of ethics and norms of behaviour, reciprocity and fraternity.' Bureaucracy—or secure employment—is a container. Part of the reason we malign bureaucracy is that we conveniently forget that we are transcended *by* organization:

> the office does not die ... it has a dignity that transcends the human being who provisionally occupies it and who must respect it. When that respect is erased, public office from the highest to the most modest is perceived as the private property of the present holder who can use it as he sees fit.
> (Supiot, 2006: 3, as cited in du Gay, 2011: 11–12)

**I have written this book in an intentionally irreverent style:** I have argued elsewhere that scholarly pursuits will benefit from cross-fertilisation, not just from adjacent disciplines but from disparate ones too. By way of illustration, in Vine (2020a), for example, I have made discernible attempts to engage with the natural sciences, particularly physics. In this book, I engage—intentionally—with arts and humanities, and develop a style—not so much sourced from these disciplines (as coverage here is often as dry as it is in the social sciences), but to reinforce the broader epistemological message. Unusually for an academic text, I use the first person pronoun and employ a candid style, particularly in respect of the more personal chapters 4–7. I am comfortable writing this way and—ultimately—I feel it is more engaging for the reader. And—let's face it—bureaucracy is usually considered dull as dishwater. This should not, however, imply that the analysis contained within is any less rigorous. On the contrary, this style allows me to flesh out the contradictions, existential pertinence, and culturally contingent aspects of the concept of bureaucracy in a way which has not yet been realised.

## So, what about Max Weber?

Perhaps more so than any other analytical concept in the study of organization, the analysis of bureaucracy has been monopolised by a single author: the 19th-century sociologist, Max Weber. Yup, Weber is unarguably the big gun when it comes to the study of bureaucracy. But I am not convinced a wholesale return to Weber is especially profitable. To this end, I am determined to avoid the trap of misplaced concreteness. This should not suggest, of course, that I have no respect for Weber's scholarship. He has produced some extremely insightful works and many of the questions I am seeking to address in this book can be traced back to his own musings. For example, and as others have noted, Weber commented that 'an abstract celebration or denunciation of bureaucracy makes little sense' (du Gay, 2005: 3). Nonetheless, if we are to stand any chance of breaking new ground, I am not convinced the rehearsal (or indeed re-interpretation) of the existing line of thought will be especially revealing. My rationale for this is sixfold.

First, one of the overarching objectives for my book is to instil a fresh approach to educating ourselves about bureaucracy. Weber is not especially illuminating in this respect, something others have noted too. For Willmott (2011: 285–6), for example,

> A condition of possibility of the ethos of bureaucracy being enacted in practice is a fuller awareness, embrace, and prizing of its values and principles by office-holders. It is to be regretted that Weber says comparable little about the fostering and maintenance of such awareness and vigilance.

I very much hope I am able to respond to Willmott's concerns; I am, after all, determined to develop a more nuanced, thorough and effective education associated with bureaucracy (see chapter 7).

Second, a rigid adherence to Weber's ideal type limits the analytical potential of contemporary research in the field of bureaucracy, not least in exploring they ways in which bureaucracy *transcends* organization. Interestingly, Thompson (1993: 200) has noted the following:

> bureaucratic structures will necessarily become more flexible, and people will be required to organize with changing groups of individuals, depending upon the issue being worked on. Greater emphasis will be placed upon inter-organizational relations, as organizations will be called upon to cooperate with each other to solve problems which extend beyond their narrow concerns.

This utterance is of fundamental import to my own endeavours. I wish to explore the ways in which bureaucracy—or at least the patterning, characteristics, and life motifs associated with it, are emerging in *pan-organizational* form (see chapter 3); and this represents a significant departure from Weber's model. Indeed, and as Casey (2004: 59) argues, 'there is emergent evidence of a raft of new activities occurring in contemporary organizations, which challenge our conceptions of bureaucratic organization.'

Third, I have no desire to be yet another scholar of organization hell-bent on mining Weber's works for something fresh. I firmly believe this resource is more or less exhausted. Yet another book about Weber and bureaucracy would more than likely amount to something unremarkable. This is not to overlook the relevance of Weber, but to note that we might productively search elsewhere if we are to say anything new or interesting about bureaucracy. So, for example, instead I consider the contributions of Nietzsche (who is rarely, if ever, invoked in discussions of bureaucracy), and note in particular what he has to say about how organization proliferates.

Fourth, while Weber was interested primarily in bureaucracy because of a broader interest in power, I'm interested in bureaucracy as an emergent or semi-agentic phenomenon. To this end, I'm less interested in how bureaucracy is wielded, and more interested in how it manifests itself. This ontological distinction is crucial.

Fifth, I feel compelled to reflect critically on the assumed relationship between bureaucracy and disenchantment. Weber (1989 [1918]: 300, cited in Casey, 2004: 65) notes:

> The fate of our age, with its characteristic rationalization and intellectualization, and above all the disenchantment of the world, is that the ultimate, most sublime values have withdrawn from public life, either into the transcendental realm of mystical life or into the brotherhood of immediate personal relationships between individuals.

This is extremely important. In my mind, both Weber and Casey are mistaken. I argue instead that it is bureaucracy itself that contains within it the kernel of existential meaning. We perennially misrepresent it as disenchanted and sterile. In reality, nothing could be further from the truth.

Finally, there is a methodological rationale for moving away from Weber. I am inspired here by the naturalist, Jane Goodall. Goodall's remarkable breakthroughs in respect of primatology came not by pursuing a formal education and following in the footsteps of earlier primatologists. No. She didn't have a university degree. Her extraordinary insights—that chimpanzees use tools, feel emotions, and engage in warfare—came from observation. We must *watch* bureaucracy and bureaucrats (including ourselves) if we are to make fresh sense of these phenomena.

## Can we finally lay Weber to rest?

Not quite. It would be foolhardy to reject Weber outright. As Clegg et al. (2016: 158) have noted of the field more generally: '[We owe] a great debt to Weber and any intellectual discussion of organization tends to draw, either directly or indirectly on his ideas.' Although I fall short of presenting a systematic review of Weber's contribution here, I feel compelled to make two important points. First, although bureaucracy did not begin with Weber, its study and systematic examination is almost always attributed to him (Gajduschek, 2003), and I cannot ignore this. Second, Weber's commentary on bureaucracy in *Economy & Society* should not be overlooked. I have no plans to rehearse that commentary here, not least because this has been done countless times before. However, I do urge my readers to consult Chapter 11 of that text (titled, simply, Bureaucracy). It is mercifully brief and worth reading. While certain sections of these musings are so well reported, they border on cliché (so, for example, hierarchy and the separation of office and person), there are aspects of his canon which have attracted less attention and it is these I deliberately draw upon later in this book. These include: existential security (p959); the guild-like closure of officialdom (p960); life tenure (p962); bureaucratic-historical longevity (p964); cultural contingency (p971); complexity (p972); the administrative 'gap' (p979); the bureaucratization of warfare (p981); and bureaucratic resilience (p987).

In sum, I want to play a small part in reversing what I perceive to be the fetishisation of Weberian bureaucracy; I'm keen to provide the field with 'experience-nourished, passionately felt, existentially authentic insights' (Magee, 2000: 98). I am therefore extremely carefully not to simply regurgitate Weber, or indeed the secondary literature it has spawned. That is not to say that I ignore it completely; on the contrary, I engage with it in what I very much hope amounts to innovative new ways.

## Bureaucracy since Weber

In a tradition dating back to Aristotle, scholars are expected to review the extant literature in their chosen field before embarking on a new piece of research. My previous declarations in respect of seeking fresh vantage points notwithstanding, I have no desire to subvert this tradition. The chapters dedicated to my review of the relevant literature (chapters 2 and 3) are focussed on an aspect of the concept I feel is most pertinent to the broader thesis: *identity*. I demonstrate why it is that we tend to feel so strongly about bureaucracy; bureaucracy represents a perceived (but rarely real) threat to our identity. What follows, then, in this section is a very brief overview of the historical study of bureaucracy since Weber.

There is now an established and familiar narrative associated with the timeline of bureaucracy studies. It goes something like this: The post-war period was a golden age for scholarship in the field of bureaucracy. This began to wane in the 1970s and 1980s. From the 1990s and especially into the 2000s it has since experienced something of a resurgence. What marks the resurgence out as distinct, however, is that it includes a body of work dedicated to the counter-critique of bureaucracy, i.e. its defence.

Of the Golden Age, Talcott Parsons's work is, perhaps, the most notable. Not only did Weber's works become accessible to the English-speaking world courtesy of Parsons's translations, but several of his contemporaries at Harvard (including Robert Merton), published extensively on the concept and its ramifications. As the century unfolded into the post-war period, and business schools began to proliferate, a focus on bureaucracy became unfashionable. New, alternative, lenses for examining organization came to the fore. As Styhre (2007: 23) notes, these alternatives included Total Quality Management (TQM), lean production, and just-in-time logistics. The rhetoric shifted away from administration and bureaucracy (associated with traditional operations) and towards commercial methodologies (associated with projects and project management), such as Agile, Scrum, PRINCE2, and Six Sigma. Ultimately, this shift would contribute to the late 20th century brand of neoliberalism. The era of post-bureaucracy had, apparently, arrived. More recently—in the early 2000s—reacting to the rhetoric of post-bureaucracy, du Gay (2000, 2005) produced two stimulating books. And, more recently still, Clegg et al. (2011) edited a collection of chapters exploring some undertheorised areas of bureaucracy in respect of management, organization and modernity.

## Anti-bureaucratic attitudes in context

The exceptions noted above, relevant coverage of bureaucracy since Weber has been almost entirely negative. This is the challenge: anti-bureaucratic attitudes are pervasive. They transcend politics, they transcend ontology, and they transcend both machismo and feminist perspectives.

*Anti-bureaucratic attitudes transcend politics.* For Heckscher (1993, writing the Foreword for Abrahmsson's book), 'at the core of both major ideological strands ... has been a fierce enmity toward bureaucracy and formal organization.' This transcendence is echoed elsewhere in the literature. du Gay (2011: 20), for example, notes that '[i]n discussions of public sector performance ... governments of many different political hues have come to the conclusion that Weberian bureaucracy is not a solution but rather a barrier to "delivery"' Styhre (2007: 54), has noted a comparable trend in respect of opposing political camps in the world of academia: 'the main steam of critique of bureaucracy derives from either neoliberal economics [often associated with the political right] or humanist orientations such as the Human Relations School' [often associated with the political left], further illustrating the cross-ideological pervasiveness of bureaucracy's critique.

*Anti-bureaucratic attitudes transcend ontology.* For du Gay (2000) there are three types of anti-bureaucratic sentiment: populist, philosophical, and entrepreneurial. Of populist anti-bureaucratic sentiment, he notes that this 'often appears to be little more than a long list of what people do not like about their relations with modern, "positive" government: "red tape", regimentation, a rising flood of forms, impersonalism and so on' (ibid. 1). Of philosophical anti-bureaucratic sentiment, du Gay writes that the bureau is routinely conceived of as the one-sided expression of an 'instrumental rationality' which can sustain its identity only through repressing and marginalising its emotional *Other*. Finally, in respect of entrepreneurial anti-bureaucratic sentiment, du Gay notes the rise of both Public Choice Theory and New Managerialism as evidence of attempts to concoct alternatives to bureaucracy. Most recently of all, Lopdrup-Hjorth and du Gay (2020: 441) have noted that 'in spite of their distinctive normative and political differences, both critical organizational scholars and right wing populists use a vocabulary characterised by a 'profoundly antithetical stance toward bureaucracy.'

*Anti-bureaucratic attitudes transcend feminist and machismo perspectives.* On one hand, we see a vehemently anti-bureaucratic attitude in the bravado-charged cultures of finance and investment banking. In these professions, risk and risk-taking, for example, are considered an imperative part of the 'city boy' identity. In a similar vein, Donald Trump has thrown his weight behind anti-bureaucratic sentiment in numerous tweets, both prior to and during his presidency. However, bureaucracy attracts comparable scorn from the other side of the fence. Ferguson's *The Feminist Case Against Bureaucracy* (1984), for example, established an ideological precedent among critical scholars. Burrell (1997: 244), too, depicts bureaucracy as a distinctly masculine manifestation of an organization and to this end casts none less than Weber as a misogynist: 'The female terms he uses are almost always denigratory.

He often talks of certain laws being for "old women" and of pacifism being for "ladies of both sexes".' (However, it should be stressed that the feminist case presented by scholars such as Ferguson and Burrell has itself attracted counter-critique; see for example Billing 1994, 2005.)

## Chapter synopses

In this chapter, I have presented an understanding of bureaucracy that prioritises its institutional logic and existential significance, rather than its legal-rational credentials. Understood this way, bureaucracy becomes indispensable to business, management, and organization. Indeed, bureaucracy *is* organization. The subsequent thesis is divided into three parts.

Part I represents the theoretical thrust of my work. It presents and builds upon a detailed explication of relevant scholarly contributions over the past century and a half, and is reliant on some fairly heavyweight macrosociological theorising. It will appeal primarily to those with a specialist interest in neoliberalism, organizational identity or institutional dynamics. Notwithstanding the apparent pervasiveness of anti-bureaucratic sentiment, I argue that an elevated vantage point enables us to see that our historical attitudes to bureaucracy are cyclical: to this end, the contemporary bias is one which is often imprecisely described as 'post-bureaucracy' (chapter 2). As part of these discussions, I suggest that the binary casting of 'bureaucracy' and 'post-bureaucracy' as epochal markers is of limited use; instead I argue that we must understand the two categories as dialectical parameters between which all organizational life unfolds (chapter 3). Non specialists may wish to simply read the opening and concluding subsections of chapters 2 and 3, before proceeding to Parts II and III of the book, whereupon I develop my specific empirical contributions.

In Part II, I deconstruct and seek to better understand the current—overwhelmingly negative—attitude towards bureaucracy: this is no easy feat since this negativity continues to transcend political hue and intellectual disposition. It is achieved, I hope, through a systematic distillation of our apparent fixation on extreme pathological manifestations of bureaucracy (chapter 4), as well as the predilection for novelists and filmmakers to continually reinforce this attitude by casting bureaucracy as a recurrent dystopian trope (chapter 5).

In the final section of the book, Part III, I chart a pragmatic way in which to move the field forward. I do this first by urging ethnographic reflection on our own experiences of bureaucracy (chapter 6) before outlining a rationale for, and ways in which to, fruitfully re-establish the systematic study of bureaucracy onto our educational apparatus, specifically on degree programmes such as business and management, political sciences, and government studies (chapter 7). I summarise and reflect on the overall thesis in the concluding chapter (chapter 8) by means of four retrospective analytical frames: pattern, paradox, balance, and sensemaking.

**PART I**

# Bureaucracy: Rave, Rant, Repeat

# 2

# BUREAUCRACY, POST-BUREAUCRACY AND IDENTITY CRISIS

On the face of it, anti-bureaucratic sentiment is pervasive. Upon closer scrutiny, however, scholarly attitudes towards bureaucracy have come full circle over the past century: from a fear of freedom in the early 20th century, switching to a fear of oppression in the post war years, before returning to a fear of freedom again in the early 21st century. This cyclical pattern is illustrated in Figure 2.1, alongside representative writers for each period.

This chapter is chiefly concerned with the manner in which the anti-bureaucratic sentiment of scholars in the mid-20th century yielded to pro-bureaucratic attitudes in the late-20th and early 21st centuries. This is the part of the (current) cycle that is of most relevance to our lives today. Before exploring this latter shift, however, I outline the pro-bureaucratic sentiment of the early 1900s, and note how it yields to the anti-bureaucratic sentiment of the mid-20th century.

## The early 1900s: from pro-bureaucracy to anti-bureaucracy

Of the pro-bureaucratic sentiment that characterised the late 1800s and early 1900s, Wilson, Weber and Fromm are presented as principal representatives. One of the first scholarly expositions of bureaucracy is found in Woodrow Wilson's (1887) *The Study of Administration*. Notably, Wilson is sparing in his use of the word bureaucracy and where he does use it, he does so with caution. In fact, on at least one occasion in his paper he uses the word as a *Schimpfort*, perhaps by way of relating to a chary readership. The broader tone of his paper, however, is one which can be interpreted as a defence of the concept. Rather than dwell on accusations of contradictory scholarship we focus instead on what this reveals: the pro-bureaucratic sentiment identified of Wilson was probably a reaction to even earlier period of negative sentiment. This of course lends support to the broader cyclical argument presented.

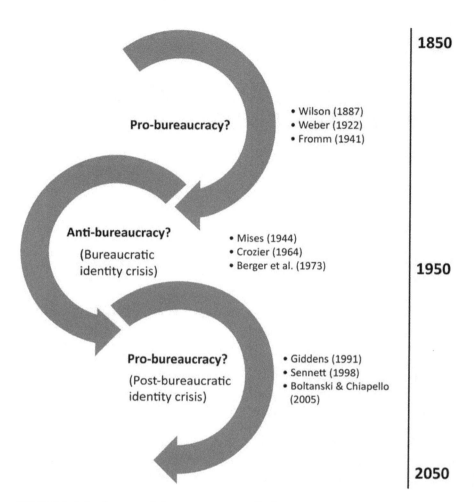

**FIGURE 2.1** Attitudes towards bureaucracy: a cyclical pattern

Given Wilson's eventual election as US president, it is unsurprising that his study of bureaucracy is trained on its political pertinence. It is, he says, 'raised very far above the dull level of mere technical detail by the fact that through its greater principles it is directly connected with the lasting maxims of political wisdom, the permanent truths of political progress' (Wilson, 1887: 210). Of greater relevance, he notes that a 'science of administration … [must] strengthen and purify its organization' (ibid. 201). Although somewhat oblique, the comment is lent greater clarity when Wilson later suggests that by comparison to the European and Prussian monarchies of his day (which by their very nature cultivated a sense of stability) American societal values (in which open and free public opinion is enthroned) demanded a sense of executive expertness in respect of administration (ibid. 207). Ultimately, for Wilson, the object of administrative study is to set 'foundations laid deep in *stable* principle' (ibid. 210, emphasis added). For Wilson, then, bureaucracy provides an important sense of stability.

A similar argument is found in Weber's works. Although not an ideological defender of bureaucracy as such (see chapter 8 for a reflection on Weber's analytical ambiguity), Weber presents—in terms of an ideal type—the virtues of the bureaucratic form, notably in respect of *security, life tenure,* and *resilience.* So, Weber speaks of bureaucracy as the 'grant of a secure existence' (ibid. 959); that 'the position of the official is held for life' (ibid. 962); and that '[o]nce fully established, bureaucracy is among those social structures which are the hardest to destroy' (ibid. 987).

The benefits of bureaucracy outlined by Wilson (at the close of the 1800s) and Weber (at the beginning of the 1900s) can be understood in a broader psychosocial sense by reflecting on Fromm's work. Contrary to how it is routinely understood, for Fromm freedom is anxiety-inducing. This argument is most famously presented in his 1941 book *Escape from Freedom* (published as *The Fear of Freedom* in the UK in 1942). While it would be a misrepresentation to suggest that either Wilson or Weber was fearful of freedom in quite the way Fromm describes, they each paint a picture of bureaucracy as a means of mitigating the disorienting challenges of a 'free' society (in Wilson's case, elicited by an absence of royal prerogative; in Weber's, by the increasing complexity of civilisation).

Fromm's work is rarely invoked in discussions of bureaucracy and yet it is remarkably fruitful in at least three respects. First, he hints at a cyclical attitudinal pattern comparable to that we have delineated in respect of bureaucracy: 'In the long and virtually continuous battle for freedom … classes that were fighting against oppression at one stage sided with the enemies of freedom when victory was won and new privileges were to be defended' (Fromm, 1985 [1942]: 1). Of this, he later asks the following question: 'Why do certain definitive changes of man's character take place from one historical epoch to another?' (ibid. 9). In response, Fromm goes on to argue in a psychoanalytical vein that our pendulous attitudes to freedom mirror the dialectic associated with primary bonds vis-à-vis individuation. So, while initially the infant is inseparable from his or her mother, slowly he or she realises a sense of independence. However, we rarely ever revel in isolation. For the vast majority of us, ties of kinship remain vital existential markers in our adult years. Fromm reflects on this observation, and extrapolates to broader social dynamics where, he notes, a sense of *complete* freedom is equally troubling. To this end, Fromm suggests that each of us is compelled to identify specific 'mechanisms of escape' (ibid. 25).

These mechanisms are threefold: (1) authoritarianism; (2) destructiveness, and (3) automaton conformity. It is the first of these, authoritarianism, for which Fromm is probably best known. Writing originally in 1941 his focus was inevitably on the interpreting and understanding the rise of Nazism. For Fromm, it was simple: the

German people felt adrift in the interwar period. The dominance associated with National Socialism provided a sense of direction, identity, and security. His second mechanism, destructiveness, refers to a latent tendency in us all to display hostile behavioural traits in the face of powerlessness. It is Fromm's often overlooked third mechanism, however, which is of most relevance to our current thesis: automaton conformity. For Fromm, automaton conformity describes the tendency for us to internalise external belief systems and adopt them as our own. In so doing, we yield to a broader discourse which helps mitigate the anxiety associated with existential isolation.

Although Fromm does not engage in a discussion of bureaucracy directly, he certainly provides us with a vocabulary for understanding how bureaucratic structures (or belief systems) help alleviate the anxiety associated with complete freedom. Fromm's contribution thus enables us to crystallise the arguments that bureaucracy provides a sense of stability (Wilson) and security (Weber). To some degree this crystallisation is reflected in studies of manumission. Contrary to expectation, slaves were sometimes reported to reject their freedom; without an established craft or livelihood, the freedom on offer would be little more than a Pyrrhic victory. Such a story is famously conveyed in *Arabian Nights* (translated into English in the 18$^{th}$ century).

But at the time of Fromm's publication, attitudes towards bureaucracy were beginning to change. The mid-20th century yielded multiple—and sustained— critiques of bureaucracy, typically focussed on its instrumental shortcomings. These came in the form of Merton's (1940) charges of trained incapacity and over conformity; Ludwig von Mises's (1944) argument that state apparatus could not operate with anything like the level of efficiency of free market pricing mechanisms; and the shortcomings Crozier (2017 [1964]) identified in respect of centralization, impersonality and dysfunction. Together, this is the sort of vocabulary most us invoke in everyday discussions of bureaucracy. These are the critiques that have come to dominate common conceptions of bureaucracy.

## The post-war period: from bureaucratic identity crisis to post-bureaucratic identity crisis

My focus in this chapter, however, is on the latter shift identified in Figure 2.1: from anti-bureaucracy to a return to pro-bureaucracy. In reviewing the evolution of the academic discourse over this period, I note that this particular sweep of the pendulum can be understood in terms of crisis. A complete reversal of identity crisis is revealed; from one which emphasised the stifling intrusion of institutional stasis, to one in which the anxieties of freedom once again take centre stage. I demonstrate how concerns centred on suppressed creativity in bureaucratic organizations ('the bureaucratic identity crisis') have yielded to concerns centred on the feelings of isolation engendered by post-bureaucratic endeavours ('the post-bureaucratic identity crisis'). This evolution is illustrated through an analysis of four pivotal texts: Berger et al. (1973) *The Homeless Mind: Modernization and*

*Consciousness*; Giddens (1991) *Modernity and Self-identity*; Sennett's (1998) *The Corrosion of Character*; and Boltanski and Chiapello (2005) *The New Spirit of Capitalism*. Other scholars have offered comparable analyses (see, for example, du Gay and Morgan, 2013), but the intention here is to move away from a preoccupation with economic superstructure and focus instead on the manner in which the fabric of our organizational landscape is evolving.

## Why crisis?

Crisis is a strong word. But, as we will see, in discussions related to identity and bureaucracy it is justified. We can fruitfully conceptualise *two* separate identity crises related to bureaucracy. The first accompanied the transition from what is regarded as traditional society to modernity. The second accompanies the transition from modernity to late modernity. Both crises, it seems, arose not simply because change is unsettling but because the agents of transition (in both cases) failed to acknowledge the important underpinnings of the extant system. For the purposes of this analysis, I forge a distinction between the *modern* crisis and the *postmodern* crisis as broad framings encompassing the identity threats to organization. As befits the orientation of this book, however, I reconceptualise this distinction in terms of the *bureaucratic* (as a phenomenon inextricably linked to modernity) and *post-bureaucratic* (as a phenomenon inextricably linked to postmodernity) identity crises. This affords a clearer focus for understanding the specifics of the trend and provides a firmer foundation for analysis.

The concepts of both bureaucracy and identity crisis transcend the texts of Peter Berger et al. (1973), Anthony Giddens (1991), Richard Sennett (1998) and Boltanski and Chiapello (2005). However, over the course of the 33 years between 1973 and 2005, the attitude towards the effects of bureaucracy on our identity is reversed. To assist the reader, prior to tackling each text in turn, I forge a continuum on which the texts are conceptually represented to illustrate the two distinct identity crises (see Figure 2.2).

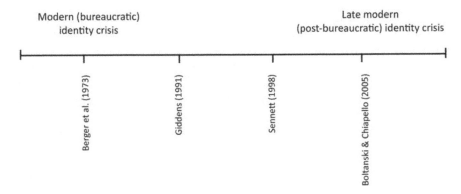

**FIGURE 2.2** Bureaucracy: you're damned if you do and damned if you don't

It should be noted that there is no clear implication in these texts that there are two separate crises; this is inferred when the four texts are viewed as a connected—but evolving—discourse. Berger et al. (writing in 1973) explore the first (bureaucratic) crisis. Inspired by Berger et al.'s exegesis, Giddens (writing in 1991) does indeed write specifically of the 'late modern age' but does not clearly distinguish between modernity and late/high/post-modernity, apart from suggesting that late/high/post-modernity is somehow the accentuation (or logical development) of the modernity that precedes it, rather than as representative of a significant departure from it. The distinguishing factor in Sennett's writing, when compared to that of Berger et al., is how concern regarding bureaucracy has completely reversed. While Berger et al. caution against the rationalising and dehumanising effects of bureaucracy; Sennett expresses concern at the loss of the stability inherent to the bureaucratic model and in so doing engages foremost with the second (post-bureaucratic) crisis. Boltanski and Chiapello (originally published in French, in 1999) suggest that the problems and subsequent critique of modernity in the 1960s is fundamentally distinguishable from that of late modernity in the 1990s. For Boltanski and Chiapello, the second and third (or 'new') spirits of capitalism are said to represent modernity and late modernity respectively, although it should be stressed that they do not use the term 'late modernity.' However, unlike Berger et al., Boltanski and Chiapello do not regard the second spirit as compromising one's existential security; instead they report that much of its critique stems from its predisposition to stifle creativity. Like Sennett, Boltanski and Chiapello orient their critique towards late capitalism, and so accordingly they occupy the outermost position on the right-hand side on our continuum. Each contribution is explored in detail below.

## Berger et al. (1973) 'The Homeless Mind: Modernization and Consciousness'

In the 1970s, Berger et al. argued that the rapid process of modernization is troubling for our consciousness. Specifically, they suggest that both technological and bureaucratic advances rupture traditions and render humanity 'homeless.' They define modernisation as the growth and diffusion of a set of institutions rooted in the transformation of the economy by means of technology: 'We ascribe principal importance to those institutions directly related to the technologised economy. Closely related to these are the political institutions associated with what we know as the modern state, particularly the institution of bureaucracy' (Berger et al., 1973: 9).

The text is therefore framed around the problem of modernisation (or more accurately 'the problem of modernity'). The book targets 'technologisation' (ibid. 23–40) and bureaucracy (ibid. 41–62) as primary concerns, and socio-cultural pluralism (defined as 'the pluralization of social life worlds') (ibid. 63–82) as a supplementary concern. As regards technology, the authors question 'the everyday consciousness of ordinary people engaged in technological production' (ibid. 23). They conclude that 'technological production brings with it *anonymous social relations*' (ibid. 31, original emphasis). Moreover, the authors reproduce the now well-rehearsed argument that 'at least in the mass-production setting of the assembly line or similar industrial contexts, social relations between workers are experienced in terms of ... anonymity' (ibid.). In this sense, then, the authors draw on scholarship dating back to Marx which critiques the alienating (and in this case 'anonymising') effects of capitalism. They develop the critique, however, by explicitly addressing the concept of bureaucracy. While for many, Weber is somewhat ambiguous in terms of his own view regarding the effects of bureaucracy (see for example, Höpfl, 2000), Berger et al. are much clearer: the institution of bureaucracy further reinforces anonymity.

In addition, then, to technologised routine and the institution of bureaucracy, Berger et al. suggest that a 'pluralization of social life worlds' is a third fundamental aspect of the homelessness they describe. A 'life world' describes the process of living 'in a reality that is ordered and that gives a sense to the business of living' (ibid. 63). Furthermore:

> Through most of human history, individuals lived in life-worlds that were more or less unified. This is not to deny that through the division of labour and other processes of institutional segmentation there have always been important differences in the life-worlds of different groups within the same society. Nevertheless, compared with modern societies, most earlier ones evinced a high degree of integration.
>
> *(Ibid. 64)*

Of course, that traditional society evinced a higher degree of integration cannot be assumed categorically. In *The Division of Labor in Society* (1893), Durkheim argued that modern industrial society elicits specific interdependencies between subjects, in a structure comparable to that of organisms in nature. In this way, modern industrial society is considered more integrated than the traditional society that preceded it. Berger et al.'s work, however, follows the conviction set out by Tönnies (1887) who favourably distinguished *Gemeinschaft* (community) from *Gesellschaft* (society). The pluralisation Berger et al. speak of is borne of the modern demarcation between public and private spheres and the pluralisation *within* each of the spheres themselves. The *modern* citizen must contend with what the authors regard as the immense complexity of the division of labour, as well as political, legal, educational and medical institutions in the public sphere; while the unity of the private sphere is challenged by the onset of domestic arrangements distinct from the traditional nuclear family. In sum, Berger *et al.* present three main institutions through which they mobilize their theory that our minds have been rendered homeless: technologised routine, bureaucracy, and the pluralisation of life worlds.

## Giddens (1991) *Modernity and Self-identity: Self and Society in the Late Modern Age*

Giddens explicitly builds on the exegesis presented by Berger et al.:

> As he [*sic*] [Berger et al.] points out, throughout most of human history, people lived in social settings that were fairly closely connected with each other ... The settings of modern social life are much more diverse and segmented ... Partly because of the existence of multiple mileux of action ... modes of action followed in one context may be more or less substantially at variance with those adopted in others ... A lifestyle sector concerns a time-space 'slice' of an individual's overall activities ... A lifestyle sector can include, for instance, what one does on certain evenings of the week ... a friendship, a marriage ... etc..
>
> *(Giddens, 1991: 83)*

However, although the analysis presented by Giddens is largely commensurate with that of Berger et al., there is relatively little agency lent to technology and none whatsoever accorded to the concept of bureaucracy. In this sense, there is clearly—consciously or otherwise—an attempt to distance himself from Berger et al. In terms of 'identity crisis' specifically—and the two-stage model I am proposing—Giddens is ambiguous as to whether his writing is about modernity or late modernity. Even the title reflects this ambiguity: <u>Modernity</u> and Self-identity: Self and Society in <u>Late Modern</u> Age (underlining added). This ambiguity is further reflected in the opening chapter. On the very first page, Giddens suggests that '[m]odern institutions differ from all preceding forms of social order in respect of their dynamism, the degree to which they undercut traditional habits and customs, and their global impact,' and yet a few pages later the same assertion is repackaged in terms of late modernity: 'The late modern world—the world which I term high modernity—is apocalyptic, not because we are heading towards calamity, but because it introduces risks which previous generations have not had to face' (ibid. 4). There is, however, some legitimacy in resisting the taxonomic urge to categorise with labels such as modern, late modern, postmodern, and so on. This ambiguity is to some degree at least explained by his suggestion that whereas postmodernity implies a departure from modernity, late (or high) modernity is very much part of the modern metanarrative (Giddens, 1991: 3). This terminological ambiguity in terms of modernity and late (or high) modernity serves to reinforce the decision to frame the transitional model presented (see Figure 2.1) in terms of bureaucracy and post-bureaucracy instead.

Terminological ambiguity aside, Giddens provides valuable material for developing an argument centred on identity crisis. Foremost are his suggestions that science is existentially troubling; that individuality is a contemporary phenomenon; and that the 'protective cocoon' has been dismantled. The risks to which Giddens here refers are conceptualised as a form of existential doubt associated principally with the prevalence of scientific enquiry:

> No matter how cherished, and apparently well established a given scientific tenet might be, it is open to revision—or might have to be discarded altogether—in the light of new ideas or findings. The integral relation between

modernity and radical doubt is an issue, which, once exposed to view, is not only disturbing to philosophers but is *existentially troubling* for ordinary individuals.

(Ibid. 21, original emphasis)

This existential angst is further mediated by the notion of 'providential reason.' Giddens identifies the drive to secularize as problematic because of the existential doubt it invariably elicits. He continues:

> Practical consciousness is the cognitive and emotive anchor of the feelings of ontological security ... The notion of ontological security ties in closely to the tacit character of practical consciousness [i.e. non-conscious']—or in phenomenological terms, to the 'bracketings' presumed by the 'natural attitude' in everyday life.
>
> (Ibid. 36)

In this sense, the 'natural attitude' in everyday life is ruptured in late modernity, and since ontological security is not something people readily recognise it presumably takes somebody of Giddens's intellectual stature to unravel. In terms of individuality, Giddens makes the observation that 'the idea that each person has a unique character and special potentialities that may or may not be fulfilled is alien to modern culture. In medieval Europe, lineage, gender, social status and other attributes were relatively fixed' (ibid. 74). Moreover:

> [T]he individual, in a certain sense, did not exist in traditional cultures, and individuality was not prized. Only with the emergence of modern societies and, more importantly, with the differentiation of the division of labour did the separate individual become the focus of attention.
>
> (Ibid. 75)

Although individuality is typically understood as a positive trait, Giddens points out that it compromises our 'protective cocoon.' For Giddens, 'the protective cocoon is the *mantle of trust that makes possible the sustaining of a viable Umwelt*. That substratum of trust is the condition and the outcome of the routinised nature of an '*uneventful*' world (ibid. 29, original italics, underlining added). Moreover: 'The capability to disturb the fixity of things, open up new pathways, and thereby colonise a segment of a novel future, is integral to modernity's unsettling character' (ibid. 133). In this way, then, Giddens charts the 'invention' of the individual. Most significantly, the very notion of individuality implies existential exposure and insecurity.

## Sennett (1998) *The Corrosion of Character: The Personal Consequences of Work in the New Capitalism*

Following Giddens, Sennett orients his critique towards late capitalism or—in his own words—'new capitalism.' In this sense—and although Sennett does not at any stage compare his thesis with theirs – his critique is the mirror image of that presented by Berger et al. Where Berger et al. expressed concern at the predictability and continuous routine of 'technologised' labour, Sennett highlights the ills of short-term flexibility. Where Berger et al. expressed concern at the dehumanising effects of bureaucracy, Sennett expresses concern at the informalities and obscuration of power in the post-bureaucratic epoch. For Sennett (1998: 23):

> The long-term order at which the new regime takes aim … was itself short-lived—the decades spanning the mid-twentieth century. Nineteenth century capitalism lurched from disaster to disaster in the stock markets and in irrational corporate investment; the wild swings of the business cycle provided people with little security. In [the] generation after World War II, this disorder was brought somewhat under control in most advanced economies; strong unions, guarantees of the welfare state, and largescale corporations combined to produce an era of relative stability. This span of thirty or so years defines the 'stable past' now challenged by the new regime.

In terms of the abandonment of routine, Sennett teaches us that the contemporary emphasis on flexibility is changing the very meaning of work, and—by implication—the words we use for it. 'Career', for instance, in its English origins meant a road for carriages, and as eventually applied to labour meant a lifelong channel for one's economic pursuits. Flexible capitalism has blocked the straight roadway of career, diverting employees suddenly from one kind of work to another (ibid. 9). Furthermore:

> At the dawn of industrial capitalism … it was not self-evident that routine was an evil. In the middle of the eighteenth century, it seemed that repetitive labor could lead in two quite different directions, one positive and fruitful, the other destructive. The positive side of routine was depicted in Diderot's great *Encyclopedia* … the negative side of regular labor-time was portrayed most dramatically in Adam Smith's *The Wealth of Nations* … Diderot believed routine in work could be like any other form of rote learning, a necessary teacher; Smith believed routine deadened the mind.
>
> *(Ibid. 32)*

Following the fears of Smith, and later Marx, the concept of Fordism (and the Tayloristic methodology it embodied) became a dirty word, particularly within critical management discourses. However, Sennett believes Diderot's original conceptualisation was misunderstood:

> Diderot did not believe routine work is degrading; on the contrary, he thought routines beget narratives, as the rules and rhythms of work gradually evolve. It's ironic that this boulevardier and *philosophe*, a creature of sleazier salons of mid-eighteenth century Paris, appears today more a champion of the

inherent dignity of ordinary labor than do many of those who have spoken in the name of the People.

*(Ibid. 44)*

This is undoubtedly controversial, but pre-empts a shift away from the concerns of Berger et al. Beyond the specifics of routine, Berger et al. presented more general concerns about bureaucracy. But Sennett seeks to reverse the critique here too:

> In attacking rigid bureaucracy and emphasising risk, it is claimed, flexibility gives people more freedom to shape their lives. In fact, the new order substitutes new controls rather than simply abolishing the rules of the past—but these new controls are also hard to understand. The new capitalism is an often illegitimate regime of power.
>
> *(Sennett, 1998: 9–10)*

In analysis reminiscent of the sort proffered by Michel Foucault, Sennett here argues that the characteristics of the post-bureaucratic world order help obfuscate the deployment of power. Moreover, the positive connotations associated with 'flexibility' conceal a reality premised on *risk*. Indeed, the concept of risk appears in both Giddens and Sennett. For Giddens, risk is inextricably linked to the emergence of the 'individual.' By way of clarification:

> All individuals establish a portfolio of risk assessment ... Thinking in terms of risk becomes more or less inevitable and most people will be conscious also of the risks of *refusing* to think in this way, even if they may choose to ignore those risks. In the charged reflexive settings of high modernity, living on 'automatic pilot' becomes more and more difficult to do, and it becomes less and less possible to protect any lifestyle, no matter how firmly pre-established, from the generalised risk climate.
>
> *(Giddens, 1991: 125–6)*

In this way, even adopting a 'risk averse' strategy is, paradoxically, risky. Giddensian risk is both institutionalised and pervasive. Sennett takes the opportunity to offer clarification in this regard commenting that the willingness to take risks is no longer meant to be the preserve of venture capitalists or extraordinarily adventurous individuals but has become a daily necessity shouldered by the masses (Sennett, 1998: 80). Sennett's concern at the onset of post-bureaucracy (or at least the discourses which propagate it) lent inspiration to the influential works of du Gay (2000, 2005) and Kallinikos (2003). Broadly speaking, these later writers argue that organizations which are—as already stated—fundamental mediators of reality are undergoing a seismic shift from traditional bureaucracies to loosely-related networks, and so our processes of identity formation and maintenance are now compromised. Further theorization in this vein is offered by Strati (2000: 4) who suggests that 'one of the principal conceptualizations of organizational life that defines it as sharply distinct from society is the notion of bureaucracy.' If, then, contemporary organizations are purporting to abandon their bureaucratic foundations, it becomes more difficult to distinguish them from the loosely-formed and distant aspects of society of which they form a part. Put simply, organizational bureaucracy constitutes a medium between the exposure of unadulterated individualism on the one hand and the anonymity of mass society on the other. Furthermore, it provides a sense of both continuity and security. Our generation's drive to cleanse systems and organizational processes of their bureaucracies therefore elicits and underscores this crisis of identity.

Sennett identifies a further challenge to bureaucracy in the form of a 'no long term' principle (Sennett, 1998: 24). Part time, temporary and flexible working patterns are oriented as short term phenomena. Of course, and as Petriglieri and Petriglieri (2010: 49 emphasis added) remind us, early life is characterised by 'a *succession* of holding environments' (nursery, junior school, and senior school). This itself is reminiscent of Lichtenstein's (1977: 197) suggestion that:

> The coexistence, objective as well as subjective, of continuity and change is what defines personal identity. It is part of everyone's identity to have been an infant, a toddler, a participant in kindergarten and in schooling, and finally a young adult. Undergoing all these changes, biologically as well as socially, and still being the same John or Joan, *is* human identity.

However, although these 'holding environments' persist in early life as Petriglieri and Petriglieri note, the assumption that Lichtenstein made in the 1970s that they continue into adult life is now in doubt. Contemporary adult work may involve working for three or four different organizations every year (see, for example, Arthur and Rousseau, 1996; Hall, 1996). For Sennett this situation has been made possible through the *normalisation* of instability. Sennett (1998: 31) comments thus: 'What's peculiar about uncertainty today is that is exists without any looming historical disaster; instead it is woven into the everyday practices of a vigorous capitalism. Instability is meant to be normal.'

In Sennett's text, then, there are clear continuities with Giddens. However, Sennett's work is sufficiently differentiated from Giddens such that it constitutes a clear reversal of Berger et al.'s 1973 contribution (the same cannot be said for Giddens' text). In this way, Sennett's thesis justifies its position towards the right-hand side of the identity crisis continuum.

## Boltanski and Chiapello (2005) *The New Spirit of Capitalism*

Unlike Berger et al., Giddens and Sennett, Boltanski and Chiapello do not write explicitly about identity. However, they are included in this analysis because their account of the changes the broader capitalist system has experienced is pertinent in terms of identity and identity crisis. Boltanski and Chiapello's *The New Spirit of Capitalism* was published in its original French just a year after *The Corrosion of*

*Character*. We find no semblance of theoretical continuity following Berger et al., Giddens, or Sennett, but this is most likely due to the fact that Boltanski and Chiapello are part of a continental scholarly tradition and were writing primarily for a French audience. The title of this work alludes, of course, to Weber's *Protestant Ethic and the Spirit of Capitalism* and, as Budgen (2000) suggests, the capitalism here described is thoroughly Weberian in guise.

By way of a brief synopsis, the text begins by examining management discourses in the 1990s. They argue that these neo-conservative discourses subsumed the liberal concerns of the 1960s. In this sense—and given the book's focus on the French iteration of the capitalist form—the student uprising of 1968 and subsequent displacing of de Gaulle's government is lent crucial agency. The authors write of the period: 'The 1960s project aimed at the liberation of *cadres* and the relaxation of the bureaucracy that developed out of the centralization and growing integration of ever larger firms' (Boltanski and Chiapello, 2005: 68). As part of the uprisings, protesters scrawled graffiti and brandished placards bearing slogans such as 'NON A LA BUREAUCRATIE' (http://www.iisg.org/collections/cards/e04-264.php); and 'We want structures that serve people, not people serving structures' (http://www.cddc.vt.edu/bps/CF/graffiti.htm). Boltanski and Chiapello recognise that such messages resonate with more recent organizational practices. In this way, then, they are able to legitimately argue that the Left's concerns of the 1960s became subsumed into the capitalism of the late 1990s. Significantly, however, they describe how the new capitalist/management discourses have sought to dismantle bureaucracy but in so doing have effectively 'dismantl[ed] the world of work' (ibid. 217). For the discontented of the 1960s, the aim of suppressing bureaucracy was regarded as a vehicle for liberation. Ultimately, its implementation three decades later rendered instead a world of insecurity (ibid. 224).

Boltanski and Chiapello's thesis is underpinned by a thematic rendering of capitalism over its recent historical course. They chart the history of capitalism as follows: the first spirit of capitalism at the turn of the 20th century is characterised by family-owned small firms which offered a sense of both trade and security to their employees; the second spirit of capitalism which characterised the post-war period offered both stability and security via the institution of bureaucracy (but stifled creativity and entrepreneurial freedom); and finally, the third (or 'new') spirit of capitalism remedies the concerns regarding individual creativity of the second spirit but strips the employee-individual of any semblance of security the previous iterations of capitalism afforded.

The authors lament the fact that the concepts of both 'capitalism' and 'class' have vanished from the spoken and written vernacular, at least in terms of their potency. Specifically, the authors believe that *critical sociology* must be replaced by a *sociology of critique* since capitalism has an uncanny 'ability to assimilate critique.' While this surely represents a triumph for the very efficacy of critique, it presents contemporary analytics with a problem; for Boltanski and Chiapello, the capitalistic internalisation of the 'events of 1968,' has rendered the contemporary workplace insecure and unjust.

## Early 21st century contributions

For Berger et al. (1973), the concern was very much focussed on the constraints associated with both technology and routine. For Giddens (1991), the focus was on the transition between these [modern] concerns and the [late modern] ones which were emerging. By the time of Sennett's publication (in 1998), these late modern concerns had become dominant. Finally, for Boltanski and Chiapello (2005), an analytical shift in focus followed, albeit very much in respect of the economic superstructure. Notably, they did not explicitly address identity as an analytical device. There are, however, more recent writers that do. Thomas and Linstead's (2002) *Losing the Plot? Middle Managers and Identity*; Barley and Kunda's (2004) *Gurus, Hired Guns, and Warm Bodies: Itinerant Experts in a Knowledge Economy*, and Standing's (2016) *The Precariat: The New Dangerous Class* for example, are all based on empirical research underscored by identity. In each, the theoretical rationale presented can be traced back to the works of Berger et al., Giddens, Sennett, and Boltanski and Chiapello.

Thomas and Linstead interview middle managers to garner an understanding of the ways in which they construct and maintain their identities such that they can secure and preserve a degree of legitimacy in the unpredictable environment of downsizing, delayering, and restructuring. The authors propose that middle management experience a kind of 'identity in flux' (Thomas and Linstead, 2002: 75). The authors further comment that identity must be understood as 'processual' and 'becoming' (rather than being). This supports the idea that identity in late modern times is precarious. Furthermore, and commenting of their subjects: 'Within each [case study] it can be seen that, due to a range of different factors, middle managers are feeling great uncertainty and insecurity over their role and status' (ibid. 78). Furthermore: '[S]everal factors contribute to [middle managers'] heightened feelings of identity instability. Insecurity, ambiguity, and confusion can be understood as a leitmotiv running through the text suggesting that these middle managers feel that they are 'losing the plot' in their organizations' (ibid. 87–8).

Conceptualised in conventional temporal terms, plot confers pre-determined narrative. A loss of plot, therefore, implies a loss of narrative. Invariably, this loss elicits a reaction, a reaction which is of significant benefit to the employer: 'As middle managers face the onslaught from the contemporary discourses of change and restructuring, there are pressures to overwork, work long hours and other forms of "presenteeism" to secure their role, purpose and future' (ibid. 89). In this sense, then, the managers' feelings of disembeddedness (characteristic of Boltanski and Chiapello's third spirit of capitalism) led to anxious attempts to resurrect a sense of identity and meaning.

Barley and Kunda (2004) focused on what they variously describe as 'itinerant' or 'contingent' workers. This classification includes part time, temporary, contracted, self-employed, and home-based labour. In this respect contingent labour is a *post*-bureaucratic phenomenon. Barley and Kunda's empirical data were drawn primarily from IT contractors. On the topic of their subjects' identity formation, they comment:

All learned to think of themselves as outsiders; what varied was how they made sense of their experience. Younger and inexperienced contractors usually felt the pain of estrangement. Many wanted to be accepted as legitimate members of the community ... 'I felt like an illegal alien,' Luke Pusher confided as he told us about his first contract ... The experience was so unpleasant that Luke soon took a permanent job to regain a sense of belonging.

(Barley and Kunda, 2004: 215)

Luke's reaction, it transpires, is unusual. As the authors further comment: 'By and large, contractors got what they wanted: they had distanced themselves from the politics, incompetence, and inequities of organizational life, which they had found so oppressive when they were employees' (ibid. 291).

However, over time, it seems these contractors discovered that the market was also a social institution. Contractors could not repeatedly locate jobs, close deals, and survive on the job unless they embedded themselves in networks of communication and obligation that were in their own way just as 'political' as the corporations they had left behind. Although they were no longer imprisoned in an 'iron cage of bureaucracy,' they found themselves suspended in webs of dependency that were no less constraining. Their newfound sense of agency and self-reliance did not mean freedom from social constraints or absence of reliance on others; it simply meant that the contractors' social dependencies had changed context (ibid.). There are direct parallels, then, to Boltanski and Chiapello's observation that although the concerns of bureaucratic imprisonment endemic to the second spirit of capitalism had been ameliorated, the 'new' spirit of capitalism is tainted instead by insecurity. The contractors' newfound freedom as agents of their own professional destiny and creativity (aspects of work lacking in the second spirit of capitalism) soon become a fundamental *concern* for the same subjects (in accordance with the ills of the third spirit of capitalism). Conceptualised another way, this is verification of a post-bureaucratic identity crisis.

More recently, still, Standing (2016) delineates a new class system appropriate for the neoliberal era. It is characterised by five layers: the elite, the salariat, the proficians, the core, and the precariat:

At the top is the 'elite,' consisting of a tiny number of absurdly rich global citizens lording it over the universe, with their billions of dollars, listed in Forbes as among the great and the good ... Below the elite comes the 'secretariat,' still in stable full-time employment, some hoping to move into the elite, the majority just enjoying the trappings of their kind, with their pensions, paid holidays and enterprise benefits, often subsidised by the state. The salariat is concentrated in large corporations, government agencies and public administration, including the civil service. Alongside the salariat, in more senses than one, is a (so far) smaller group of 'proficians.' This term combines the traditional ideas of 'professional' and 'technician' but covers those with bundles of skills that they can market, earning high incomes on contracts, as consultants or independent own-account workers. The proficians are the equivalent of the yeomen, knights and squires of the Middle Ages. They live with the expectation and desire to move around, without an impulse for long-term, full-time employment in a single enterprise. The 'standard employment relationship' is not for them. Below the proficans, in terms of income, is a shrinking 'core' of manual employees, the essence of the old 'working class.' The welfare states were built with them in mind, as were the systems of labour regulation. But the battalions of industrial labourers who formed the labour movements have shrivelled and lost their sense of social solidarity. Underneath those four groups, there is a growing 'precariat,' flanked by an army of unemployed and a detached group of socially ill misfits living off the dregs of society.

(Standing, 2016: 8–9)

And, notably from the point of the present thesis, Standing describes the precariat thus: 'Besides labour insecurity and insecure social income, those in the precariat lack a work-based *identity*' (ibid. 14, original emphasis). And he continues:

The precariat lives with anxiety—chronic insecurity associated not only with teetering on the edge, knowing that one mistake or one piece of bad luck could tip the balance between modest dignity and being a bag lady, but also a fear of losing what they possess even while feeling cheated by not having more. People are insecure in the mind and stressed, at the same time 'underemployed' and 'overemployed.' They are alienated from their labour and work, and are anomic, uncertain and desperate in their behaviour.

(Ibid. 23)

This chapter has demonstrated both how scholarly attitudes towards bureaucracy have come full circle over the course of the past century, and how two separate identity crises related to bureaucracy have manifested themselves. With a focus on delineating the context, history, and theoretical underpinnings of the latter of these two crises (the post-bureaucratic identity crisis), in the next chapter I turn attention to its ramifications. These include (1) a resurgence of trade guilds and professional associations; (2) a conscious rendering of self as reflexive project; (3) projectification, by which I mean the growing tendency for organizations, work, resources, and deliverables to be configured as [temporary] projects rather than [permanent] operations; (4) desecularization and—with it—the re-establishing of the place of worship as a primary organizational unit; and (5) the appeal—both within the workplace, and beyond—of the discourses and practices of New Age spirituality. Ultimately, and as we will see, these responses demonstrate a fundamental shift in our organizational geography.

# 3

# BEYOND POST-BUREAUCRACY

A brave new organizational geography?

In chapter 2, I systematically reviewed the evolution of the relevant scholarly discourse since the 1970s, focussing on four representative texts: Berger et al. (1973) *The Homeless Mind: Modernization and Consciousness*; Giddens (1991) *Modernity and Self-identity*; Sennett (1998) *The Corrosion of Character*; and Boltanski and Chiapello (2005) *The New Spirit of Capitalism*. A complete reversal of identity crisis was revealed; from one which emphasised the stifling intrusion of institutional stasis, to one in which the anxieties of freedom take centre stage. It was demonstrated that the concerns regarding suppressed creativity in bureaucratic organizations (configured as the bureaucratic identity crisis) have given way to concerns centred on the feelings of anxiety engendered by post-bureaucratic organization (configured as the post-bureaucratic identity crisis). As part of this phenomenon, a significant deficit of institutional belonging was identified.

In this chapter, I identify and explore several macrosociological responses to the post-bureaucratic identity crisis. These include: (1) a resurgence of trade guilds and professional associations; (2) a conscious rendering of self as reflexive project; (3) projectification, by which I mean the growing tendency for organizations, work, resources, and deliverables to be configured as (temporary) projects rather than (permanent) operations; (4) desecularization and—with it—the re-establishing of the place of worship as a primary organizational unit; and (5) the appeal—within the workplace and beyond—of the discourses and practices of New Age spirituality. In the chapter's summary discussion, it is argued that together these responses demonstrate a fundamental shift in our organizational geography; a shift which has important and far-reaching pedagogical implications, particularly in respect of business and management.

## Responses to the post-bureaucratic identity crisis

Bureaucracy mitigates uncertainty. As Styhre (2007: 56) notes, 'When firms are bureaucratized, uncertainty and conflicts are controlled by the imposed bureaucratic order, arranging the activities into specialist fields and clear domains of responsibility.' As this 'imposed' order is relaxed, and the supposedly 'post-bureaucratic' agenda begins to prevail, the resultant anomie (in the form of identity crisis) elicits several reactions. As I will go on to argue, each represents an attempt to re-establish the continuity, security, and linearity associated with bureaucracy. To some degree, at least, this is evidence that bureaucracy does not so much die in the post-bureaucratic order but simply manifests itself slightly differently (although, ultimately, whether or not you see it as new evidence of bureaucracy, or evidence of continuity, security and linearity is unimportant; the point is that there is a bureaucratic will or urge that refuses to die).

Taken collectively, responses to what I have conceptualised as the post-bureaucratic identity crisis can be identified as emerging within the discourse of which the aforementioned key texts form an integral part. Below, I identify these responses commenting in particular their validity, limitations and—ultimately—the specific manner in which they reveal a re-articulation of bureaucracy. In some respects at least, these 'responses' can be understood as a re-fashioning of bureaucracy.

### Response 1: Trade guilds and professional associations

Although guilds date back to antiquity (Brouwer, 2002: 95), they began to flourish in Europe during the Middle Ages. By the time of the Industrial Revolution, however, their numbers and influence started to diminish as they were regarded as a hindrance to free trade and, specifically, technological advance. According to Sennett (2008: 68, emphasis added): 'Medieval guilds did not tend to emphasise individual differences within a town's workshops; the guild's collective effort of control names *where* a cup or coat was made rather than *who* made it.' More significantly, Kieser (1989: 540) argues that 'Medieval guilds were not yet formal organizations but formed important predecessor institutions in the evolutionary process that led to the emergence of organizations.'

With the bureaucratic underpinnings of the modern organizational form now under threat (thereby engendering the sense of identity crisis I have already described) there is some evidence that work guilds are undergoing a revival. This is particularly interesting if we recognise, as Sennett does, that 'the guild network provided contact for workers *on the move* ... Elaborate ritual did the work of binding the guild members to one another' (ibid. 68, emphasis added). Is the impermanence and disembeddeness of post-bureaucratic society comparable to the itinerant work practices of medieval tradesmen? Is, therefore, the work guild an appropriate surrogate for the lost bureaucratic institution? In *The Death of the Guilds*, Krause (1996) argues that although today's white collar professional associations (such as those of the legal profession) are invariably much larger than the guilds of medieval Europe, 'their meetings have had some of the same bonding, ritual character' (Krause 1996, cited in Sennett, 2008: 246). Barley and Kunda (2004: 294), meanwhile, observe of their contingent subjects (by this, they include part time, temporary, contract, and self-employed workers) a concerted effort 'to forge a unique kind of professional practice point to incipient patterns of occupational lines.' In this way, where contingent workers might once have sought affiliation with an employer, they are now (self-)organizing along occupational lines. They suggest that an approach to overcoming the disembeddedness of the itinerant economy is to 'encourage professional associations ... to serve as employers-of-record' (ibid. 315). The reference to employer-of-record is significant in terms of a reaction to the post-bureaucratic identity crisis outlined. A specific example, in this case from The Professional Association of Contract Employees (PACE) helps illustrate this:

> PACE, an affinity group, operates ProTrac, which provides pass-through employer-of-record services for contractors. Contractors become ProTrac employees ... For a markup of 5 percent, ProTrac not only provides payroll and tax services, but also offers contractors access to a variety of benefits, including group health insurance and [retirement] plans. Although ProTrac is structured as a 'for profit' affinity group, existing professional associations and even professional unions could assume a similar role.
>
> *(Ibid.)*

ProTrac thereby constitutes an organizational umbrella. As an employer-of-record, the clerical element of the bureaucratic 'traditional' employer is resurrected. Equally, the provision of healthcare and retirement plans, for example, rekindles at least part of the stability and security characteristic of the bureaucratic configuration. Of course, the stability and security to which Barley and Kunda refer is represented primarily as functional rather than existential, but functional integration is a prerequisite for effective existential defences. In this vein, the term 'affinity group' hints at the subtler elements of ProTrac's apparent benefits. Ultimately, it is, perhaps, no surprise that guilds and guild-like collectives are experiencing a resurgence during this period of post-bureaucratic identity crisis. After all, Weber (1968 [1922]: 960) himself noted the 'guild-like' character of officialdom.

## Response 2: The self as reflexive project

Having examined in detail the Giddensian understanding of (self-)identity (specifically in relation to how his thesis can be seen in terms of identity *crisis*) in chapter 2; in this section the focus shifts to explore more closely Giddens' broader theorisation as a *response* to identity crisis. For Giddens (1991: 53, original emphasis), '[s]elf-identity is not a distinctive trait, or even a collection of traits, possessed by the individual. It is the self as *reflexively understood by the person in terms of his or her biography.*' Giddens suggests that in contemporary society the continuity, predictability, and security associated with pre-modern life has had to be substituted. Of course, at first glance at least, this appears to represent a response not to the post-bureaucratic identity crisis, but to the earlier bureaucratic identity crisis. However, as will be demonstrated, it provides important context for a broader argument. For Giddens this substitution is provided by the self in terms of establishing and maintaining a sense of personal history. This particular interpretation is justified in terms of an internalisation of scientific reflexivity. By way of clarification, Giddens continues:

> in the context of a post-traditional order, the self becomes a *reflexive project*. Transitions in individuals' lives have always demanded psychic reorganization ... But in some cultures, where things stayed more or less the same from generation to generation <u>on the level of the collectivity</u>, the changed identity was clearly staked out—as when an individual moved from adolescence to adulthood. In the settings of modernity, by contrast, the altered self has to be explored and constructed as part of a reflexive process of connecting personal and social change.
>
> *(Ibid. 32–3, original emphasis, underlining added)*

We are reminded here that the notion of the 'individual' is a modern construct. Ironically, perhaps, the external institutionalisation of reflexivity is mirrored internally at the level of the individual. Giddens identifies 'the lifespan as a distinctive and *enclosed* trajectory' (ibid. 146: emphasis added). He goes on to suggest that the individual is reified by 'turning his back' on external sources of meaning such as the life cycle of generations, the ties of kinship, other pre-existing relationships and the permanence of physical place. For Giddens, then, the *self as reflexive project* is understood as the means by which we are each compelled to 'narrativize' our own life so as to sustain some semblance of meaning and existential security in an uncertain world. In a world characterised by job security and stability, there is little need to engage in these narrativizing activities; in the post-bureaucratic world where individuals rarely stay put in one company for long the concept of career—as a narrativizing device—takes on a vital role.

In his seminal study, *Career as a Project of the Self and Labour Process Discipline*, Christopher Grey (1994) applied Giddens' theorisation as an analytical device to assist in understanding the concept of career. Etymologically, the term comes from the Latin word *carrera*, which means race. Significantly, the OED defines career as 'course or progress through life (or a distinct portion of life).' In the absence of institutional and bureaucratic stability, then, career becomes a surrogate (and valuable) form of self-continuity. For Grey (1994: 1467–8):

> Giddens (1991) is ... concerned to demonstrate that the condition of 'high modernity' is associated with new modes of self-identity in which the self is construed as a project ... Specifically, what is at issue is how career, as part of the project of the self, can constitute labour process discipline ... The project

of self-management links ... past, present and future though the vector of the self ... through a unified project of self-management, the self comes to bear upon itself in all settings and on all occasions. The project of self-management might be said to consist of the construction of our lives as ... institutions.

As with the emergence of professional associations, we see direct parallels in terms of compensatory measures as regards the lost artefact of the bureaucratic 'job for life.' Of course, the concept of career is synonymous with bureaucracy. However, where for Weber (1968 [1922]: 963) progress within a bureaucracy involved 'fixed career lines' for which ongoing tenure is assured and promotion expected, Grey's *career as a project of self* involves the navigation of a much more precarious employment relationship in which opportunities for promotion are fiercely competitive, and failure to achieve promotion invariably involves redundancy (at least in the case of chartered accountancy, the empirical focus of Grey's paper). Grey (1994: 1482) argues that 'self-management through career is a more productive and economical form of management control than disciplinary power, with its costs and unintended consequences, could ever be.' However, the ramifications of his findings extend beyond this Foucauldian application. An 'occupational' career implies, of course, that work will transcend multiple—most likely, numerable—employers over its course. And in describing this course as a 'career,' we can lend a sense of progressive purpose to its execution, even where this involves some degree of *post-hoc* rationalisation where apparently disjointed career changes are formally justified in the interests of maintaining some semblance of personal track. The growing importance of the curriculum vitae is also relevant in this regard. Miller (1993: 521), for example, argues that the curriculum vitae is 'a form of autobiographical practice ... centrally involved with the construction and presentation of a self in a particular occupational context.' It might legitimately be argued that an 'occupational career' reflected in the discourse of a curriculum vitae thus represents an attempt on the part of the employee to *re*institutionalise life, at least in part. This argument is lent further credence if we juxtapose it with the observation made by Weigert and Hastings (1977: 1173, 1174) that organizations, at least in the 1970s, served an 'archival function' in the sense that they were receptacles or 'biographical museums' for shared memories. Ultimately, the pair suggested that 'bureaucracies perdure beyond the time measured by a member's biography. Business corporations, sports teams, symphony orchestras, armies, even entire societies survive members' biographies and remain somehow the same' (Weigert and Hastings 1977: 1175–6).

Of course, at the time of Weigert and Hasting's publication, the concerns associated with what we are describing as the post-bureaucratic identity crisis had yet to unfold. Where once organizational members were able to secure a discernible sense of identity from their employer, this is less commonplace today; hence the need to institutionalise the concept of career, a career which invariably transcends multiple employers over its course. It is 'the existence of a career structure with promotions' which has become significant 'whilst providing simultaneously a vehicle or vessel for those aspirations' (Grey, 1994: 1482). The metaphor of a 'vehicle or vessel' is striking because, like institution or bureaucracy, it implies a protective enclosure. However, where the traditional bureaucracy was relatively stable, Grey's concept of the vehicle or vessel is, by definition, in flux. Furthermore, where investment in organizational belonging was a distinctly social (or sociable) affair in bureaucratic times, investment in one's own narrative by way of career is less so. For Clegg (2011: 220), the post-bureaucratic career is illustrated most notably by the activities of the project manager:

> What is distinctive about contemporary post-bureaucracy is that the major mechanism of the career has undergone a substantial change. The typical bureaucratic career was an enclosed phenomenon, classically contained within one organization. Post-bureaucracy differs significantly on this dimension. The inherent political dynamics of post-bureaucratic organizations are condensed and concentrated on the figure of the project manager, circulating from project to project, alliance to alliance, and network to network, torn between the *habitus* of their professional background and the reporting needs of the situation in which they are currently located.

It is to the concept of projectification that we now turn.

## *Response 3: Projectification*

Following its controversial beginnings in the Manhatten Project, project management has become an integral component of the business and management canon. The Project Management Institute defines a project as 'a temporary endeavour undertaken to create a unique product, service or result' (https://www.pmi.org/about/learn-about-pmi/what-is-project-management). Of course, definitions such as this hint at a more ancient lineage. Certainly, there is no reason why the construction of the Egyptian pyramids, for example, should not—retrospectively, at least—be conceptualised as a project (and it is interesting to note that for many—though not all—commentators, bureaucracy underpinned ancient Egypt). Indeed, for Jensen (2012: 9), 'People have always had projects. Caesar had projects, Napoleon had projects. Columbus also had a project. The difference is that today everyone speaks about their projects. They speak of everything they do as projects.' He continues: 'What is really at issue [today] is a transition in principles of organization and forms of social intercourse, which makes living in the project society an altogether different experience.' Today, projects and project management have become pervasive. This contemporary surge is 'typically explained by reference to the increasing recognition of "the project" as a versatile, flexible and predictable form of work organization' (Hodgson and Cicmil, 2006: 113), as well as its apparent suitability for service-sector work when compared to traditional operations-based work (see, for example, Standing 2016: 38). More generally, the project is seen both as precursor and agent of what has become known as the knowledge economy and hence for many, projects are regarded as the all-encompassing institutional currency of 'the organization of the future' (ibid.). Indeed, so influential is this new type of work, Jensen (2012) goes so far to refer to this as epoch-defining, that is *homo projectus*.

Building on recent critical interpretations of project management, I explore the typically unseen (and unanticipated) implications of this transition towards a culture of business in which projects have become normalised. Project work is another form of what Barley and Kunda (2004: 9) have described as contingent labour: 'an array of short-term arrangements including part-time work, temporary employment, self-employment, contracting, outsourcing, and home-based work.' To this end, it seems the alleged instrumental advantages of project-based work have come at a significant cost to the individual since such contingent employment is impermanent, insecure, stress-inducing and fails to afford participants a sense of organizational identity. Aside from the social psychological (not to mention ethical) ramifications of this phenomenon, a more nuanced understanding of the actualities of project work might go some way to explaining why despite the expansive academic and practitioner literatures geared towards project management models, methodologies, and specialist software, so many projects fail (Hodgson and Cicmil, 2006); that is they do not actually meet scheduling, cost and/or quality criteria.

At first glance, at least, most definitions of 'project' appear rather prosaic. There are, however, several characteristics that transcend various definitions that are acutely relevant to our broader thesis. A selection of definitions follows (emphases added):

'A *temporary endeavour* undertaken to create a *unique* product, service or result'
*(Project Management Institute, www.pmi.org/about/learn-about-pmi/what-is-project-management)*

'*Unique, transient endeavours* undertaken to achieve a desired outcome'
*(Association of Project Management, www.apm.org.uk/resources/what-is-project-management)*

'A *temporary organization* that is needed to produce a *unique* and predefined outcome or result at a given time using predetermined resources'
*(Office of Government Commerce, 2005)*

'A project is a *unique* set of coordinated activities, with a *definite starting and finishing point*, undertaken by an individual or organization to meet specific objectives within defined schedule, cost and performance parameters.'
*(British Standard 6079–1: 2)*

The common themes gleaned reveal an underlying temporality, a venture into the unknown, transience and impermanence. In turn, these all hint at a sense of existential uncertainty. It should come as no surprise, then, that project management is in crisis:

> In the closing decade of the 20th century, project management was challenged more seriously than in any previous period. Despite the levels of research founded on the presumptions of instrumental rationality in decision-making and control, it is increasingly apparent that accepting and applying such orthodoxy does not eliminate project failures, nor does it guarantee project success.
> 
> *(Hodgson and Cicmil, 2006: 114)*

I here suggest that this is part of a broader neoliberal crisis. The ramifications of projectification have been felt not just in the academic literature, but in the populist management press too. In 2011, recruitor.com published a piece on contingent labour. They wrote:

> Ah, contingent labor: a word beloved almost as much as human capital or incentivize … In 2011, the joys of temp labor have finally been brought to the professional masses. So much so that we all seem to be contingent laborers, strangers passing each other in a corporate night(mare). It's not that there is no care for the collective spirit of the employees that make up a company, it's that at most companies there just is no collective spirit. We don't owe anything to each other anymore, right?
> 
> *(www.recruitor.com)*

For Jensen (2012: 70–2):

> Paradoxically, the projectual human may experience the absence of structure as a repetitive, monotonous humdrum … Singles who keep throwing themselves into new love projects after every wrecked attempt a starting a relationship may begin to experience this as a repetition intruding upon their lives as a condition rather than the individual having made a conscious choice of living life without a steady relationship. [...] My current boyfriend is … The fact that you cannot be sure of anything is the only thing you can be sure of.

In this way, project society *normalises* uncertainty, transience, and passage. Projects become a form of self-surveillance:

> Insecurity is engrafted into the general devolution of control to self-control in the project society. Whereas the disciplinarian society used to monitor people from a central point, e.g. a watch tower, surveillance is no longer necessary to the same extent. Why? Because it is in the individual's own interest to do things as well as possible with the aim of getting new projects. The only thing that is to be controlled in the project society is self-control.
> 
> *(Ibid. 84–5)*

So, whereas Grey suggested that it is career that constitutes the new form of (self-surveillance), for Jensen it is projects. However, there is no contradiction here: *both* interpretations are valid since career is itself a project of sorts. The perennial concerns of surveillance—originally cast as totalitarian motifs (think *Brave New World*), are now recapitulated in the post-totalitarian world. It takes Foucauldian analytics to the next level! This, as we will see in chapter 5, is all too often overlooked in dystopian fiction.

What, then, are the broader ramifications of projectification? What we have seen is the emergence of *coworking* among project workers: 'Coworking is a style of work which involves a shared working environment, sometimes an office, yet independent activity. Unlike in a typical office environment, those coworking are usually not employed by the same organization' (1$^{st}$ Global Coworking Survey).

Coworking is the social gathering of a group of people, who are still working independently, but who—ostensibly, at least—share values, and who are interested in the synergy that can happen from working with people in the same space. For some, this resonates with Maffesoli's work:

> [W]e seem to be facing a veritable eruption of an instinctive kind, a sort of *vis a tergo*, causing people to gather together for almost any reason; the only important thing being, in the final analysis, that all should bathe in affectual ambience ... a new account of the social is being sketched out that puts its entire emphasis on fusion without asking why it is happening.
> (*Maffesoli 1991: 10–11*)

I am currently engaged in research which seeks to help resurrect Durkheim's much neglected concept of collective effervescence. There is still work to do, but my provisional findings suggest that a contemporary application of both Durkheim and Maffesoli reveals an existential need for togetherness and bureaucratic routine and discipline. In short, I get the feeling that for many of us, our experience of project work has elicited a nostalgia for the certainty, permanence, security, and fellowship of traditional bureaucracy. It is perhaps unsurprising, then, that for Clegg (2011; 220), project management is the 'core of politics in post bureaucracy.'

## *Response 4: Desecularization*

In his broader musings in respect of self-identity, Giddens predicted that participation in other non-economic (communal) organization forms—specifically religion—would experience a revival: 'for reasons that are to do precisely with the connections between modernity and doubt, religion not only refuses to disappear but undergoes a resurgence' (Giddens 1991: 195). It is to the phenomenon of *de*-secularization, then, that we now turn.

It wasn't until 1999 when Peter Berger published his short, edited volume (*The Desecularization of the World*), that the word 'desecularization' formally entered the scholarly canon. As such, terminologically at least, the trend is a relatively recent one. In the short time since, however, the term (and related ones, such as 'postsecular') has been fiercely debated. Noticeably, Berger does not define 'desecularization.' It is reasonable, however, to deduce that it describes the reverse of secularization. But the concept of secularization itself represents contested conceptual terrain. Stark and Bainbridge (1985), for example, have argued that secularisation is a self-limiting phenomenon, precisely because science and other naturalistic systems of thought will never be able to adequately satisfy the human needs that religion addresses. In this sense, secularization is itself presumed to be a recurring or cyclical process. Of course, the process of desecularization isn't mentioned here explicitly; rather it is implied. Despite this, we might usefully represent this process metaphorically in terms of a pendulum periodically swinging back and forth between secularization and desecularization. The two phenomena are intrinsically linked. More recently, McLennan (2010) in 'The Postsecular Turn' has argued that it is most appropriate to regard

> postsecular reflexive enquiries as *intra*-secularist rather than anti-secularist; that is to say, they form part of the intellectual process that has been dubbed the 'secularization of secularism' itself, rather than straightforwardly extending the revival of religion into the heartlands of Western theory.
> 
> *(McLennan 2010: 4)*

In this vein, McLennan suggests of postsecular endeavours: 'There is a bitter irony: secularism requires and even produces "religion" as its own discourse and political condition of existence' (ibid. 5). It is on this understanding of desecularization (conceptualised as a *response* to the broader triumphs of secularism) that I examine the resurgence of religion.

As Dawson (2006: 113) notes, 'Giddens spends little time directly addressing religion in his work but he is not surprised that it has survived as an important social institution well into the modern era.' In this sense, Giddens provides an appropriate rejoinder to the theme of desecularization. Towards the end of his seminal text, Giddens comments thus:

> We see all around us the creation of new forms of religious sensibility and spiritual endeavour. The reasons for this concern quite fundamental features of late modernity. What was due to become a social and physical universe subject to increasingly certain knowledge and control instead creates a system in which areas of relative security interlace with radical doubt and with disquieting scenarios of risk.
>
> *(Giddens, 1991: 207)*

Giddens concedes that the reflexive project of the self is not entirely a solitary endeavour since the resurgence of religion presumably involves some degree of social intercourse. Following Giddens, Sennett identifies something interesting and unexpected in respect of the unemployed subjects in his study. In response to the contemporary, flexible, and discontinuous tendency of the dispossessed form of capitalism:

> the one community engagement the men [Sennett's precariously employed subjects] do pursue with ever greater vigor, is membership in and stewardship of their local churches. In [the United States], fundamentalist and evangelical forms of Christianity have been sharply on the rise.
>
> *(Sennett, 1998: 130)*

This is clearly significant. A few years after the publication of Sennett's text, in *Bait and Switch*, Ehrenreich (2005) went undercover as an investigative journalist to explore the lives of out-of-work white collar 'workers.' Like Sennett, and Giddens before him, Ehrenreich discovers an interesting relationship between (job) insecurity and religious participation. She comments:

> This was not my first venture into the extensive territory where Christianity, so called, overlaps with the business culture. As it happens, that area of overlap has been expanding rapidly in recent years, to include work-based ministries; employee prayer groups, some at major companies like Coca-Cola and Intel; networks of Christian businesspeople and other community leaders; and a growing number of overtly Christian businesses ... According to the New York Times, there were fifty coalitions of workplace ministries in 1990; today there are thousands. Job seekers are likely to encounter the Christian business culture at events like the Norcross Fellowship Lunches—ostensibly business meetings that turn out to be worship services. Or they might be drawn to a church-based meeting, advertised as a networking event for the unemployed, that is in fact an occasion for proselytizing.
>
> *(Ehrenreich, 2005: 131–2)*

The interpretation invited here suggests that these Christian groups are seeking to attract new recruits by deception. In part this may be true but in stressing this particular interpretation Ehrenreich apparently overlooks data imparted earlier in her ethnography:

> [For Ron, a representative of a job agency Ehrenreich visits] the secret ... is 'to make the search process like going into the office, whether that means going to the library, to a friend's house, or to our office'. Furthermore, you have to have someone to 'keep you accountable', meaning a surrogate boss figure. 'We're used to having bosses, being responsive to someone, so you've got to create the same dynamic.'
>
> *(Ibid. 89)*

Ron's assessment of the situation is interesting: job seekers are predisposed to attend these religious seminars because they want to feel the protective cloak of an organizational form which they are used to; a form of attire with which they are familiar. In this interpretation, the religious guise of the meetings is largely incidental. And this is the interpretation of Ehrenreich's data that I prioritise: it is about *bureaucracy*. Indeed, it is also reinforced by another of Ehrenreich's subjects, Lisa, encountered at another church 'networking' meeting:

> I believe that Jesus is my Lord and Savior. My journey to this place of peace and joy was brought about through trials and tribulation. I found myself at the door of the Career Ministry as a seeker and often wondered what I was seeking for—I came looking for a job and found life! … I am a Human Resources professional with 11+ years of experience in the service, retail and hospitality industries.
>
> *(Ibid. 134)*

Evaluation of this statement yields two important insights. First, the religious preamble is suffixed with the 'real' reason Lisa is present—she's looking for a job. The religious framing of the meeting means she is compelled, however, to hone her conduct accordingly. Second, Lisa describes her Christian experiences as premised on the notion of a journey (of 'trials and tribulation'); her religion is thus internalised as part of her career in the self-reflexive terms delineated in Grey's (1994) thesis. In that same paper, Grey explores the moulding of biographical continuity undertaken by university students to procure a desirable graduate appointment in an accounting firm (such as justifying the selection of particular degree programmes that elicit 'good career options' and the accumulation of extra-curricular activities which demonstrate 'responsibility'). Ehrenreich lends voice to a comparable tactic, only here the biographical continuity is accorded to the church. In reflecting on Lisa's experience, among others, Ehrenreich writes:

> The old narrative was 'I worked hard and therefore succeeded' or sometimes 'I screwed up and therefore failed'. But a life of only intermittently rewarded effort—working hard only to be laid off, and then repeating the process until aging forecloses decent job offers—requires more strenuous forms of explanation. Either you look for the institutional forces shaping your life, or you attribute the unpredictable ups and downs of your career to an infinitely powerful, endlessly detail-oriented God.
>
> *(Ibid. 142)*

In this sense, then, the Church *normalises* (in much the same way as Sennett describes the requirement bestowed upon us that 'instability is meant to be normal'), the post-bureaucratic flexible work patterns that characterise neoliberalism. By way of further illustration, Ehrenreich (ibid. 146) recounts a conversation with another of her subjects:

> "So where will you be working", I ask.
> "At my old place, where I got laid off a year ago".

"How do you feel about going back there? I mean after they laid you off".
"Oh, no problem". He smiles beatifically. "They didn't need so many people then, and now they do".

'So this,' Ehrenreich concludes,

> is the new ideal Christianized, 'just in time', white-collar employee—disposable when temporarily unneeded and always willing to return with a smile, no matter what hardships have been endured in the off periods. Perhaps one of the functions of the evangelical revival sweeping America is to reconcile people to an increasingly unreliable work world: you take what you can get, and praise the Lord for sending it along.
>
> *(Ibid.)*

Davie (1994: 200) theorises along similar lines:

> [O]ne way of enduring in a fragmented and rapidly changing context (global or otherwise) is to embrace an all-encompassing world view and to live—often in an admirably disciplined way—within this ... Taken to extremes this tendency results in a series of competing fundamentalisms, a feature of late capitalist development, though one that bewilders many of its commentators. Such fundamentalisms take a variety of forms: some religious, both Christian and non-Christian, and some secular, including within the latter category—to give but two examples—certain types of feminism or radical expressions of regional identity.

The discipline, then, of *organized* religious participation constitutes a compensatory means of salving the disembeddedness of late capitalism. In times of post-bureaucratic identity crisis, the 'discipline' once associated with the bureaucratic organizational model finds in religious participation an alternative conduit for its expression. This is further evidenced by Dawson (2006: 107): '[r]eligions ... are organizations that provide general compensators based on belief in the supernatural.' Dawson is frustratingly vague when it comes to defining precisely what he means by compensation, other than to say that 'religions deal in the most general of compensators: ultimate relief from suffering' (ibid.). Provisionally, however, this broad remit suggests that we can find in religion a source of recompense for the post-bureaucratic identity crisis.

Analytically, *de*secularization—like secularization—represents contested terrain. However, as we have seen, there are empirical glimpses of religious revivalism in the works of Giddens, Sennett, Ehrenreich, and Davie. From these works we can see that there is undeniably a link between the post-bureaucratic identity crisis and religious resurgence. However, the one part of the world which remains fervently secular—even for Berger (1999)—is Western Europe. But although traditional patterns of religious behaviour have not (yet?) undergone a resurgence in Western

Europe, there are increasing numbers of Western Europeans (and others in the developed world) interested in what is loosely described as New Age spirituality, and it is to this phenomenon we now turn.

## Response 5: 'New Age' spirituality

The term 'New Age'—together with similar formulations such as 'new times,' 'new era,' or 'new world'—is typically used to convey the idea that a significantly better way of life is dawning (Heelas, 1996: 15) For Sutcliffe (2003: 3), although a genealogy for the 'New Age' can be traced to the late 1930s, it is often conflated with the relatively recent concept of 'mind, body and spirit.' Both Heelas (ibid.) and Sutcliffe (ibid.) recognise that the term is controversial, and used both constructively and derogatorily by both referents and non-referents. Mindful of this, I here deploy the term primarily to mean contemporary; as in contemporary spirituality. This allows me to distinguish between the spirituality of traditional religion on the one hand and the spirituality that has—apparently—evolved from non-institutional contexts in the latter part of the twentieth century on the other. I further acknowledge, however, that the label 'New Age' resonates with an outlook, approach to, or interpretation of, life characterised by both *esotericism* (Hanegraaff, 1998) and *spiritual heterogeneity* (Holloway, 2000). It is also understood to be both *post-Christian* (Houtman and Aupers, 2007) and, perhaps most notably, underscored by a unique *lingua franca* which places an emphasis on the human (and planetary) condition and how it can be transformed (Heelas, 1996: 2).

In organization and management studies, while scholars rarely venture into the realm of the study of traditional religion (exceptions include Casey, 1995; Höpfl, 2000; and McGrath, 2005, 2007), research relating to spirituality—and especially *workplace* spirituality—is more commonplace. A brief overview of this literature yields at least four distinct areas of research; spirituality and organizational effectiveness (Dehler and Welsh, 1994; Garcia-Zamor, 2003); 'Spiritual Management Development' (Frost and Egri, 1994; Fairholm, 1996); critical interpretations of spirituality in organizations (Bell and Taylor, 2004; Dent et al., 2005; Izak, 2010); and the sociology of workplace spirituality (Casey, 2002). It is this final category that is of most relevance to our present thesis. The most interesting coverage in this respect is to be found tucked away in the final chapter of Casey's (2002) *Critical Analysis of Organizations*. In that chapter ('After postmodernism'), Casey discusses the ways in which both selves and organizations have responded to postmodernism, and, as we have seen, the identity crisis it—or, in our case, post-bureaucracy—has spawned. Casey frames this response in terms of workplace spirituality: 'The emergence of current forms of spirituality at work finds expression among individual employees as well as in deliberate corporate sponsorship and encouragement of spiritual sensitivities' (ibid. 151). Furthermore, 'in addition to bringing one's mind and body to work … one is now permitted, if not required, in a growing number of organizations, to bring heart and soul as well' (ibid. 150). Most interestingly, however:

Encouraging soulful, mystical equanimity as a cultural value both appeals to dispirited, overworked and potentially downshifting employees, and endeavours to rekindle their devotion and service to their work and organization in increasingly precarious global conditions. The potential freedoms offered by managed desecularization to jaded employees whose professional identity and sources of motivation and value in their work performance have been eroded or truncated by corporate instrumental saturation are, management intends, harnessed and utilized by the corporation.

*(Ibid. 178)*

For Casey, then, workplace spirituality emerged as an interest both at the level of the individual employee (as a means of recompense for the identity stripped as part of the conditions endemic to late modernity) and engineered from above (as a means of control). However, Casey herself acknowledges that this approach to research focuses on what she terms 'unchurched' spiritualities (ibid. 176). Given that her analytical focus is on workplaces, which are both practically and organizationally distinct from churches, this is to be expected. However, and in anticipation of the pan-organizational association model developed later in the chapter, I regard 'churched' spiritualities (in the sense that spirituality, like religion, is succumbing to organizing tendencies) as equally relevant. This is also something I go on to explore in more detail in chapter 6, reflecting on my own experience at the Findhorn Foundation.

Moving beyond the spirituality literature spawned specifically by scholars of management and organization, Heelas underpins his work with the concept of *self*. Indeed, while at the outset he acknowledges the heterogeneity of the New Age movement (he illustrates this by contrasting images of New Age travellers and New Age yuppies), he comments that:

Beneath much of this heterogeneity, there is a remarkable constancy. Again and again, turning from practice to practice, from publication to publication, indeed from country to country, one encounters the same (or very similar) *lingua franca* to do with the human (and planetary) condition and how it can be transformed ... This is the language of what shall henceforth be called 'self-spirituality.'

*(Heelas 1996: 2)*

This emphasis on 'self' pervades the literature on spirituality. Heelas himself prefaces Chapter 1 with two quotations: 'It all starts with self' [Shirley MacLaine] and 'My intention for your experience of religion is that it becomes a religion of the self' [Ron Smothermon]. Heelas apparently echoes the rendering of identity by Giddens, and so it makes no sense to speak of spirituality without inserting the 'self-' prefix; spirituality is fundamentally about the conceptualization of self. However, unlike 'self-identity' (in which the self is conceptualized as a reflexive project), Heelas goes one step further: 'New Agers make the monistic assumption that the Self itself is *sacred*' (ibid., emphasis added); hence the uppercase 'S' in 'Self-.' The etymological links between the two authors hint at a more fundamental relationship. As Dawson (2006: 112) implies, there is considerable continuity with the Giddensian concept of the self as reflective project since 'privatised spirituality reflects the inward turn to find the guiding thread of [our] lives.'

Despite these definitions of spirituality centred on the concept of 'self,' evidence of the post-bureaucratic identity crisis can be found in the work of Heelas. Notably, the second section of his book is dedicated to understanding the 'Appeal' of the New Age movement. This section itself is broken down into two chapters, the first of these 'Chapter 5: Uncertainties of modernity' is crucial to our thesis. Heelas draws an interesting distinction between the 'iron cage' (the Weberian metaphor) and the 'crumbling cage' (a metaphor he himself sources from Gehlen, 1980) hence lending further support to the model presented in the previous chapter which described and sought to account for the chronological shift between the identity concerns of modernity (the bureaucratic identity crisis) and the identity concerns of late modernity (the post-bureaucratic identity crisis). While the familiar concerns of the metaphorical 'iron cage' underpin the bureaucratic identity crisis, the concerns of the 'crumbling cage' underpin the post-bureaucratic identity crisis.

> Those populating the campuses during the 1960s had (by and large) been educated in terms of liberal, humanistic values. And this goes a long way in explaining why so many (relatively speaking) came to perceive the mainstream as 'straight' and oppressive. Accordingly, numbers dropped out, rejecting the restrictive certainties of the conventional life world for the opportunities of the counter-culture. But there ... many found the uncertainties of life beyond structure too much to bear. And this explains why some turned to the 'secondary institutions'—including 'mystical religions'—which were springing up within the counter culture, and which were providing better-informed and organized ways for providing identities.
>
> *(Ibid. 139–40)*

There are clear comparisons to be made here to Boltanski and Chiapello's historical rendering of the third (or 'new') Spirit of Capitalism (which emerged in response to the supposedly staid and predictable bureaucratic life that characterised mainstream society in the 1960s). However, for Heelas, 'secondary institutions' have become brokers of identity. This is especially important. Furthermore:

> If ... '[m]an's [*sic*] fundamental constitution is such that, just about inevitably, he will once more construct institutions to provide an ordered reality for himself,' then it makes absolute sense to understand the development of the New Age accordingly. In other words, it can be argued that New Age 'secondary institutions' have been developed, and have appealed because they provide identity provisions for those who have been set adrift in the counter-culture.
>
> *(Ibid. 143–4)*

There is an irony here, especially if we recognise the authority of Boltanski and Chiapello: the progenitors of today's New Agers were the very individuals who gave rise to the post-bureaucratic identity crisis in the first place. There is a frustrating ambiguity to the position Heelas adopts, since he uses the concept of *self-spirituality* throughout his text, but here acknowledges the significance of spiritual (or New Age) *institutions* as a compensatory device for the lost protective casing of bureaucratic organization forms. The unresolved tension is that Heelas claims both that (self) spirituality is (organized) religion's *Other*, and that New Age secondary *institutions* have evolved for the reasons he describes. He does not explore the possibility, for example, that New Age spirituality may be undergoing a cultural shift. Since his publication, the situation remains much the same. Casey, as we have already seen, focused on 'unchurched' spiritualities and the small amount of extant research that does exist for the Findhorn Foundation, despite acknowledging the fundamental significance of institutionalised spiritualities, struggles to see beyond the prevalent discourse of spirituality which is conceptualized as a self-oriented/ inward-looking/individualized/personalized phenomenon.

Carrette and King (2005) make similar observations in their highly provocative *Spirituality Sells: The Silent Takeover of Religion*. The authors argue that following the 'erosion of traditional community allegiances, "spirituality" has become a new cultural addiction and a claimed panacea for the angst of modern living' (ibid. 1). However, although a panacea for the 'erosion of traditional community allegiances,' like Heelas and Casey before them, Carrette and King see spirituality in fundamentally individualist terms. Indeed, the pair defines spirituality as the *privatisation* of religion. The term 'privatisation' is significant, not just by means of emphasising the personal over the communal, but it resonates too with the free market. Indeed, it is this aspect of spirituality—as a discernible commodification underwritten by the profit motive—that constitutes the focus of their text. Interestingly, however, toward the end of their book, they impart the following observation: 'In an attempt to resist the privatization of spirituality ... we seek to support alternative models of "spirituality" that pay attention to ... *community*' (Carrette and King, 2005: 171–2, emphasis added).

In this way, where Heelas and Casey both admit to the significance (at least in terms of research potential) of exploring post-privatised spirituality, Carrette and King are actively seeking to engender this sort of configuration. However—and again like both Heelas and Casey—they do not explore this avenue either empirically or theoretically.

Finally, the small body of literature that has explicitly focused on spiritual *institutions* themselves reinforces the individualistic bias seen in Casey, Heelas, and Carrette and King. For van Otterloo, for example, who studied several 'New Age centres' in The Netherlands, '[t]he varied and highly flexible organizational forms the Centres have taken appears to be well suited to the transfer and elaboration of the knowledge and methods aiming at *selfspirituality*' (van Otterloo, 1999: 199, emphasis added). Of course 'self' is a social construct as Giddens has demonstrated, but self in the discourse of spirituality and even within these spiritual *communities* is reified, as Kapoor's study of Auroville in India demonstrates:

> One of the obvious contradictions that one comes across in Auroville is the fact that the community is inspired by the ideals of human unity, the highest values and the quest for perfection to go beyond the human to the 'supernatural' state, yet the residents of Auroville are characterised by extreme individualism.
> 
> *(Kapoor, 2007: 637)*

Unfortunately, although Kapoor identifies the tension between community and a discourse characterised by 'extreme individualism' she does not explore it further. Most recently, Wood's (2008) study of The Esalen Institute in California—perhaps unsurprisingly—reveals a similar self-orientation: 'Approximately 20 per cent of Americans today resist traditional religious classification and practice a *personalised*, eclectic faith. California's Esalen Institute reflects this development' (Wood, 2008: 453, emphasis added).

Predictably, the same tendency is reported of the Findhorn Foundation, a New Age community in Scotland. Sutcliffe (1995, 2000, 2003) has published several pieces based on his week-long ethnographic experience at Findhorn in 1995. In terms of his analysis, Sutcliffe corroborates the extant theories of spirituality as a self-oriented form of religiosity. Although Findhorn's community status suggests otherwise, for Sutcliffe (2000: 228, emphasis added) 'the authority of the group ... remains contingent upon, and ultimately secondary to, that of its individual constituents. The group *merely* serves to gather, affirm, and sooner or later disseminate these individuals.'

In sum, then, the extant research in respect of New Age spirituality can be interpreted as a response to the post-bureaucratic identity crisis in a manner comparable to Giddensian self-identity, i.e. *self-spirituality*. So, for Casey the focus is on what she refers to as *unchurched* spirituality, for Heelas on *self-* spirituality, for Carette and King as *privatised* spirituality, Kapoor as *extreme individualism*, for van Otterloo as *selfspirituality*, for Wood as *personalised faith*, and for Sutcliffe spirituality is about *the authority of the self*. However, it can also be understood in a very different sense. While these authors imply that spirituality is organized religion's individualised/privatised Other, in the wake of the post-bureaucratic identity crisis what we are seeing is that a sense of organization—or community establishment—is beginning to emerge in the discourses of spirituality too An alternative interpretation to the '*self*-spirituality' default therefore suggests that the group is very much the focus, even if the lingua franca of New Age spirituality implies otherwise (a classic case, if you like, of language misconstructing the 'reality' we perceive). So, what some of these authors hint at—that there is a pervasive group-based logic that apparently defies individualistic assumptions about spirituality—I unpack in more detail. Indeed, during my own extensive ethnographic experience at the Findhorn Foundation (fifteen years after Sutcliffe's), it was precisely the group and organizational dynamics that constituted the appeal of spirituality, *not* the self. I reflect upon this research in detail in chapter 6. Suffice it to say, what we are witnessing is shifting organizational landscapes.

## Shifting organizational landscapes

For Clegg (2011: 213), '[N]ew organizational forms are many but united by one thing—they are all conceived in opposition to the classic model of bureaucracy.' A cursory glance at the chapter on structure in any management or organizational behaviour textbook will amply demonstrate this. However, though certainly true when looked at in isolation, when we take a step back and observe organizations collectively, a sense of bureaucracy once again begins to emerge as part of the broader organizational landscape. Before elaborating on this model, let us consider Kallinikos's assessment at the dawn of the 21st century:

> [T]here is ... evidence to suggest that current socio-cultural and technological changes converge to the re-drawing of the prevailing boundaries of the *private* and *public world*, work from leisure, family and community. Under these conditions, the very forms by which individuals have traditionally been tied to social institutions are bound to change. New forms of individual involvement in organizations (e.g. flexible and temporary employment) develop to accommodate the shifts in social institutions, values and lifestyles... At the same time information and communication technologies become an important agent of organizational and occupational change. The precise ways, though, by which organization forms are connected to these developments remain a contested terrain. Neither the organizational forms nor the mechanisms that bring them about are sufficiently studied or clear. The appreciation of the impact of these changes on the prevailing forms of organization would seem to require the serious reconsideration of the social institution of bureaucracy in ways that step beyond stereotyped images of it.
>
> *(Kallinikos, 2004: 15)*

Sixteen years have passed since Kallinikos penned these words but to the best of my knowledge, until now, his call for clarification has gone unaddressed. Bureaucracy is (re)manifesting itself in new pan-organizational forms. Bureaucracy thus echoes the Deleuzeian motif of *Difference and Repetition*. It is repeating itself, but in a subtly altered guise. It is the institutional equivalent of Philip Glass's *Metamorphosis*. For Glass, his musical composition retains a signature rhythm but is evolving all the time. So, in our case, several responses to the anxiety experienced as a result of the post-bureaucratic identity crisis have thus been identified. Notably in each of the responses identified we can see how what I am tentatively describing as pan-organizational structure (or, more accurately, pan-organizational association) begins to more accurately reflect the contemporary organizational landscape (see Figure 3.1).

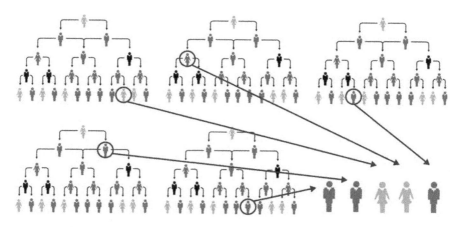

FIGURE 3.1 Pan-organizational association

In respect of the *resurgence of guilds and professional associations*, employees, who previously identified with their employer as part of a conventional organization structure, are increasingly identifying with guild-type professional associations, which in effect transcend multiple organizations. In this way, a sense of belonging or collective is achieved by grassroots organizing along occupational rather than employer lines.

In respect of the *self as reflexive project*, the attempt on the part of the individual to make sense of her career as a logical progression between organizational identity spaces, draws across multiple hierarchies.

In the case of *projectification*, an almost identical shift is noted in respect of the establishment of project teams, most of which are constituted of individuals drawn from multiple other organizations. Notably, the project teams themselves become sources of organizational identity. This, of course, enables us to interpret afresh Tuckman and Jensen's (1977) suggestion that group disformation (upon the completion of the task or project; sometimes referred to as the 'mourning' stage) is inevitably anxiety-inducing. Interestingly, Raisenen and Linde (2004: 117, as cited in Styhre, 2007: 89–90), suggest that '"In multi-project organizations today, projects are no longer the exceptional, unique and innovative work form of a new world order. Instead, project management is being subjected to the forces of organization rationalisation, resulting in a bureaucratization of projectified activities".' This lends further credence to the validity of the pan-organizational association model in respect of projects and projectification. Interestingly, Jensen (2012: 64–5, original emphasis) notes that:

> [s]ecurity and repetition are intimately connected in the experience of time: tomorrow will be more or less the same. Providing for one's own safety is

therefore also a matter of making sure that things remain the same ... [But now] repetition is no longer possible. When activities unfold as projects, they unfold as something that does not repeat itself.

Now, this is interesting. Since projects are, by definition, unique (and so by implication security and repetition become alien concepts), it is through a pan-organizational association that project workers seek out a sense of repetition and, by association, security.

In the case of *desecularization*, churches are apparently helping to assuage the anxiety caused by the 'inbetweeness' of different work organizations and constitute a proxy organization themselves. Leaving to one side the theological ramifications, desecularization plainly demonstrates a desire to rekindle a sense of organizational participation and belonging in and around a place of worship, both literally and discursively. Ehrenreich's data is truly remarkable in this sense

And, finally, in the case of *New Age spirituality*, communes and other collectives are doing likewise. Indeed, it is our very understanding of spirituality which appears to be evolving. However, despite the high volume of research since the time of Heelas' 1996 publication, the ambiguous position between 'self-spirituality' and 'spirituality-as-institution' remains either ignored (as in the cases of van Otterloo and Wood) or undertheorised (as in the cases of Kapoor and Sutcliffe). I argue that we are beginning to witness the emergence of *post-privatised* spirituality (or 'spirituality-as-institution') as part of a response to the post-bureaucratic identity crisis. I apply the prefix 'post-privatised' to describe a form of spirituality distinct from the apparently dominant understanding of spirituality (typically prefixed with 'self-') as the personalised/individualised/privatised alternative to religion. In support of this argument, I draw a comparison to the evolutionary changes that characterised 19th century *spiritualism*. According to Walliss (2006), spiritualists offered a 'religion' that was democratic rather than authoritarian; they claimed to offer proof for beliefs, such as belief in an afterlife; and they offered a vision of the Creator and the universe that was both personal (albeit ordered) rather than abstract, and inspirational rather than purely intellectual. But—and perhaps most importantly—Walliss notes that spiritualism 'fed into the *individualistic* ethos of the period by not only making potentially anyone a conduit for the supernatural but by seemingly guaranteeing the survival of the individual personality beyond death' (Walliss, 2006: 35, emphasis added). The parallel with New Age spirituality-as-individualised is striking. However, as Walliss comments further on:

> [A]lthough the antebellum Spiritualists were fundamentally opposed to organized forms of religiosity and emphasised instead the charisma of the individual medium, over the course of the last 150 years, the movement—in the UK at least—has ultimately succumbed to organizing tendencies and, in Weberian terms, the routinisation of mediumistic charisma.
>
> *(Ibid. 41)*

Walliss does not speculate on why they succumbed to organizing tendencies (and hence the relevance to the broader focus on bureaucracy), but it is this trend I have explored in contemporary forms of spirituality. In Vine (2018a), for example, I argue that the anxiety caused by fragmented family and work lives—which are symptomatic of the post-bureaucratic identity crisis—have compelled people not only to engage with New Age spirituality discourses but, more importantly, to do so in increasingly institutionalized/organized contexts. This coalescence around organizational units is of fundamental significance. Walliss's notion of 'tendency' is significant, too, as it implies that there is a predisposition to organize, irrespective of circumstances.

For each of the fives responses to the post-bureaucratic identity crisis identified, there is a clear and present desire for organizational belonging. The crisis of post-bureaucracy does not spell the end of organization, less still bureaucracy; rather it marshals a new organizational landscape. On the one hand the neoliberal assault on full time employment in place of part time work might seem to spell a sense of anomie (and many commentators have noted precisely this), on the other—and given the protean nature of bureaucracy and the broader 'pan-organizational structure' I present—the change is understood not as good or bad; just different.

The broader point is vital, particularly in respect of management pedagogy. Our university programmes, textbooks and case studies continue to assume a conventional rendering of organization. This is not to say that they fail to explore different manifestations of the organization. On the contrary, tall, flat, networked, and fluid structures are all routinely examined at length. But this apparent diversity misses a broader metric; it is the organizational geographies themselves which are in flux. It is hoped that the changing organizational landscape identified in this chapter will help dis-embed this analytical focus such that the teaching of organizational behaviour, for example, will explore not just conventional employer-based organizational structures (in all their diversity), but begin to examine these alongside organizational behaviours in religious, familial and occupational contexts, paying attention in particular to the extent to which organization in these different spheres of life is both interrelated and proxied, especially in times of crisis. Finally, attention to the organization of career is warranted, focussing principally on the ways in which it transects each of the spheres identified. In this way, our collective understanding of organization will be significantly enhanced. What is most interesting here is that even in cases of supposedly post-bureaucratic organization forms, bureaucracy is alive and kicking. For Styhre (2007: 96)

> Rather than being 'a move away' or 'a negation' of bureaucracy, the management practices of the post-bureaucratic organization may, on the contrary, be the 'final and perhaps most complete achievement' (Salamanm, 2005: 163) of the bureaucratic ethos. Contrary to the grandiose claims formulated on the demise of bureaucracy, much empirical evidence suggests that the bureaucratic organization form and its procedures are still in use.

Think about it. Even in the case, say, of network organizations, the first thing collaborators do is share contact details, create a shared space (usually via a cloud service) and agree a common timetable and schedule of operations. This is bureaucratic. I see it first-hand every time a group of my MBA students work together on a group project. Bureaucracy is, it seems, essential when faced with uncertainty. 'In the face of … ambiguities, managers resort to what is well-known and familiar, namely management practices that are firmly established as legitimate practices within the company, industry or profession' (ibid. 98). Invoking the words of celebrated system theorist, Russell Ackoff, Clegg (2011: 220) presents a similar argument, this time stressing a defence of hierarchies:

> Democracy is founded on a circular form of power because anyone who has authority over others is subject to the collective authority of these others; hence its circularity. But Ackoff is also a realistic thinker. He reminds us that divided labour must be coordinated and multiple coordinators must be coordinated; therefore, where complex tasks are involved, hierarchy cannot be avoided.

Indeed, Clegg is one of several theorists to note that the opposite of hierarchy (in the form of post-bureaucracy) is routinely more frustrating and alienating than hierarchy itself.

In sum, configured as *responses* to the post-bureaucratic identity crisis, this chapter lends significant weight to the argument that we reside not in a post-bureaucratic world, but in a world where bureaucracy has manifested itself in different ways by virtue of its protean character (including, of course, *across* multiple organizations—as illustrated in the pan-organizational model presented).

# PART II
# Understanding Bureau-phobia

# 4

# UNDERSTANDING BUREAU-PHOBIA PART I: PATHOLOGICAL BUREAUCRACY

In very broad terms, chapters 2 and 3 developed the argument that bureaucracy and post-bureaucracy are not simply states to be distinguished temporally, but parameters between which our organizational—and social—lives unfold. It was further remarked that bureaucracy has a protean ability to re-establish itself in supposedly post-bureaucratic configurations. In this part of the book, we shift focus so as to develop an enhanced understanding of why so many of us are fearful of bureaucracy. In this chapter, certain pathological manifestations of bureaucracy are explored. To this end, I examine three specific concepts: institutionalisation, the jobsworth, and the Holocaust. Unsurprisingly, perhaps, manifestations of the excesses of bureaucracy such as these have typically been cast as pathological. The fundamental problem in this respect is that we routinely make the mistake of conflating everyday bureaucracy with these pathological tendencies; this comes at the expense of our ability to acknowledge bureaucracy's considerable assets. And this is particularly unfortunate since more precise analysis of this pathological casting reveals a much greater degree of nuance; institutionalisation, the jobsworth, and even the extraordinary tragedy that was the Holocaust can each be interpreted and understood rather differently.

## Institutionalisation

Readers of Berger and Luckmann's (1966) seminal study, *The Social Construction of Reality*, will be familiar with their concept of institutionalisation. For them, the term is used abstractly to refer to the process by which we slowly institutionalise— or reify—traditional customs to the point that they become received wisdom, and hence 'fact' or 'real.' Reality is thus said to be socially constructed. While their understanding of institutionalisation is certainly relevant to discussions of bureaucracy and existential security, their approach focuses on the concept as an abstract epistemological process rather than, more specifically, the behaviours and dynamics within—or directly associated with—institutions (as 'bricks and mortar' organizations). The present discussion is of course different.

In several respects, the word 'institution' pervades the study of organization. First, institution is frequently used synonymously with organization. Second, the association of the word with its psychiatric manifestation has proven a particularly pertinent metaphor for damning undesirable organizations, especially for those versed in Foucault's work. Third, the concept of institutional theory (when understood in respect of institutional isomorphism) reminds us that organizations are the products of external forces. Fourth, for those of us sensitive to interpretative methodological approaches, we have long acknowledged that part of our remit is to reverse the 'institutionalised' approach to learning our students have inherited from their pedagogical experiences at school, so as to ignite more *critical* faculties (this is one area in which Berger and Luckmann's reading of institutionalisation is relevant). Finally—and perhaps most importantly in respect of the present thesis—the concept of institutionalisation has found application in our field in an almost entirely negative sense: institutionalisation implies the inculcation of dysfunctional—even sinister—organizational values. However, institutionalisation is not always the negative concept it is often thought to be. On the contrary, institutionalisation is imperative to our existential wellbeing. To this end, readers are urged to recall the importance of *re*institutionalisation, briefly discussed in the previous chapter.

MBA students enrolled on an Organizational Behaviour module at my own university were recently asked to complete a formative assignment. The brief read as follows: In no more than 750 words, please address the following questions: *In what ways are 'institutionalisation' and 'jobsworths' considered problematic manifestations of organizational behaviour? To what extent is this negative view justified? Are the two concepts connected in any way?* The assessment yielded some remarkable insights. What surprised me most was that the definitions cited emphasised not the negative, but the routine aspects of the institutionalisation. To this end, it seems, institutionalisation is formally defined quite innocuously as the enculturation of organizational members. Only a select few including, interestingly, the third definition listed by the *OED*, revealed a dysfunctional reading of the concept (and even here, it was firmly located as a subsidiary definition in respect of a clinical 'institution,' rather than institutions more generally). Prior to setting this assignment, I had naively assumed that institutionalisation was habitually understood as an undesirable process. After all, we live in a world in which concepts such as *institutional racism* carry highly negative connotations. Moreover, as an academic I have been primed to exhibit a critical mind-set in my own research and to cultivate the same in my students. This bias was illustrated in my cohort-wide written feedback comment: *In respect of institutionalisation, some of you made the mistake of simply presenting a perfunctory dictionary definition of the concept (these usually identified the concept as the cultural assimilation of an organization among its members). All too often you overlooked the dysfunctional aspects of the concept, which were crucial to this assignment.*

At the time, I was determined for my students to recognise the dysfunction associated with the concept. But now, in this book, I'm doing the opposite. So what has changed? It was when reading *Power and Organizations* by Clegg et al. (2006) that the penny dropped. In chapter 6 ('The Heart of Darkness'), the authors begin by noting: 'In this chapter we will ... elaborate the curious absence of Goffman, Foucault, and Bauman and the concept of total institutions from most organization theories' (ibid. 143). What? Surely we hear *nothing but* accounts of Goffman, Foucault and Bauman in our field? What I then realised, however, is that Clegg et al. are representative of an earlier generation of scholars. My generation is the fruit of theirs and has taken a rather different route through the university education system, one which put critical readings at the heart of its syllabus (whereas for the previous generation, mainstream—most likely behavioural approaches—dominated their university education in the 1960s and 1970s.) With these different contexts in mind, it is thus when I read something today more conventional about organizations and organization theory that it strikes me as distinctive, even exotic. It may sound peculiar but I find mainstream commentary refreshingly different. These days, it seems, and as I've commented elsewhere (see Vine, 2020a), we're all expected to be critical; so much so, that the word appears to have lost any discernible sense of meaning. In the present discussion, at least, it is significant because it enables me to examine the concept of institutionalisation with fresh eyes. So, while I am fully cognizant of their negative tendencies—at the extremes—I am slowly recognising the value of the more mundane, prosaic, and bureaucratic aspects of organizational life. To paraphrase *Guns N' Roses*, the institution reminds me of a warm, safe place. As far as this book is concerned, the fact that formal definitions of institutionalisation accentuate not dysfunction but enculturation is entirely relevant. In a concrete sense I was learning from my students.

## What did my students teach me?

It wasn't simply that my students marshalled me towards formal dictionary definitions of the concept. No, there was more to it than this; they unpacked and made sense of these definitions before developing lines of thought quite distinct from those that underpinned my own critical schooling. Many students began by invoking the online Oxford Dictionaries definition of institutionalisation: 'The action of establishing something as a convention or norm in an organization or culture' (Oxford Dictionaries, www.lexico.com/definition/institutionalization). Some then went on to note that the term is occasionally used negatively to describe certain employee behaviour. For example, one noted that Oxford Dictionaries also defined institutionalisation as 'Harmful effects such as apathy and loss of independence arising from spending a long time in an institution.' However, another went on to question this negativity and in so doing invoked the support of an unlikely ally:

[I]s [institutionalisation] entirely negative for an organization? Not necessarily. For example, Belbin refers to nine key team roles essential to produce an effective high performing team and there are some similar characteristics of the *Implementer* to an institutionalised employee. Implementers are likely to be reliable and turn ideas into actions. However, [Belbin] also suggests that they 'can be inflexible and slow to respond to new possibilities' and 'might be slow to relinquish their plans in favour of positive changes'.

So, was Belbin—unwittingly—a defender of bureaucracy? Even if we regard the Implementer's behaviour as dysfunctional there is, perhaps, a peculiar *functionality to its dysfunction*. For another student, the preferred definition of institutionalisation was sourced from businessdictionary.com: 'Institutionalization ... aims at integrating fundamental values and objectives into the organization's culture and structure.' Once again, the definition serves as a reminder that institutionalisation is not necessarily dysfunctional. Is the world of scholarship now so tainted by a critical consensus that we are prevented from recognising this? Are we so determined to flatter a preconceived ideological belief system that we are blind to countervailing arguments?

Beyond the array of definitions—both positive and negative—associated with institutionalisation, the most interesting reflection on these assignments is how many students recognised the importance of the concept of *balance*. Of the 19 students that submitted assignments, the suggestion that balance was key in terms of understanding institutionalisation was specifically stated by 11 of them. So, for example, most noted that while on the one hand embedded structures and routines provide a clear sense of role, responsibility, and expectation, on the other, an institutional environment which is over-bearing will likely hamper creativity and arrest development of individuality. In sum, and as many of my students observed, the concept of institutionalisation is complex and ought to be approached without prejudice. To a similar end, Kallinikos distinguishes 'total institutions' from 'non-inclusive bureaucracy':

> The far-reaching significance of modulating the individual-organization relationship in terms other than inclusive emerges clearly in the background of the comparison of bureaucracy with the organizational form that Goffman (1961) once called *total institutions*, that is, mental hospitals, prisons, monasteries, army barracks, religious sects and so on. In contrast to the non-inclusive coupling of the individual to the organization underlying bureaucracy, total institutions are based on the structural principle of inclusion. Individuals are contained in the organization, they are in other words 'inmates.' Total institutions impose their austere order on the entire personality of their members. They do not distinguish between personality and collective. The term 'individual,' as we know it, is alien to this form of organization. Total organizations thus provide an instructive contrast to bureaucracy.
>
> *(Kallinikos, 2004: 22)*

Institutionalisation does not, or at least should not, imply that individuals are being subsumed into total institutions. One of the defining characteristics of bureaucracy is the separation of person and role. While bureaucracy *institutionalises*, then, it is not all-consuming. Now, while I recognise that others have gone so far as to at least partially defend the viability of total institutions (see Clegg et al., 2006: 184, for example), I feel that it is necessary to distinguish between the 'institutionalising bureaucracy' on the one hand, and the 'total institution' on the other. In my mind, we too often make the mistake of conflating the two, and this is especially true of novelists and filmmakers, explored in chapter 6.

## The jobsworth

The jobsworth is a fascinating creature. It is for this reason that it is all the more remarkable that so little research exists on this perennial feature of organizational life, compared to—say—the concept of 'work to rule' which has been extensively explored in industrial sociology, among other fields. There is of course a close relationship between institutionalisation and norms that regulate behaviour. It can certainly be argued that the behavioural norms associated with 'jobsworthiness' typically emerge in an institutionalised environment. But what exactly is a jobsworth? Unlike the multiple and varied definitions of institutionalisation, the definitions—and broader understanding—of jobsworths demonstrated by my students were entirely negative. Some students cited McNeill's (2004) discussion which suggests that if somebody is considered a 'jobsworth' it is because they are unhelpful by insisting that rules are adhered to unnecessarily, making simple tasks more difficult. Oxford Dictionaries is more succinct: the jobsworth is: 'an official who upholds petty rules even at the expense of humanity or common sense.' Others, still, used examples to illustrate the sort of behaviour one can expect from a jobsworth. Watson's (2006) illustration was popular and reproduced by several students:

> The activities of a 'jobsworth' or 'bureaucratic personalities': [are demonstrated by] the warehouse labourer who was told to 'get those boxes moved out of the gangway before you go home.' The labourer then went on to move what contained fragile goods outside into the yard. The goods, the story goes, were then destroyed in the overnight rain.
>
> *(Watson, 2006)*

What did my students note about origins of the concepts of jobsworths and jobsworthiness? Of this point, in particular, my feedback to the students was as follows:

> While most of you demonstrated a good understanding of the concept (especially in respect of the fact that its usage is both proverbial and pejorative), it was interesting to see such a wide variety of claims regarding the derivation of the concept (everything from Merton's 1940 seminal text, Bureaucratic

Structure and Personality, to the BBC programme That's Life!, were credited with the term's origin).

Unsurprisingly most students took the opportunity to comment on their own experiences of jobsworths. Notably, none described themselves as having engaged in such behaviour; the concept was firmly located within the realm of the *Other*. This was interesting and part of me would like to share their experiences with you. However, I do need to draw the line somewhere in respect of confidentiality, especially as so many of my students appeared to border on a vitriolic attack of their organizational nemeses. I feel more confident, however, sharing my own experience of jobsworthiness. Like the accounts presented by my students, I am *Othering* the concept. However, the anecdote does not reflect negatively on the organization involved. On the contrary, it reveals a significant learning experience on my part. I have, however, taken the precaution of pseudonymising the jobsworth in question.

## My experience of jobsworthiness

When I worked for the Electoral Reform Services in the early 2000s, my nemesis was a bloke called Matthew Matterson. I worked hard for the organization, including weeknights and weekends, tending to our growing client base. I would often drive the length of the country at very late notice to address an urgent matter. Matthew was in charge of the company warehouse, yard, and car park. In times of crisis, and when all spaces were occupied, I would be forced to park on a verge. This did not go down well. No sooner had I left my car and arrived at my desk, I would have the Deputy Chief Executive drop by at my desk. 'Matthew says you've not parked properly.' I'd respond: 'Well it's that, or wait another 20 minutes until I've found a public parking space. The client will not be impressed.' 'Go and move your car,' she ordered. In my mind, there was absolutely no logic to being told to move my car. It wasn't blocking anybody and moving it meant that I was less productive. And the client would get pissed off. But Matthew didn't see it that way; I was in contravention of the rules and that's all the mattered. What surprised me most, however, is that more often than not the Deputy Chief Executive sided with Matthew, even though she was acutely aware of the commercial ramifications of time spent finding a public parking space. She even commented one day that she regarded Matthew's jobsworth behaviour positively; he was, apparently, 'an indispensable resource.' With hindsight, I can better understand her position. While my parking outside a delineated parking space made no discernible difference to the functioning of the car park, it clearly wouldn't be workable if all staff did it. Besides, the organization could not be seen to turn a blind eye to Tom, or anyone else for that matter. I'm pretty sure the organization valued my hard work and paid me reasonably well for it; however, it certainly wasn't going to let me work by my own rules. The company recognised that Matthew's behaviour rendered him a jobsworth (I certainly wasn't the only one to label him as such). Equally, however, it realised that his preoccupation with the rules—while potentially destructive on some levels—meant that he could be relied upon to uphold a sense of procedural equity. And, as Weber teaches us, equity is a crucial part of an effective bureaucracy.

## Understanding jobsworthiness

The concept of the jobsworth can be understood in several ways. One approach casts jobsworths as an inevitable and unmitigated ramification of bureaucracy's dysfunction. This argument is normally attributed to Merton (1940). As King and Lawley (2016), have noted, here jobsworthiness is understood as trained incapacity; employee behaviour is so heavily regulated by procedures and norms that the worker no longer has a sufficient sense of agency to think or act individually, or to take any form of initiative. A second approach suggests that people rationally adopt a jobsworth approach to make it easier to get through the working day (see, for example, Watson, 2006). A third approach, attributed to Bullock and Grimley-Evans (2004), suggests that jobsworths have great respect for the written law, but a limited ability to read the world in which they inhabit. In this sense, jobsworths demonstrate deficient cognitive faculties. Should, then, the jobsworth be defined as an individual with an atypical awareness of reality? Is the jobsworth's sensorium comparable to people who are colloquially (and often pejoratively) known as 'on the spectrum'? Does the very fact that we have a word for jobsworth—let alone revel in poking fun at them—reveal a neurotypical bias? A fourth interpretation is found in McNeill (2004): jobsworthiness represents a fear of change. McNeil draws upon the work of Simon Naudi, a managing director of a training company dealing with difficult colleagues, and Cary Cooper, a professor of organizational psychology and health. McNeil concludes that jobsworthiness is an example of 'uncooperative behaviours that mask a fear of change,' and that it typically occurs when an employee feels powerless. A fifth approach is found in Jay and Templar (2004: 119). They suggest that individuals who exhibit jobsworth-like behaviour are usually feeling insecure or unappreciated.

But what if anything unites these disparate approaches to understanding the jobsworth? In all cases—even that which suggests jobsworths have a limited awareness of reality—it seems that his or her behaviour is in some way a manifestation of the organizational context in which he or she is found. With this in mind it seems that contrary to popular belief, jobsworths rarely revel in their disruptiveness but act the way they do precisely because they are organizational subjects.

## What is the relationship between the jobsworth and bureaucracy?

For Linsenmeier and Wortman creativity and independence are important traits in organizational settings:

> a person who slavishly conforms to the opinions of his superiors, or to the norms and values of the company, may run the risk of eliciting negative reactions... individuals who accept all the values and norms of an organization should be regarded as organizational failures. According to Schein, 'The conforming individual curbs his creativity and thereby moves the organization toward a sterile form of bureaucracy'.
>
> *(Wortman and Linsenmeier, 1977: 151)*

This is relevant both in terms of institutionalisation and the jobsworth. Institutionalisation (or at least, *socialisation*) creates jobsworths. In the same publication, Wortman and Linsenmeier refer to research by Jones, Jones, and Gergen (1963) and Jones, Stires, Shaver and Harris (1968). Of these, they conclude that people can even get 'extra credit' for resisting the urge to be conforming when it is obvious that they have something to gain by impressing the target individual. Perhaps, then, jobsworths lack the skills of effective ingratiation. Instead they see ingratiation as a straightforward linear logic: 'these are the rules, if I continually reinforce them, my superiors will like me.' More perceptive individuals—who recognise nuance above and beyond linear logic—will inevitably regard jobsworths as unintelligent, or at least, lacking relevant social skills. A familiar point of comparison is speed limits. If authorities wish for you to travel at no more than 60kph, they will most likely erect 50kph speed limit signs. This is because it is generally accepted that motorists drive slightly faster than the formally indicated limit. This is an unwritten rule, if you like, with which most—but not all—of us are familiar. It is worth reflecting on the frustrations many of us experience when we encounter a driver in front of us or—worse still—several cars in front of us, sticking doggedly to the speed limit. The driver, we assume, is unaware of the manner in which the authorities interact with their subjects. Those adhering to the speed limits and most likely those who do similarly in respect of bureaucracy are jobsworths. To be a jobsworth, then, implies that you do not have an especially sophisticated understanding of social dynamics; it implies an inability to see the 'bigger picture.' Merton noted this sort of behaviour in 1940. The relevant passage is worth quoting in full:

> in order to ensure discipline ... sentiments are often more intense than is technically necessary. There is a margin of safety, so to speak, in the pressure exerted by these sentiments upon the bureaucrat to conform to his patterned obligations, in much the same sense that added allowances (precautionary over-estimations) are made by the engineer in designing the supports for a bridge. But this very emphasis leads to a transference of the sentiments from the *aims* of the organization onto the particular details of behaviour required by the rules. Adherence to rules, originally conceived as a means, becomes transformed into an end-in-itself; there occurs the familiar process of *displacement of goals* whereby an instrumental value becomes a terminal value. Discipline, readily interpreted as conformance with regulations, whatever the

situation, is seen not as a measure designed for specific purposes but becomes an immediate value in the life-organization of the bureaucrat. This emphasis, resulting from the displacement of the original goals, develops into rigidities and an inability to adjust readily. Formalism, even ritualism, ensures with an unchallenged insistence upon punctilious adherence to formalized procedures. This may be exaggerated to the point where primary concern with conformity to the rules interferes with the achievement of the purpose of the organization, in which case we have the familiar phenomenon of the technicism or red tape of the official. An extreme product of this process of displacement of goals is the bureaucratic virtuoso, who never forgets a single rule binding his action and hence is unable to assist many of his clients.

*(Merton 1940: 563, original emphases)*

Here we have Merton's proto-jobsworth, the *bureaucratic virtuoso*, in all his glory. On reflection, then, it seems the jobsworth is an inevitable ramification of bureaucracy; a necessary evil. However, we need to tread carefully. Does our perennial damning of the jobsworth reveal a sort of neurotypical imperialism? In all probability, it is neurodivergent individuals that are likely to exhibit jobsworth-like behaviour. In effect, poking fun at jobsworths thus compounds the sense of ostracisation experienced by this group. As I've argued elsewhere (see, for example, Konnovs and Vine, 2019), in the wake of taboos associated with gender, race, sexual orientation, and transgender identity, neurotypical biases are likely to become increasingly taboo in the future. Our attitude to the jobsworth may well change as the *ethics of the day* evolve.

## The Holocaust

The most extreme example of bureaupathology is undoubtedly the Holocaust. Zygmunt Bauman's 1989 book *Modernity and the Holocaust* was one of the most influential texts I read as an undergraduate in the 1990s. I continue to use the text in my own teaching. While I have no plans to systematically revisit Bauman's thesis here (if you've not read it, you ought to), I wish to comment on it in respect of bureaucracy. In my mind, what it did do more so than anything else was cultivate in its readership both fear and hatred of bureaucracy. The subject of Bauman's text represents the pinnacle of bureau-phobia. Now, while I am by no means the first to challenge Bauman's portrayal of bureaucracy (du Gay, for example, did this in 2000), I do feel its inclusion here is warranted in respect of bureaupathology and, I hope to introduce some fresh material in terms of the broader effects Bauman's thesis has had.

On reading Bauman's book, my students typically conclude thus: *bureaucracy is not just ineffective; it's downright evil.* What exactly is Bauman's argument? He notes that while most believe 'that the Holocaust was an *interruption* in the normal flow of history' (Bauman 1989: viii, emphasis added), in reality nothing could be further from the truth. In 2001, while I was studying for a masters in Organization Studies at the University of Warwick, we were invited to respond to the following essay question: *Examine the view that 'The Holocaust represents a major triumph of management technique and a total failure of human values.'* As I began working on this assignment, I slowly developed a fascination with both modernity and bureaucracy. The Holocaust is a baffling phenomenon. Unlike the dead of earlier genocides; the witch-hunts of Europe; the Indians of the Americas; the European butchering of indigenous Tasmanians, the Holocaust occurred in post-Enlightenment Europe. Consequently, historians, sociologists, and psychologists since the event have been prone to dismiss the genocide as an aberrance; as something largely detached from both post-Enlightenment progression and human nature. For Bauman, however, the Holocaust was enabled by a discernibly post-Enlightenment modernist mentality. As Sofsky (1997: 111, emphasis added), has stressed, 'mass murder demands organization. Repeated killing is ... an activity with all the distinguishing features of *work*.' For Sofsky, 'effective' genocide is arranged methodically; according to plan; over time; oriented to a goal; and marked by bureaucratic efficiency and routine. In essence, the Holocaust was facilitated and sustained by means of industry; 'factories of death.'

Bureaucracy was certainly instrumental in maximising the effectiveness of Holocaust management. Bureaucracy, in the organizational sense, rationally facilitates specialisation, formalisation (organizational rules), hierarchy, salary, and a loyalty and respect for colleagues (*esprit de corps*). Effectively, bureaucracy enabled the genocide in two ways. First, although the Nazi mob was fuelled by fury, fury can only be maintained briefly; it is short-lived. Conversely, bureaucratic principles are long term and continually nourish the cause. Second, by establishing a hierarchical regime coupled with the various dehumanising tasks the Nazis faced, bureaucracy distances and depersonalises mass murder.

The managerial initiative at play here is plain to see. It was crucial in distancing participants from their actions. As Figure 4.1 illustrates (reproduced from the book), Bauman shows how a distinctly modernist mentality helped render 'the Jew' as a commodity. This was initiated by the State's gradual introduction of legislation prohibiting the employment of Jews; employers were, inevitably, forced to dismiss them. Without a means of income, they were subjected to expropriation. This gave rise to the abysmal conditions in the ghettos. Already at the mercy of the Nazis, the Jews were exploited and starved; this, says, Bauman disguised 'inhumanity as humanity' (ibid. 191), which eventually 'justified' their complete annihilation.

Notably, the managerial initiative evident in this process is principally *linear*, reflecting the close alliance of Holocaust management and modernism. For those involved in this process, the Jews had become commodities and so their death was largely inconsequential; it was as though they had never existed. As Bauman (1989: 122) notes, the Jews found themselves in a situation 'more akin to that experienced by a subordinate group in a power structure, than as victim of an ordinary genocidal operation.' There is a managerial essence to the Holocaust and it is this that constitutes the distinguishing feature of the Holocaust when compared to pre-modern genocide.

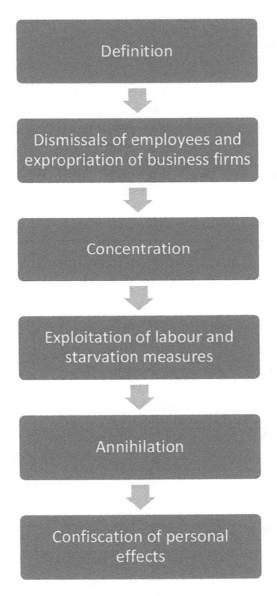

**FIGURE 4.1** The neutralisation of moral responsibility towards Jews in Nazi Germany
Source: Bauman, 1989: 190.

## 78 Understanding bureau-phobia

This linear process occurs within the machinations of bureaucracy which, in effect, both distances and depersonalises mass murder. However, and as Bauman suggests, this hierarchical arrangement (both in terms of command and process) was not enough to completely detach the perpetrators from their moral conscience. It was the substitution of technical for moral responsibility and the separation of tasks that would achieve this. 'In a [technological-bureaucratic] society, the effects of human action reach far beyond the vanishing point of moral visibility' (Bauman, 1989: 193). The compression of time and space is clearly at work here too. The technological actions of the SS outstripped their (already diminished) moral predisposition. Bauman illustrates the manifestation of this technical responsibility with an account of a Nazi technical expert's memo. The memo proposes improvements to mobile gas vans. The expert suggests that the manufacturers of the vans should shorten the wheelbase of the vehicles since the larger loading areas in the existing vehicles meant that there was wastage (both in terms of gas and time) to fulfil the executions:

> A shorter, fully loaded truck could operate much more quickly. A shortening of the rear compartment would not disadvantageously affect the weight balance, overloading the front axle, because 'actually a correction in the weight distribution takes place automatically through the fact that the cargo in the struggle to the back door during the operation is always located there. Because the connecting pipe was quickly rusted [because of] the fluids, the gas should be introduced from the above, not below. To facilitate cleaning, an eight to twelve-inch hole should be made in the floor and provided with a cover opened from outside. The floor should be slightly inclined, and the cover equipped with a small sieve. Thus all fluids would flow to the middle, the thin fluids would exit during operation, and thicker fluids could be hosed out afterwards.'
>
> *(Cited in Bauman, 1989: 197)*

The detached and thoroughly dispassionate tone of the extract demonstrates how effective the bureaucratic structure was in substituting a technical conscience for a moral one. Bauman refers to this phenomenon using the concept of '*lucrotropism*—a sort of gravitational pulling force of the highest return on capital' (ibid. 103).

To lend theoretical weight to his arguments, Bauman reflects on the seminal work of Stanley Milgram. Milgram's experiment on obedience was in part motivated by a desire to better understand Nazi genocide. Is the obedience observed in the laboratory in any way comparable to that seen in Nazi Germany? 'The answer must be that while there are enormous differences of circumstance and scope, a common psychological process is centrally involved in both events' (Milgram, 1974: 192). It is clear that in observation of both experiment and Holocaust, the subjects demonstrate 'the same limitless capacity to yield to authority and the same use of identical mental mechanisms to reduce the strain of acting against the helpless victim' (ibid. 192). And, of course, authority is a cornerstone of bureaucracy. The Holocaust provides a most pertinent example of obedience to authority; for Bauman, at least, it is thus bureaucracy *par excellence*.

So, what is the pedagogical value of Bauman's thesis? Most students—including my own—read it as a chilling critique of bureaucracy and it is easy to see why. But this is an oversimplification. I remain to be convinced that it discredits bureaucracy *per se*. The management of the Holocaust certainly involved complex organization and was therefore inevitably bureaucratic. The crucial point, however, is, while bureaucratic techniques were pivotal to the administration and management of the Holocaust, bureaucracy did not *cause* the Holocaust. The Holocaust was facilitated not by bureaucracy, but by the effective deployment of scientific management techniques. Now, conscious of Adler's (1993) persuasive defence of Taylorism, I do not wish to suggest that such techniques are inherently evil either, but it is these more so than bureaucracy that facilitated the Holocaust. In the 1990s post-modernism ruled the scholarly roost. It is perhaps unsurprising, then, that many of my lecturers were hell-bent on casting modernity and, specifically, bureaucracy as moral wastelands. But this is to overstate their agency; bureaucracy is morally inert, yes, but that doesn't imply that it is immoral or even amoral. As Giddens (1972: 38–9, original emphasis) has argued:

> Charisma, is, as a 'pure type,' wholly opposed to the routine, the *alltäglich*. Traditional and legal domination, on the other hand, are both forms of everyday administration, the one being tied to the other being bound by abstractly formulated universal principles. The charismatic leader, 'like … every true leader in this sense, preaches, creates, or demands *new* obligations.' It is for this reason that the 'charismatic element' is of vital significance in a modern democratic order; without it, no consistent policy-making is possible, and the state relapses into leaderless democracy, the rule of professional politicians without a calling.

Here Giddens argues that bureaucracy is not possible without the charismatic leader.

> Bureaucratisation […] while elevating the conduct of human affairs to a peak of technical efficiency, cannot itself generate the capacities involved in 'genuine' leadership. In the democratic order, [Weber] saw both the need and the possibility to create the charismatic element necessary to the modern political leader.
>
> *(Ibid. 54–5)*

To the extent that the Holocaust was bureaucratic, it too required the charismatic leader (in its case, Hitler) to make it possible. And it is in Hitler of course where we find a sense of agency. Although outside the remit for this book to comment systematically on the nature of that agency, Magee's account of Hitler's motivation must be one of the most compelling. Magee argues that the Holocaust was Hitler's way of bringing about a sense of political stability. He says: 'if one thing more than another can be said to have started the seeds of the Holocaust germinating in [Hitler's] mind it is probably his interpretation of events involved in Germany's collapse at the end of the First World War' (Magee, 2000: 362). While the Germans—including a young Hitler—were away fighting this war in other countries, back home in Germany and without much resistance (since the resistance was away fighting), the socialists, many of whom were Jews, began to seize control. In Hitler's mind, and as he argues in *Mein Kampf*, the Holocaust was a means of preventing this from happening again. It was a 'logical' means of ensuring what Hitler regarded as political stability in the future. The fact that bureaucratic methods were implicit in the delivery of the Holocaust is unremarkable. If anything, we should be surprised if the Holocaust *hadn't* involved bureaucratic methods. Nazi bureaucracy had no agency in and of itself.

What is therefore missing from Bauman's otherwise excellent book is a sense of context. On the one hand, yes, modernity and modern management 'caused'—or at least facilitated the Holocaust, but for this one atrocity how many times has modernity and modern management technique *improved* welfare, when compared to pre-bureaucratic alternatives? Think about the degree to which the bureaucratic concepts of equity, impartiality, (job) security, and—as I am arguing in this book—existential security are woven into the very fabric of our institutionalised lives. Contrariwise, think about the degree to which we feel a sense of anomie when such arrangements are threatened with change (see chapters 2 and 3). As Clegg (2011: 164) notes:

> Excesses of instrumental rationality (organizing) and disregard for substantial rationality (human rights) can lead to barbarism. But the opposite also holds. Disorganization and chaos, or a lack of instrumental rationality and over-concern with substantive rationality, such as are furnished by racism and fundamentalism, can provoke similar disastrous consequences.

In accepting Bauman's thesis without qualification, we are both making a huge generalisation and confusing correlation with causation. Such acceptance also seems to ignore—completely—the fact that so much critique of bureaucracy is centred on its *in*efficiency, rather than its efficiency. If as these critics argue, bureaucracy is inefficient, then why is the Holocaust—widely regarded as an efficient means of slaughter—being attributed to it? If Bauman was a postgraduate student, these comments would be slapped down in red ink. A final rebuttal can be found in more recent discussions of Weber, ethics and bureaucracy.

> Weber clearly rejects any suggestion that the principles of bureaucratic organization are honoured and properly applied when office-holders automatically carry out instructions and refrain from voicing any objection. To do so would be to exemplify an 'ethic of adjustment' or of 'conviction.' Enacting the bureaucratic ethos demands of the diligent office-holder that s/he assess the

legitimacy of the directives, not simply accept them or follow only those that accord with his or her convictions. The ethos of the office requires the bureaucrat to raise objections when receiving a directive that s/he considers wrong.

*(Willmott, 2011: 282)*

We are thus compelled to consider the charge that bureaucracy lacks concern for morality. Paul du Gay's research has already—and quite persuasively—contested this charge. It is not unreasonable, for example, to cast the impartiality of the bureau as an ethic. And, it must be stressed, there is no comparable ethic for post-bureaucracy.

Critique aside, we have learned some important lessons from Bauman's thesis. First, it reveals an extraordinarily level of sophistication in respect of micro-sociological detail. Second, it demonstrates how scholars—even some of those at the very top of their game—cannot escape the fact that they are products of their time. Bauman's research came at a time when anti-bureaucratic sentiment was rife in academic journals. Bureaucracy has long had a bad press, and knowingly or otherwise, Bauman reproduced this ill feeling.

## Reflecting on bureaupathology

What have we learned from these three—very different—manifestations of bureaupathology? Are they *necessarily* extreme manifestations of bureaucracy? Or must we discern a greater degree of complexity? Take the Holocaust. What do we see here, aside of course from the obvious humanitarian disaster? We see evidence of bureaucratic tension and paradox. The Jews, Bauman argues, through the mediating effects of bureaucracy unwittingly implicated themselves in genocide. We also note the extent to which Bauman went to show that, since the Holocaust was executed in accordance with and extraordinary level of efficiency, it *must have been* bureaucratic in nature. And yet, how many countless critics since have lampooned bureaucracy for precisely the opposite: its *in*efficiency. The Holocaust was undeniably horrendous but it cannot—and should not—be blamed without qualification on bureaucracy. And what of the more prosaic matter of institutionalisation? What do we see here? We see evidence of bureaucratic tension and paradox. When we think of institutionalisation we tend to think of it in negative terms: psychiatric dominance and institutional racism. Indeed, institutionalisation is almost always interpreted in a negative sense. Is this fair? If, as I am arguing more broadly, bureaucracies provide for us a sense of existential security and ontological belonging, surely institutionalisation is one such ramification of this? A more nuanced reading of the concept reveals something rather different: institutionalisation is containing and describes the broader process by which our identities are negotiated, formed and affirmed. And, finally, what about the jobsworth? What do we see here, aside of course from the potential for comedic value? Yet again, we see evidence of bureaucratic tension and paradox. On the one hand he—and I use this pronoun deliberately—is a frustrating manifestation of all that is problematic with administrative sciences. On the other, and as my boss so poignantly put it, the jobsworth is an 'indispensable resource' in articulating an organization's broader duty to uphold a sense of processual equity. Furthermore, as we've seen, there is a very good chance that the jobsworth's behaviour is attributable more to a *neurodivergent* set of traits, and less to bureaucracy. So why, then, have we been so naïve? Why do we continue to cast these bureaucratic artefacts in exclusively negative ways? One reason, I think, is to be found in the unlikely world of the arts.

# 5

# UNDERSTANDING BUREAU-PHOBIA PART II

Dystopian bureaucracy

In the previous chapter, we examined what are perceived to be extreme manifestations of bureaucracy. In each case, we noted that these preconceptions rarely reflect reality. In this chapter, we explore the manner in which these preconceptions of bureaucracy continue to propagate in the arts, specifically in novels and films. Broadly speaking, my argument in this chapter is that bureaucracy is culturally *mis*represented. If we accept the position that fiction is a discursive device that contributes to the construction of culture and society, then the fact that bureaucracy remains one of the most prevalent and pervasive dystopian motifs in both literature and film is at least part of the reason it is considered normal to chastise the concept in everyday discourses.

In earlier chapters, I began to develop the argument that bureaucracy is neither good nor bad. Bureaucracy just *is*. Although academicians are beginning to recognise this, novelists and filmmakers have yet to cotton on. In novels and films, bureaucracy is just bad, pure and simple. In some respects, this bias is bizarre. Our world has generated some extraordinary literary and cinematographic talents. Both media have yielded works that reveal remarkably creative and intellectual insights; from the political commentary of William Shakespeare to the postmodern celluloid delights of David Lynch. For some reason, however, as a literary or cinematic device bureaucracy continues to represent a stock dystopian motif. But why should this matter? Surely novels and films are, after all, about entertainment? Well, as cultural theorists have long recognised, books and films are part of the discourse in which we are immersed; they construct our beliefs about the world around us. Consider how very young children learn about the world beyond their immediate sensory experience; even in an era of interactive electronic entertainment, the bedtime story remains a cherished part of most children's daily routine. Storytelling is the first abstract formal learning method we encounter as human beings. It is also probably transcultural; perhaps even an immanent part of the human condition.

Stories mould the way we think about the world from a very young age. Child development researchers such as Wang and Leichtman (2003) have compared the sorts of stories that children in different cultures around the world are read, as well as the sorts of stories the children themselves tell. What these studies tend to note is that in Western storytelling the concept of the protagonist/hero/heroine is a fundamental trope, whereas stories in the East (especially China), tend to have plots which emphasise the virtues of social engagement and collective action. The point is that a sense of individualism (both in terms of identity and economic outlook) is cultivated in the West from an early age; contrariwise, a sense of community and togetherness is routinely cultivated in the East. More specifically, narratives (which are, in essence, sequences of events) presuppose and *reinforce* particular cause-and-effect relationships. They also construct unconscious biases, prejudices, and discriminatory attitudes. Consider the familiar 'narrative' of the nuclear family, which—of course—constructs what we perceive to be a 'normal' pattern of kinship. However, for some historians including Berger (2002), the nuclear family is a relatively recent 'invention,' which became prevalent in England from the 13th century onwards, but uncommon elsewhere. Indeed, for Berger it is considered to be a crucial enabler of Industrialisation.

In the social sciences, we are slowly beginning to recognise the pedagogical importance and potential of the humanities. Fine art (Strauß, 2017), theatre (Beirne and Knight, 2007) and storytelling (Boje, 2008) all have an important role to play. In 2018, for example, the University of Suffolk, where I work, hosted its first Storytelling Conference. It was, apparently, the first such conference in the UK. It attracted a diverse, international audience and proved to be surprisingly popular across a multitude of academic disciplines; from anthropologists to radiographers. Now, I am assuming that the majority of the readers of this book are engaged in some way with social scientific endeavours, either as academics or as students. What I am proposing is that a more sophisticated understanding of our attitudes towards bureaucracy will be realised by engaging analytically with the humanities. For some, this is will be a reasonable request. For others, particularly those schooled in positivist epistemologies, the request may seem farcical. At the very least, these individuals may be reticent about engaging with techniques borrowed from the humanities. I am therefore compelled to present justification for doing precisely this. I wish to persuade such readers not only that the study of the arts, in general, has the potential to bear fruit in the social sciences, but that the study of dystopian fiction, in particular, is remarkably revealing, especially from the point of view of the current thesis.

## What is dystopia?

When we speak of dystopia, we are simultaneously—and paradoxically—speaking of utopia. This is because it is typically from utopian intentions that dystopian ends materialise. On the face of it, then, dystopia represents an opposite to utopia. However, to consider dystopia as an entity distinct from utopia (let alone its opposite) is a misnomer. Dystopia and utopia are inextricably linked. A lay interpretation of this might, for example, note that one person's utopia is another's dystopia, or where utopia becomes saturated by ideological fanatics, it often degenerates into dystopia. A more nuanced approach will, however, recognise this tendency across *all* utopian aspirations. Utopia and dystopia ought not to be characteristic of opposing poles on a straight continuum; rather they ought to be considered as highly volatile counterpoints on opposite ends of a shape reminiscent of a horseshoe. In this way, their conceptual rendering is comparable to the way in which the political spectrum is often presented when ideological nuance is taken into consideration.

## To what extent is dystopian fiction an influential pedagogical device?

Managers—and organizational men and women more generally—are no different from the rest of us; they read fiction. In fact, as Clegg (2011: 214) has noted, 'Successful managers seek insight from a range of sources: they will read widely—not just business publication but books and articles on social trends, history—even science fiction.' Notably, a large proportion of dystopian stories are categorised as science fiction, not least because they involve speculation on societal and organizational *futures*. Interestingly, the relationship between science fiction and organization studies has attracted scholarly attention. Corbett (1995), for example, studied representation of technology and organizational futures in science fiction films. Later, Smith et al. (2003) edited a collection of chapters which together explored the broader—and multifaceted—relationship between organization and science fiction films such as *Blade Runner* and *Star Trek*. Following in these footsteps, one of my current PhD students is exploring the reported influence of dystopian science fiction on management style and decision-making among executives.

However, for Russell-Smith (1914: 12), utopias (and, by implication, dystopias) are generally regarded as 'literary curiosities which have been made respectable by illustrious names, rather than as serious problems which troubled the age at which they appeared.' Contrary to Russell-Smith's position, I argue that methods repurposed from the humanities are not just matters of idle curiosity but supply the fertile seeds of true analytical passage. On a practical level, literary utopia has long been considered an effective means of influencing societal futures. In a didactic sense, then, utopia is powerful device:

> There is plenty for it to do other than write party manifestos … it can satirize and criticize, it can clarify standards and expectations; it can conduct thought experiments, to try out new possible arrangements of social life; it can pick out and project hopeful trends, re-working them in a picture of future society that draws us on by the force of its imaginative realization.
> 
> *(Kumar, 1991: 98)*

That the 'literary genre [of utopia] ... is in fact a mixture of remote distance from, and fierce familiarity with, the real world of politics and society ... gives it its distinctive hybrid quality' (ibid. 96). Literary utopias keep alive the principles of hope. For utopia contains the quality, '[to] teach desire to desire, to desire better, to desire more, and above all desire in a different way' (Thompson, 1955: 791). It is here suggested that the dystopian might seek to influence social reality in a comparable way, albeit in a precautionary sense. Related to this are Mannheim's (1955 [1936]: 199) carefully chosen words:

> [E]very age allows to arise ... those ideas and values in which are contained in condensed form the unrealized and the unfulfilled tendencies which represent the needs of each age. These ... elements then become the explosive material for bursting the limits of the existing order. The existing order gives birth to utopias which in turn break the bonds of the existing order, leaving it free to develop in the direction of the next order of existence.

For Mannheim, utopia—and by implication, dystopia—serves an important practical purpose: it helps guide the existing age and enables society to evolve. Where in the past satirical utopias and dystopias helped keep governments in check, their ideological and ethical leverage can now be trained at organization. In this sense, both utopia and dystopia might directly influence social and corporate practice. The fundamental problem, however, is that although academic output in respect of bureaucracy has evolved to meet a new power nexus (the post-bureaucratic rhetoric), fiction hasn't. And fiction, as previously noted, has the readership and effect that academics can only dream of.

## Dystopian fiction and bureaucracy

Graeber (2016: 26–7) suggests that 'all bureaucracies are to a certain degree utopian, in the sense that they propose an abstract ideal that real human beings can never live up to.' If we accept the argument that dystopian ends invariably follow utopian aspirations, Graeber's point vis-à-vis the distinct flavour of dystopian fiction in respect of bureaucracy begins to make sense. Indeed, and as Graeber (ibid. 52) later comments:

> [H]aven't great novelists often written compelling literature about bureaucracy? Of course they have. But they have managed to do this by embracing the very circulatory and emptiness—not to mention idiocy—of bureaucracy, and producing literary works that partake of something like the same mazelike, senseless form. This is why almost all great literature of the subject takes the form of horror-comedy. Franz Kafka's *The Trial* is of course the paradigm ... but one can cite any number of others ... It's interesting that just about all these works of fiction not only emphasise the comic senselessness of bureaucratic life, but mix it with at least an undertone of violence.

Clegg et al.'s paper, 'Kafkaesque power and bureaucracy,' published in the same year as Graeber's book, lends further context. The writers invoke an argument by Warner (2007): Kafka depicted the reality of bureaucratic organizing rather than producing a surreal commentary in which people were trapped by the rituals, routines, and rules of bureaucracy. The authors note that the subjects of their research exhibit the very same characteristics Kafka describes in his novels: 'Lost in a mechanism that they cannot comprehend, they experience senselessness, disorientation and helplessness, lacking any clear course of action with which to escape perceived injustice, organizational perversity, personal disorientation and power abuse' (Clegg et al., 2016: 160).

This is of course *precisely* how Kafka and countless others represent bureaucracy; but bureaucracy can also—and should also—be represented differently to this. We must not discount the possibility that Kafka's work is itself active in conditioning our collective attitudes towards bureaucracy; after all, fiction constructs every bit as much as it reflects. More pertinently, consider each of the characteristics described: senselessness, disorientation, helplessness, the inability to escape perceived injustice, organizational perversity, disorientation, and power abuse. Where have we come across comparable labels before? Each of these words could undoubtedly be used to describe the sense of anomie associated with the *post*-bureaucratic identity crisis (see chapter 2). Fiction is both persuasive and beguiling. I cannot, however, fault the authors of the paper for this bias. No—they were merely reporting on their subjects' *perceived* aspects of Kafkaesque bureaucracy. The point is, I think, that the public psyche is primed by the arts to interpret experiences of bureaucracy this way, but has no comparable priming in respect of post-bureaucracy.

So, what then of the novels and films that explore bureaucracy? As noted, the vast majority of dystopian fiction is 'bureaucracy-bashing,' whereas very little is 'bureaucracy-defending' (the Savage's infamous quip in *Brave New World* that: 'I'll make you be free whether you want to or not,' being a notable exception). Why is this? Below, I consider the historical utopian/dystopian literature, before examining more recent—20th century—technological utopian/dystopian literature. I then go on to explore contemporary utopian/dystopian literature by recourse to Amazon's current top 10 best-selling dystopian novels. I conclude, finally, by exploring the specific contributions of science fiction novelist J. G. Ballard. As we will see, bureaucracy represents a perennial dystopian theme throughout the history of the genre, whereas adhocracy (or synonymous concepts) is ignored completely.

## Bureaucratic themes in dystopian classics

More's *Utopia* (More, 1998 [1516]) is genre-setting and thus represents an important frame of reference. The text is composed of two parts, the first of which transitions from fact to fiction through the conversation between More himself, a voyager called Raphael Hythloday, and (interestingly) a civil servant called Peter Giles. Book II consists of Hythloday's travels and experience on the island of Utopia, and here the authoritarian character of the utopia becomes clearer. 'To keep cities from becoming too sparse or too crowded, they have decreed that there shall be six thousand households in each, with each household containing between ten and sixteen adults' (ibid: 55). More's island is further characterised by patriarchy (p44), homosocial identity (p50), and ubiquitous surveillance (p60). There is, of course, disagreement as to whether More intended his fictional society as desirable. Most analysis suggests, in part at least, that he did. Such a society was reasonably ambitious in More's time, a period characterised by monarchical rule and despotism. 'More's own society was rigidly hierarchical and highly regulated, so Utopia may not have seemed as restrictive to him as it does to us' (Logan and Adams, 1998: x).

The utopian premises of More's society are routinely invoked as the dystopian subject matter of early 20th century authors. Of these latter authors, most combine unrestrained technological advance with bureaucratic dominance. Huxley's *Brave New World* (1931), for example, presents a clear challenge to the social utopia presented by More. The world Huxley describes shares similar 'virtues' to More's utopia: there is no war, no official torture, no terrorism, no hunger, no crime, and no conflict. Bureaucratic techno-authoritarianism reigns, however. As Huxley (2004 [1959]: 4) himself comments, *Brave New World* is 'the nightmare of total organization.' Indeed, the plot unfolds in a world in which the industrialist, Henry Ford, is considered god-like. The religious connotations inherent in the peoples' profession, 'Our Ford' and their timely making of 'the sign of the T,' are especially noteworthy.

In the much celebrated novel *Nineteen Eighty-Four* (1999 [1949]), George Orwell explores the totalitarian ramifications of surveillance. Under the jurisprudence of the ubiquitous Big Brother, this surveillance is achieved through pervasive propaganda, the thought police, and even the development—or rather the diminishment—of the spoken language as a mechanism of social control: 'The purpose of Newspeak was not only to provide a medium of expression for the world view and mental habits proper to the devotees of Ingsoc, but to make all other modes of thought impossible' (Orwell, 1999 [1949]: 236). For both Huxley and Orwell authoritarianism was ripe for satire. For both, strict regimentation and surveillance emerge as definitive dystopian motifs. Notably, both writers lived during a period in which the social experiment of state socialism—with its huge bureaucracies—was beginning to unfold; this of course presented a formidable target for literary critique, something that is particularly evident in the work of Orwell.

*Player Piano* by Kurt Vonnegut (2006 [1952]) foresees technological catastrophe following the unconstrained advances in automation and computerisation. Each member of society carries an identity smart card on which comprehensive personal records are recorded. 'Computers regularly sift through these details, and anyone who is found doing a job that can now be done by machine joins the unemployed' (Carey, 1999: 442). As humanity slowly becomes subordinated to technology, a resistance group emerges and in its credo declares that:

there must be a virtue in inefficiency, for man is inefficient, and Man is a creation of God ... You perhaps disagree with the antique and vain notion of Man's being a creation of God. But I find it a far more defensible belief than the one implicit in intemperate faith in lawless technological progress—namely, that man is on earth to create more durable and efficient images of himself, and hence, to eliminate any justification at all for his own continued existence.

*(Vonnegut, 2006 [1952]: 302)*

Further implications of the controlled supplanting of humanity with technology are found in Forster's *The Machine Stops* (1909). In Forster's fiction, the delineated future is one in which a nebulous 'Machine' controls every aspect of human life as an early anticipation of the potential for artificial intelligence. Accordingly, human life has itself become mechanical and dehumanised. Invariably, the 'Machine' is representative of both bureaucracy and industrial alienation more generally.

## Bureaucratic themes in bestselling dystopian fiction

At the time of publication, Amazon's top 10 bestselling dystopian novels were as follows (synopses in parentheses courtesy of Amazon):

1. *The Handmaid's Tale* (It is set in a near-future New England in a totalitarian state resembling a theonomy that has overthrown the United States government.)
2. *The Fever King* (In the former United States, 16-year-old Noam Álvaro wakes up in a hospital bed, the sole survivor of the viral magic that killed his family and made him a technopath. His ability to control technology attracts the attention of the minister of defence and thrusts him into the magical elite of the nation of Carolinia.)
3. *Nineteen Eighty-Four* (The novel is set in the year 1984 when most of the world population have become victims of perpetual war, omnipresent government surveillance and propaganda.)
4. *The Rise of Magicks* (After the sickness known as the Doom destroyed civilisation, magick has become commonplace, and Fallon Swift has spent her young years learning its ways. Fallon cannot live in peace until she frees those who have been preyed upon by the government...)
5. *Ready Player One* (It's the year 2044, and the real world is an ugly place. Like most of humanity, Wade Watts escapes his grim surroundings by spending his waking hours jacked into the OASIS, a sprawling virtual utopia that lets you be anything you want to be...)
6. *Of Blood and Bone* (They look like an everyday family living an ordinary life. But beyond the edges of this peaceful farm, unimaginable forces of light and dark have been unleashed.)

7. *The Fifth Season* (The first novel in a new series by award-winning author N. K. Jemisin where a mother struggles to find her daughter in a post-apocalyptic world.)
8. *Brave New World* (Set in London in the year AD 2540 (632 A.F.—'After Ford'—in the book), the novel anticipates developments in reproductive technology, sleep-learning, psychological manipulation, and classical conditioning that combine profoundly to change society.)
9. *Extracted Trilogy* (The end of the world has been avoided—for now. With Miri and her team of extracted heroes still on the run, Mother, the disgraced former head of the British Secret Service, has other ideas… While Mother retreats to her bunker to plot her next move, Miri, Ben, Safa and Harry travel far into the future to ensure that they have prevented the apocalypse. But what they find just doesn't make sense.)
10. *The Rule of One* (In the near-future United States, a one-child policy is ruthlessly enforced. Everyone follows the Rule of One. But Ava Goodwin, daughter of the head of the Texas Family Planning Division, has a secret— one that her mother died to keep and her father has helped to hide for her entire life.)

Of these top 10 dystopian novels, in all but one (*Of Blood and Bone*), bureaucracy constitutes a discernible theme if not in name (in the case of *The Handmaid's Tale, Nineteen Eighty-Four*, and *Brave New World*), then in associated trope. So, in the case of *The Fever King* the pervasive theme of 'technopathy' is, in some respects, a contemporary re-rendering of the all-pervasive existential entrapment and control earlier writers associated with bureaucratic process. I'm thinking here of the eponymous Hal of *2001: A Space Odyssey*. In the case of *The Rise of Magicks*, one of the novel's initial frames of reference is that the prevailing government is distinctly totalitarian. For *Ready Player One*, the Oasis (the virtual 'utopian' world created as a retreat from the grim realities of the real world) transpires to be a world characterised by complete control. For *The Fifth Season*, social stratification—and its associated rigid division of labour—is all-consuming. In the *Extracted* trilogy, totalitarian governments develop time-travelling technology for their own—presumably dishonourable—ends. And, finally, *The Rule of One* couldn't be more damning of bureaucracy if it tried. The story centres on the ostensibly debilitating effects of a fictional one-child policy in modern day United States.

The pertinent point is, of course, that *none* of these novels in any sense hints at the potential debilitating effects of post-bureaucracy; of a world *without* order. Whereas we have seen some excellent defences of bureaucracy in the world of academia in recent decades, this sentiment has not yet manifested in fictional form.

## Are things any different beyond the bestseller lists?

Amazon's bestsellers are a strange mix of the classics (written prior to the scholarly research which began to challenge post-bureaucracy), and contemporary pop-fiction (unlikely to explore intellectually innovative themes). Have writers with greater intellectual credence done anything to address the imbalance? J. G. Ballard died in 2009. A year later, I took the opportunity to evaluate his lifeworks for a paper which would form part of conference funded by the Sage journal, *Organization Studies*, celebrating his life. The paper was called 'From Ballardian bureaucracy-bashing to *post*-bureaucratic identity crisis: will the real dystopian please stand up?' Unusually for an academic conference, it was held in a subterranean bar in London's trendy Hoxton. The venue was well chosen; it had a distinctly dystopian post-apocalyptic theme.

Techno-bureaucratic dystopia features prominently in Ballard's work: from the existential centrality of record-keeping in 'Minus One' (Ballard, 1963), to the mind control mediated through giant bill boards in 'The Subliminal Man' (Ballard, 2009 [1963]). There is also architectonic bureaucracy in 'The Concentration City' (Ballard, 1957) and *High Rise* (Ballard, 1975), and the concept of the mind dominated by a highly pervasive media in *The Atrocity Exhibition* (Ballard, 1970). But does Ballard help remedy this deficit in respect of bureaucracy-defence? Regrettably not. Like the classic 20th century novelists and the writers of pop-fiction in the early 21st century, Ballard stuck rigidly to bureaucracy-bashing. Perhaps more so even than his contemporaries, his examination of bureaucracy is gloriously hate-filled. What I think is so interesting about this is that, bureaucracy aside, the other hugely popular trope in dystopian fiction is the post-apocalypse. Technically, historically, and etymologically, the post-apocalypse refers to 'the revelation.' But what exactly is being revealed? In one respect, the concept of revelation represents the perfect opportunity to explore the shortcomings of post-bureaucracy. But do novelists do this? No, instead they fixate on bureau-pathology, technological failure, environmental disaster and so on. A connection is *never* made between an absence of bureaucracy and its likely ramifications.

Given this discernible influence, we find ourselves today paradoxically facing another type of dystopia: one in which bureaucracy is absent. Do we therefore require a new dystopian genre? It is perhaps worth noting that of Ballard's stories that dealt with bureaucracy, all were written (and most were published) in the 1960s or 1970s. Although Ballard lived until 2009, is it possible that he chose to publish no more in this vein because he was beginning to have a change of heart? Perhaps—rather than write stories that explored post-bureaucratic dystopias (which might have undermined the message he sought to convey in his earlier texts), he simply chose to keep quiet. We will never know. However, to the extent that the 'hyper-organizational spaces' (Zhang et al., 2008) of *Cocaine Nights* (Ballard, 1996) and *Super-Cannes* (Ballard, 2000) are representative of the social commentary that characterised his later material, then there doesn't seem to have been the shift that we might have hoped for: the spatial and organizational materiality that characterises these novels fails in any sense to transcend the all-too-familiar tropes of dystopian order and control. We are left with a fundamental problem, a deficit. This deficit can be illustrated via a simple diagram (Figure 5.1).

**92** Understanding bureau-phobia

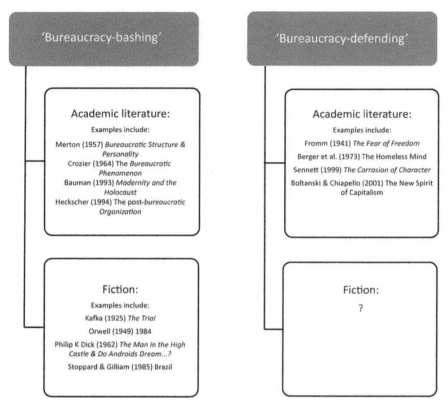

**FIGURE 5.1** The representation of bureaucracy in academic literature and fiction

So, how might this deficit be addressed? One writer without Ballard's intellectual baggage is Jonathan Franzen. His work provides a small glimmer of hope. In my mind, Franzen is the one novelist who does tackle the concept of post-bureaucracy (although he doesn't use the term, as such). Franzen's much anticipated novel, *Freedom*, was published in 2010. The highly acclaimed author is noted for his cogent ability to capture the concerns of the contemporary human condition in fictive form. In tackling the concept of freedom head on, the novel's theme explores the paradox first described in the 1930s by Erich Fromm in his seminal work, *The Fear of Freedom* (for a discussion of Fromm's contribution, see chapter 2). For Franzen, the freedom of contemporary times is cause for self-pity and is, apparently, an agent of undoing in the Western world:

> Where did the self-pity come from? The inordinate volume of it? By almost any standard, [Patty—the story's protagonist] led a luxurious life. She had all day every day to figure out some decent and satisfying way to live, and yet all

she ever seemed to get for all her choices and all her freedom was more miserable ... she pitied herself for being so free.

(Franzen, 2010: 181)

Reviewing the book for London's *Evening Standard*, Philip Delves Broughton wrote:

> This is the key theme of the book, and the reason for the title. We pampered creatures of the 21st century are ruined by our own freedom. Instead of it bringing us happiness, it brings us only uncertainty. Having eschewed the certainties and disciplines of earlier generations, we find ourselves lost and adrift, propelled by the lingering emotions of childhood into futile searches for meaning.
>
> (Evening Standard, 7 September 2010, p.23)

The book is already regarded by some, including *The Guardian*'s Jonathan Jones (2010), as the novel of the century. The message Franzen delineates is undeniably an important one. A shift towards the neoliberal (or neo-conservative) tendentious values of freedom has serious consequences.

## What now?

Dystopian fiction has long used bureaucracy as a principle trope. But why is it that dystopian fiction has tended to focus on the shortcomings of bureaucracy (typically understood in terms of bureau-pathology), but ignored completely those shortcomings associated with post-bureaucracy (particularly in respect of the existential isolation it engenders)? If we accept the argument that fiction is an active agent in crafting and constructing the fabric of our lives (including, of course, of work and organizational lives), this is a serious deficit. Our lives are enmeshed in discourses which are co-constructed and recapitulated by narratives and stories; our approach to—and consumption of—bureaucracy is no exception.

Dystopian fiction does more than entertain. Ballard and his contemporaries are not prophetic; rather their tales are cautionary and effectively so. With this in mind—and if we accept Boltanski and Chiapello's broader thesis (see chapter 2)—then Ballard constitutes part of the counter cultural revolution. In this sense, his work is a fundamental agent of change. What implications does this have for the study of organization and indeed beyond? Do the post-bureaucratic concerns outlined require a literary vehicle comparable to the significant canon dedicated to bureaucratic concerns, by way of redressing this discursive imbalance? Why is there not a literary canon dedicated to the concerns such as dislocation, perpetual flexibility, and so on? Why does fiction perennially misrepresent bureaucracy? Writers and filmmakers are normally champing at the bit to explore a new way of looking at the world. So why not in the case of post-bureaucracy? I don't portend to have the answer, but I have developed a provisional rationale. There are several points I'd like to emphasise.

First, bureaucracy since Weber has been intricately associated with the machine metaphor and this, I suspect, is seductive, particularly in celluloid form. Each of us 'is only a single cog in an ever-moving mechanism which prescribes to him an essentially fixed route of march' (Weber (2001 [1948]: 228). The machine metaphor is one which instantly conjures a sense of the foreboding. We are humans, we cry! We are *not* machines! The visual imagery dating back to at least Fritz Lang's *Metropolis* of 1927 stays with us. Machines = bad. Human beings = good. If anything this binary ethic has been further galvanised by current—critically oriented— discussions in the field of Artificial Intelligence (AI). Critics of AI, it seems, are determined to preserve what they regard as the sanctity of the human condition. This position ignores arguments to the contrary: the broader security associated with routine, ritual and tradition, and more specific microsociological utterances such as 'temping bliss' (see chapter 6), and the peculiar delights of mechanocomorphism. As noted earlier in this book, I myself am especially fond of the physicality and repetition of splitting logs for firewood in autumn in readiness for the winter ahead.

Second, it seems writers of fiction and filmmakers mistakenly see in bureaucracy a sense of *complete order*. As Law (1994: 1), notes 'perhaps there is ordering, but there is certainly no order.' Bureaucracy *orders* but it is never complete. In fact, it is precisely because bureaucracy is about [incomplete] ordering and not [complete] order, that it is so resilient. There is always potential for ordering; we are creatures that strive for order. Dystopian fiction trained on bureaucracy makes the fundamental mistake of assuming that bureaucracy is about 'pure order' rather than 'ordering'; this is comparable to the inability to distinguish between institutionalisation and total institutions encountered in chapter 4; the former denotes 'ordering,' the latter 'pure order.'

Third, writer and filmmakers appear to be hell-bent on casting bureaucracy as dystopian as they reflect on 'real-world' events. Graeber (2016: 92) notes the following:

> [L]et's return for a moment to that '68 slogan: 'All power to the imagination.' Which imagination are we referring to? If one takes this to refer to the transcendent imagination—to an attempt to impose some sort of prefab utopian vision—the effects can be disastrous. Historically, it has often meant creating some vast bureaucratic machine designed to impose such utopian visions by violence. World-class atrocities are likely to result.

This is interesting. It implies, I think, that we are predisposed towards casting bureaucracy as dystopian because of our experience of real-world events, notably state socialism. But state socialism—at least in its Soviet manifestation—ended a generation ago. Regrettably, our novelists and filmmakers appear not yet to have acknowledged this.

Fourth, where bureaucrats *are* cast as protagonists, the value of the bureaucratic context itself never constitutes the take-home message.

Bureaucracy, after all, has been around for thousands of years, and bureaucratic societies, from Sumer and Egypt, to Imperial China, have produced great literature. But modern North Atlantic societies are the very first to have created genres of literature where the heroes themselves are bureaucrats, or operate entirely within bureaucratic environments.

*(Graeber 2016: 74–5)*

It isn't clear who Graeber has in mind when he refers to these 'hero-bureaucrats,' but I think I know what he's getting at. He's hinting at the Erin Brokovichs of this world i.e. those who achieve great things within the machinations of the corporation. I guess he's probably onto something, but—unlike the bureaucracy-as-dystopia motif, films such as *Erin Brokovich* are memorable not for their specific treatment of bureaucracy, but for the protagonists themselves. Despite Graeber's inference, such films do not mould our collective beliefs about—and attitudes towards—bureaucracy.

Finally, perhaps fictive defences of bureaucracy, however well crafted, simply aren't sexy enough. Ironically, it is dystopia's bleakness that constitutes its appeal. Bauman (2017: 58) notes in *Retrotopia* that:

> our sci-fi films and novels are more and more catalogued in the sections of horror movies and gothic literature. These days we tend to fear the future, having lost trust in our collective ability to mitigate its excesses, to render it less frightful and repellent, as well as somewhat user friendlier. What we still, by inertia, call 'progress' evokes … fear of an impending catastrophe.

Bauman suggests that this bleak outlook is down to the fact that we have lost faith in the future and so increasingly look to the past for inspiration and (re)invention. But does Bauman's argument overlook the suggestion that dystopia makes for a more engaging story than utopia? Science fiction has become increasingly bleak in its outlook and in part at least this is most probably because we find a perverse sort of pleasure in bleakness. If, as a form of entertainment, dystopia is more profitable than positive renderings of future worlds, then rather than cultivate a body of fictive literature that celebrates the 'secret joys' (to use Graeber's words) of bureaucracy, we're probably better off cultivating comparable *post*-bureaucratic dystopian narratives These will most likely be just as bleak (albeit for different reasons), and hence as profitable.

Reflecting on this fictive deficit I was reminded of a superb paper called 'Autonomy as utopia and dystopia.' In it, the authors, Knights and Willmott (2002: 59, 60) explore the

> contemporary conventional wisdom of western culture: the understanding that autonomy is an unalloyed virtue, a version of utopia to be pursued without qualification precisely because it is viewed as unequivocally desirable and virtuous. The modern association with individual or collegial freedom, self-

determination and self-expression give autonomy its laudatory and seductive appeal ... Mindful of how the other utopian visions—from Plato to More or from Hitler to Skinner—entertain practices that are, arguably, oppressive, we should be attentive to the potential of autonomy to be dystopic in the name of self-determination.

Utopias are active literary devices. This is because utopias are technically—and empirically—unrealisable; instead their value lies in their pedagogy. 'Our concern [is] to interrogate the identification of autonomy as a commonsense utopia: an unquestioned aspiration that may never be wholly realised but is nonetheless regarded as a desirable, virtuous goal' (ibid. 77). In one fell swoop, Knights and Willmott note that the opposite of bureaucracy is universally regarded as a utopian end. This observation is of course the counterpoint of my broader point that post-bureaucracy—or anti-autonomy—never gets the dystopian treatment it so clearly warrants.

# PART III
# Towards a New Education in Bureaucracy

# 6
# A BUREAUCRATIC BIOGRAPHY

David Myatt has described himself variously as a Neo-Nazi, an Islamic Fundamentalist and a scholar of Ancient Greece. Perhaps more so than most he knows the value of autoethnography. For those unfamiliar with its purpose, value, and reliability, I open this chapter with the following quote, courtesy of Myatt:

> Wisdom arises from personal suffering; or personal experience is the genesis of true learning' Myatt defines *pathei-mathos* by saying: 'The Greek term πάθει μάθος derives from the *Agamemnon* of Aeschylus (written *c*. 458 BCE), and can be interpreted, or translated, as meaning learning from adversary, or wisdom arises from (personal) suffering; or personal experience is the genesis of true learning.'
>
> ('David Myatt,' Wikipedia, *accessed 28th February 2019*)

Personal experience is the genesis of true learning. I rather like that. I include this chapter for two reasons. First, to the best of my knowledge, the academy has yet to produce a scholarly autoethnography of bureaucracy. Second, one of my regrets about the classical literature of bureaucracy (and this, I think, is true of many social concepts) is that we don't really have a feel of what bureaucracy was actually like in times gone by, including of course, Weber's. Arguably, this is because anthropological methods were not especially well regarded at the time. The distinct flavour of bureaucracy at the dawn of the 20th century will thus forever be out of reach to us. By including this chapter, I hope to give scholars of the future a feel of bureaucracy in the early 21st century. In so doing I am, as they say, contributing to the ethnographic record.

In 1964, and on the opening page of *Modern Organizations*, the eminent sociologist Amitai Etzioni (1964) penned the following:

> Our society is an organizational society. We are born in organizations, educated by organizations, and most of us spend much of our lives working for organizations. We spend much of our leisure time paying, playing and praying

in organizations. Most of us will die in an organization, and when the time comes for burial, the largest organization of them all—the state—must grant official permission.

Over half a century has passed since this utterance. But what has actually changed? Arguably, each of us leads a life underscored by organization. Each of us has a biography shaped by successive organizational environments and, by implication, shaped by successive bureaucracies; a 'bureaucratic biography,' if you like. This is how I validate an autoethnographic account of bureaucracy. Our rendering of life is both as producer and consumer of bureaucracy; this experience is invaluable. The data presented in this chapter help develop two arguments: First, often contrary to expectation, biographies of bureaucracy reveal *both* negative experiences (in terms of inflexibility, nonchalance, and pettiness) and positive experiences (in terms of equity, enculturation, comfort, warmth and belonging, 'temping bliss,' and ethics). Second, a tentative appreciation for bureaucracy appears to emerge slowly, over time.

## 'Self as datum'

As an ethnographer and organizational anthropologist, in this chapter I present an 'autoethnography *a posteriori*' (Boncori and Vine, 2014) exploring and reflecting on my own experiences of multiple bureaucracies. The chapter begins with my early recollections of organizational life in a North London nursery in the early 1980s, and then through a sequence of 'secure' bureaucratic educational environments. From here I then plunge into the world of work: as an employee, a freelancer, and small business owner. I then reflect on my current role as mediator between my students and the university's bureaucracy, as Executive MBA Programme leader at Suffolk Business School. Finally, I reflect on the bureaucracy of births, marriages, and deaths, in the form of my own wedding; the birth of my daughter, Sophie, last year; and the death of my mother, in 2012.

## Bureaucracy: from one secure bureaucratic holding environment to another

### *Dinosaurs Playgroup (1980–1981)*

I was three years old. The playgroup was called Dinosaurs. Kids love dinosaurs. Apparently. My memories are obviously hazy and it is difficult to disentangle what I remember from the time, from later memories of looking at photographs or listening to recounted anecdotes courtesy of my parents. But this should not distract from their relevance. Although very young I'm pretty certain that I remember a discernible sense of dis-ease regarding the singing of the classic nursery rhyme, *Baa Baa Black Sheep*. This was north London and an ethnically-diverse area, Hornsey. It was controversial because some parents considered it racist. My mum volunteered at the nursery and one of the parents complained that another parent had referred to her son's 'black eye' erroneously. 'It's a *bruised* eye,' the parent stressed. I would imagine that the original utterance was said innocuously, but I can't be sure. What's relevant about all of this? Well, strangely, I think it was my first experience of the dynamics of an ostensibly secure bureaucratic environment. Whereas at home, such disagreements were dealt with through the *ad hoc* informal machinations of family discourse, here such disagreements were mediated more formally: the nursery issued a letter to parents, delineating what was considered appropriate vocabulary. Such officialdom was, apparently, considered 'ridiculous' by many of the lower middle class—white—parents, including my mum. My mother was no racist but presumably felt that this was undermining a tradition. She was herself the daughter of a Polish refugee and claimed to be a cheerleader for diversity. What I found interesting, however, was that she seemingly resented other people's rights to feel offended by what she herself considered inoffensive. Certain feelings were apparently legitimate, others—she felt—were not. The point about the black/bruised eye fell into the latter category. What astonished me, however, was this was the first time that I noted a discrepancy between my mother's reading of the world and 'the world as it was.' It is, after all, the bureau that mediates and makes official. The bureaucracy determined that the labelling of a 'black eye' was—at least, potentially—racist. On the face of it, this anecdote is about that most dubious (and analytically imprecise) of concepts, political correctness. However, what it reveals at a deeper level is that it is the bureau that mediates and creates the 'ethics of the day.' As Patriotta (2003: 181, cited in Styhre 2007: 81) notes of bureaucracy: 'Controversies recede into the background and legitimate knowledge is sealed into organizational black boxes.' Now, while I'm sure there is still some disagreement over the nursery rhyme today, it is interesting to see how things have changed. This was the bureau creating the 'official' discourse.

What more can I say about my experience at Dinosaurs? I certainly recall it serving as a form of organizational identity-formation (and, of course, subsequent dis-integration.), most likely my first. I met Jesse Campbell, who would become a childhood friend there. His parents were more readily-identifiable as North London literati. His mother, Jane, had been privately-educated and used expressions like 'frightfully punctual.' I loved how she spoke. His Dad, the late child psychologist, Dr David Campbell worked at the Tavistock Clinic. Jesse and I got on very well at Dinosaurs. We played there and at each other's home. Our play was creative and inventive; inspired, even. After a year, school-wise, we went our separate ways. My parents wanted a Catholic education for me. Jesse's parents didn't. He went on to Coleridge Primary School and then a liberal-oriented independent school in Hampstead (known colloquially as the private school for children of affluent Guardian readers). I went on to Our Lady of Muswell primary school and then St. Ignatius College. Inevitably, both rather conservative; neither a bastion of progressive, free-thinking. Jesse's education was clearly quite different. Although we stayed friends while of primary school age, we lost touch in our teens. But as chance would have it, we bumped into one another in October 1997 in *The Cooler*, a nightclub in a subterranean part of Warwick University's students' union. Each of us inebriated, it was a jubilant reunion. We were both Freshers at the same university. I was studying at Warwick Business School; he in the Department of Philosophy. To this end, I imagine we were each products of our early environments, and notably the organizational bureaucracies to which we had each been subjected were—to some degree—influential in this respect. Regrettably, the relationship between culture and bureaucracy tends not to be explored in the literature. Indeed, for the most part, bureaucracy tends to be considered as *a*cultural. It isn't. Far from it. I must of course be extremely careful not to reify bureaucracy; the point is subtler. Bureaucracy validates experience. Bureaucracy validates prevailing norms. Bureaucracy validates culture. We were both members of Dinosaurs. Now, while I can't say for sure whether or not Jesse's parents sided with the concerns of the complainants in respect of the *Baa Baa Black Sheep* (and the subsequent black/bruised eye) debate, as educated, progressive thinkers I would imagine they did. Mine didn't. At least not until the letter in question was circulated. Bureaucracy therefore helped shape my parents' attitudes; it 'contained' the culture at Dinosaurs.

## *Our Lady of Muswell Roman Catholic Primary School (1982–1989)*

On to my primary school. I loved my primary school. I was a confident, bright kid and felt secure there. I was probably a pain in the ass. Anyway, I was part of a class. I was part of a school. I was part of a national education system. Each week I took home a letter, the purpose of which was to keep parents up to date. My friends didn't just have forenames but surnames as well. Siblings—across year groups—could be identified by common surnames. Registers were taken at the very beginning of class every morning, like clockwork. Students were listed alphabetically by surname. As Vine, I was always the penultimate student's name to be read out. I always wanted to be one of the first names to be read out but not necessarily the first; the third or fourth would do. Although 'low-ranking' in terms of surname, I was one of the older kids in the class (being born in December) and I felt an extraordinary sense of pride about this. I was always one of the first to have her or his birthday each year. Moreover, my birthday was near Christmas and I noticed that people tended to be in a jubilant mood at this time of year. I also remember wondering why the school year started in September. Why not in January? That would make more sense. If the new school year did begin in January, would I be one of the youngest in the class? Would that have made a difference to the person I would go on to become? Would it have made a difference to my identity? The answer is *probably* since bureaucracy co-constructs culture. Within the class, we were also divided into groups. Ostensibly, these groupings were based on academic ability though this wasn't entirely obvious at the time. We sat on tables in these groups. We always sat in the same chair. Each of our desks bore our name. I became friends with those people I sat adjacent to. I leaned to spell their names.

They would become influences on me and me on them. The organization—the bureaucracy—was part of me and I was part of it.

## St. Ignatius College (1989–1996)

Secondary school was a ball ache. I think it probably is for most kids. I spent most of my time at secondary school either terrified or frustrated. And I ended up as Head Boy. God only knows what it was like for others. In fairness, this may just be that the teens are a difficult period in anyone's life. As a bureaucracy, however, St. Ignatius was—I suppose—not dissimilar to other senior schools: letters to parents, streams, houses, subject choices, examinations, university applications. Oh, and rugby. I played rugby for all seven years. I didn't really like it to be honest but each time I tried get out of the team, I failed. And I'm not quite sure why. I guess I felt a sense of responsibility to the team. Or perhaps it was shame. At one point, I approached our coach and explained to him that I wanted to quit the team as I felt my schoolwork was suffering as a result of the commitment. His response: 'Vine, I can't make you stay in the team.' He then walked away. What the fuck did that mean? I honestly didn't know. It worked though. I begrudgingly continued to play for the team. It wasn't even as though I was much good. To this day, I'm not quite sure why there was so much pressure on me to remain. But looking back twenty-five years later, Mr Barrett's words begin to make sense. What he meant, I think, is that while he personally could not make me stay in the team, his office could. The *bureau* could. The school—as organization—could. Nothing more needed to be said. The school had invested in me and wanted a return on that investment.

## The University of Warwick (1997–2001)

I had a full grant to study at Warwick. It wasn't really warranted. My dad owned a small advertising agency and my mum was a senior pharmacist at a private hospital in London. Somewhere along the line, however, there must have been a tick in the right box and this qualified me for the full grant. I'm not sure exactly why I qualified for it. I think it may have been that my parents were divorced. *Are your parents divorced?* Yes. That works out at £12,000 grant. Like any self-respecting student in the 1990s, I pissed every penny of it up the wall. (What was clearly intended to create a sense of equity didn't quite work on this occasion.) It was at Warwick, however, that I explored the concept of bureaucracy in a scholarly context for the first time. Professor Gibson Burrell had an enormous influence on me. I'd not met somebody with his scholarly curiosity before. On our Advanced Organizational Behaviour module, he introduced us to Bauman's work on the Holocaust (see chapter 4). Could it really be that the Holocaust was facilitated by modern *bureaucratic* methods of management? This was a monumental mindfuck. Interestingly, and perhaps inevitably, it is the bureaucratic elements of Warwick I remember most fondly. I still recall the smooth texture of the wood veneer on the office window where we nervously queued to collect our assignment grades and feedback. I still remember the style, format and even the feel of the feedback pro forma. It was a photocopied affair with a large box for verbatim feedback. I still recall the peculiar sense of comfort, warmth, and belonging when sat late at night on the fourth floor of Warwick's library. I loved being surrounded by books. I would dream about the knowledge they contained and that even if I sat here for everyday for the rest of my life, I couldn't possible read them all.

## *Electoral Reform Services (2001–2007)*

I joined Electoral Reform Services in 2001, as a temp. I had just completed my Master's degree and needed some cash. I was stuffing envelopes alongside a team of other precariously employed individuals. One of these was an eccentric bloke who described himself as a 'serial-temper.' He was an out of work writer in his 50s, but apparently loved working for a temp agency. Why, I asked. Through the repetitive work, he suggested he could obtain what he referred to as 'temping bliss.' He would plug in his headphones, stuff envelopes to the rhythm and realise his own personal sense of nirvana. The critical management academic in me wanted to deconstruct this and attribute it to false consciousness, self-deception or denial. To this day, however, I am convinced not only that he was speaking honestly but that temping bliss is a genuine experience. And not, as Pentland and Router (cited in Styhre 2007: 188) imply, simply as 'grammars of action' from which the skilful and knowledgeable co-worker can hone individual practices. No. There is something deeper here; something that goes to the heart of the experience. Think about it. It is no coincidence that so many hobbies (which are, of course, undertaken as a form of relaxation or escapism), follow a repetitive/routine logic: stamp-collecting, bird-watching, knitting, model-making, and so on. This of course flies in the face of the expectation that many of us today are compelled to embrace careers characterised by change and dynamism. It is here that I invoke Chandler's (2012) paper, 'Work as Dance':

> I have no wish to romanticize work, to ignore the degradation of labour ... or to argue that repetitive work produces pleasure as frequently as dance does. I do, however, want to suggest that this is at least a possibility—and that even degraded work might, by very nature of its repetitiveness and rhythmic qualities, be experienced by those doing it as more or less pleasurable at times. At the very least we might be drawn along in work, and remember the distinction ... made between tedium and traction—with the opportunities for traction provided by repetitive, cyclical work providing a degree of satisfaction (or at least pseudo-satisfaction) as an alternative to tedium.
>
> *(Chandler, 2012: 9)*

Is it really possible to pair bureaucracy with dance? Ultimately, such connections do make sense once we begin to regard bureaucracy not as *a*cultural (as it so often assumed), but as something with discernible anthropological pertinence. Graeber (2016: 44) deliberately sets out to understand what is appealing about bureaucracy.

However, I'm not convinced he achieves this, and I think part of the reason he fails to do so is because he doesn't fully acknowledge what we've described here as 'temping bliss.' Kallinikos (2004: 14), meanwhile and as we have already noted, defends bureaucracy. Nevertheless, he feels compelled to defend bureaucracy from those who 'associate ... bureaucracy with routine, initiative-stifling office work and an introvert organizational culture of rigid administrative procedures and redundant complexity.' He does so by suggesting that bureaucracy is misrepresented when described as such. I'm not convinced by this defence. Better surely to acknowledge that this is indeed what some aspects of bureaucracy are like—at least in terms of how bureaucracy is *experienced*—and then focus on the merits of repetition. Personally, I regard routine and paperwork as salient; as vital existential aspects of organizational life.

Back to the story. It turns out that I was damn good at stuffing envelopes. So good, in fact, that the Deputy Chief Executive noticed. We began chatting and few weeks later I found myself working as a project coordinator with a fair bit of responsibility. Now, I present this slightly differently on my CV and biography. I say (quite persuasively, I think) that I had a pre-existing interest in psephology and managed to find work at the Electoral Reform Services. This is I think a conscious attempt to 'narrativize' and provide a trajectory for—my career (see chapter 3). It's mostly bullshit, of course. But that is what is expected. Right?

Electoral Reform Services was, to all intents and purposes, my first experience of a commercial bureaucracy. I recall being stubbornly anti-bureaucratic. The organization used a job specification system. Each job for each client was allocated a job number, and a pro forma had to be completed in each case (the 'job spec,' as it was known). Over the course of my employment, this transitioned to an online system. I hated it. I would find ever more elaborate ways of circumventing the system. I had been employed to manage a new type of project and these pro formas were not geared towards them. The organization was used to managing elections and ballots, but my job was to manage voter registration projects. It felt like I spent half my time resisting the system. I created alternative online job management programmes tailored to the voter registration projects I was managing. I shared these with the necessary personnel. They appreciated this but wanted a job spec as well! This struck me as insane. Why the hell was I having the duplicate this information? I figured it was an unnecessary and thoroughly bureaucratic—in the pejorative sense—process. At the time, I assumed that I was alone in the universe; the only person ever to have found themselves in a situation where the bureaucratic expectations of the organization didn't neatly fall into place with my own operational aspirations (this was, after all, my first 'proper' job). Until the day I left the organization in 2007, I refused to yield to the status quo. God only knows how much time and effort I spent resisting the firm's bureaucracy. In hindsight, it was a poor strategy on my part. I should have simply completed the relevant paperwork each time. It would have been far less taxing, and—notably—less stressful for all involved.

And in hindsight, I understand why the pro formas in question were so important for others in the organization. Although all the information other personnel required was available in the bespoke system I had created to manage my voter registration projects, other departments (notably, marketing, HR, and accounts) were all used to working in accordance with the traditional job specs, and no doubt had their own local systems in place for harvesting the information they needed from these job specs to fulfil their specific part of the process. This might seem quite obvious to most readers, but as a 22-year-old graduate (and especially one who had been indoctrinated with respect to the evils of bureaucracy on my degree programmes), it was a perspective I hadn't encountered. So obsessed was Warwick with instilling a critical mind-set in its students (which it did extremely well), it had neglected to provide its students with a perfunctory understanding of bureaucracy. I was unprepared to yield to the system which the organization used (and in so doing expected everybody else to yield to *my* system). This, I suspect, is a common reason for bureaucratic frustration. We have a tendency to assume that our encounters with specific types of paperwork, rules and regulations are down to ineffectual or apathetic staff elsewhere in the organization. My experience since suggests it is because ways of doing things must inevitably involve compromise. Perhaps with the exception of the original architect of an organization's 'system,' all other organizational actors have had to compromise. Why should we be treated any differently?

Reflecting on this early experience in a commercial organization, bureaucracy seems to represent an institutional check on selfish orientations; it's a sort of moral compass. I felt that trying to adapt my projects to suit the administrative apparatus of the organization was a waste of my time. I was, at the time, convinced that others should yield to my way of doing things rather than the other way round. But as I have matured, I have begun to regard the 'trappings' of bureaucracy as a rather beguiling—and effective—form of ethics.

A final point about my nature of my employment at Electoral Reform Services. When I was first offered a job as a project manager, I was originally asked whether I wanted permanent work or contract work. Permanent would work out at £13/hour, contract at £15/hour. It was a no brainer. Not only would I get paid a higher hourly rate, but I could work 12 hours a day and get paid for each of them! I spent the next four years figuring out as many ways as possible to stay late (or start early). I did so, not so much because I was greedy (although I readily admit I was motivated by cash). No, I did so because I was acutely aware that, irrespective of how hard I worked, I was disposable. Four years later, exhausted, it eventually dawned on me that a salaried position—although less lucrative on a month-by-month basis—was probably the better bet. The virtues of full time, secure work had become clear. When my contract was next up for review, they again tabled the option of a permanent position. This time, I took it.

### *The University of Essex (2007–2011)*

In 2007, I began my PhD at the University of Essex. I was fortunate enough to win a full doctoral scholarship. Despite this golden hello, my then attitudes towards the nature of bureaucracy made for a pretty miserable experience. There are several anecdotes worth recounting here in respect of bureaucracy. The first concerns Essex Business School's administration office. Notably, the Essex Business School 'Admin Office' was only open on a Tuesday afternoon. It was never open when you needed it to be. Why a Tuesday afternoon? In my mind, the bureaucrats were at the top of the pyramid. Why not the academics? Why not the students (the customers)? I had arrived at Essex with a naïve (and somewhat patronising) belief that administrative staff were there to support academics and should even be slightly in awe of them. Forget it. As PhD students, we were encouraged to work as Graduate Teaching Assistants. My first task was to mark 228 scripts on the *Introduction to Management* module. It was a soul-destroying task. It took me two whole weeks. I was exhausted. I queued patiently on the Tuesday morning when the office was open to return the scripts to the administrators. The administrators were responsible for recording the grades, coordinating their moderation, and then returning the scripts to the students. I eventually got to the front of the queue, handed over the enormous box to the woman seated on the other side of the desk. 'They're not in alphabetical order,' she said nonchalantly. She may as well have had a cigarette hanging out of her mouth and rollers in her hair. 'Er, no,' I replied. 'We won't accept them until they're in alphabetical order.' Sure enough, the contract I was working under stated that the responsibility of academic staff was to return scripts to the office in alphabetical order. It was another half hour's work to get them in order, by which time the office would be closed. 'You'll have to return next week,' she said.

I was seriously pissed off. Once again, in hindsight, I am able to see things from the Office's point of view. If it took half an hour of my time to get the scripts in order, then presumably it would take half an hour of one of an administrator's time. At some point, the bureaucracy had decided—quite sensibly, in fact—that the academic should be responsible for alphabetising the scripts. Why? Well, he or she would be handling each of them anyway and—while doing so—could (it turns out) quite easily slot them into alphabetical order. It was, inevitably, a lot more difficult to do this retrospectively. Of course, the administrator I spoke to could have been more polite. She could have even explained why it was that the academic is expected to alphabetise them. But, then, she was most likely underpaid and under-appreciated herself.

The second anecdote concerns the PhD student study area. It had been nicknamed 'The Factory.' We all rather liked this name, but had no idea where it originated. The metaphor worked on a number of levels, and was especially pertinent given that Essex Business School styled itself as a hotbed of critical management scholarship. I enrolled in September 2007, and this was, apparently, the first year in which international PhD students outnumbered home-grown ones. By the time I left in 2011, there were virtually no British nationals on the doctoral programme. The PhD programme (like the undergraduate and postgraduate taught programmes before it), had become a cash cow. PhD students were no longer there to enrich the scholarly reputation of the university, but were another stream of revenue. It *was* a factory.

The third anecdote. While studying at Essex, I lived 7 miles away in Brightlingsea. Typically, I cycled to campus, but on rainy days I would drive. However, I resented having to pay to park: 'I'm an impoverished PhD student. Why must I pay?,' I thought. In my third year, the University decided to outsource the management of the car parks to a private organization. In typically pseudo-socialist style, I rebelled and encouraged my fellow students to rebel too. Fines were being issued left, right, and centre. I myself succumbed to a £50 fine having parked with one of my rear tyres on one of the white lines which delineated the parking spaces. This was, apparently, a contravention of the rules. I was furious. I appealed to the university but they said they had no power to intervene. I was so frustrated that I went to one of the banks on campus and withdrew the equivalent of £50 in 20 pence pieces and took them to pay the clampers. If this pissed them off (as I'd intended), they didn't show it. They were probably used to it.

The final anecdote. When I formally submitted the hard copy of my PhD thesis in 2011, the clerk gave me a receipt. A piece of paper. That was it. Interestingly, she commented that there is no fanfare. I think she was trying to empathise with what I had achieved. But, frankly, it was the piece of paper I was after. The last thing I wanted was a big band. Indeed, it was this piece of paper that I clung on to until I finally received a letter from the University of Essex addressed to *Dr* Tomasz George Vine. That was a special moment with immense bureaucratic implications.

## *The Findhorn Foundation (2009–2010)*

The Findhorn Foundation, a New Age 'intentional community'—or commune—in Scotland, became the ethnographic case study for my doctoral research. My mother had recently become fascinated by New Age subcultures and Findhorn was a powerful brand in those circles. I was curious to learn more about it. I solicited permission to live and work with the commune. I was expecting an exotic way of life completely detached from conventional organization. As the research came to a close, however, it was not the differences that were remarkable but the likenesses. I have commented extensively on this research elsewhere (see, for example, Vine, 2018a, 2020b). Here follows abridged coverage trained on our current discussions of bureaucracy. Notably, a sense of the bureaucratic was intuited from the outset of the research.

On the 16th February 2009, I sent an email to Findhorn introducing myself as a doctoral student interested in studying their community. I received the following response:

> Dear Tom. Thank you for your enquiry. The best start here is to participate in Experience Week. It is the basic building block upon which our other programmes and explorations are built. You will find much about us on our

website www.findhorn.org. I hope this is helpful. Donald (For Findhorn Foundation Enquiries)

I was struck at the apparent modularity and formality of involvement: 'Experience Week ... is the basic building block upon which the other programmes and explorations are built.' This sounded light years away from my preconceptions: communes were supposed to be *informal* counter-cultural collectives! But unlike the vast majority of communes established in the 1960s and 1970s, of which very few survived, Findhorn *had* survived. The formality, however, did necessitate a financial outlay on my part. Even with a discount for those on low income (including students, such as myself), the fee for 'Experience Week' was £395, paid online. The whole transaction was comparable to booking a hotel or flight. For Carrette and King (2005: 15) this would undoubtedly constitute evidence of the 'commodification of religion'; for me, however, it was my first taste of the formalisation of New Age spirituality. All particulars (full name, date of birth, address, nationality, contact details, and so on) were required before the transaction was complete. I was also required to submit a personal statement which described my 'spiritual background' and rationale for enrolling on Experience Week. Suffice to say, as a doctoral researcher, I had plenty to declare.

Upon arrival in Scotland for *Experience Week* there was continued evidence of this formalised approach to organizational life, as recorded in my field notes:

> I arrived at the Visitors Centre at the Findhorn Foundation at the time stipulated. I introduced myself to the woman at the desk. Her appearance was entirely conventional; I think I had been expecting tie-dye attire and facial piercings. With an air of no nonsense professionalism, any remaining prejudice began to fade. Without prompting, she asked me if I was Tom Vine ... They were expecting me. 'Before proceeding any further,' she said, 'I must ask you to verify [and, it transpired, sign off] the personal details you supplied online'.

Her insistence that the details for next of kin must be accurate made me feel a little uneasy; my private prejudices momentarily resurfaced as I contemplated the grisly fate of Howie in *The Wicker Man*.

Bureaucracy, it seems, is pervasive even in the most unlikely of circumstances: even at a proverbial 'hippie commune.' But this was a bureaucracy with a difference. Over the course of the ethnographic research, I noted some unusual manifestations of what were essentially bureaucratic artefacts. So, for example, during Experience Week, the work timetable participants received was handwritten, and in places charmingly illustrated. This, I think, illustrates a way in which Findhorn is not trying to be *post-bureaucratic*, as such, but to re-enculturate bureaucracy. Moreover, when interviewing one of the managers at Findhorn, Alfie, I asked him to comment on the nature of the structure at Findhorn. It was, perhaps unsurprisingly, presented as an inverted pyramid. He explained that the Findhorn management structure is hierarchy, but with a difference:

You know in the outside world there's this management pyramid structure like this [he gestures]. Well what we did … a long time ago is that we just took this pyramid and kind of tipped it upside down [he gestures again] so it puts everybody who was at the bottom, at the top. So the chair … her responsibility is to support the managers … the managers' responsibility is to support the focalisers [a term used describe a role comparable to that of supervisor] … the focalisers are there to support all the staff and students in their departments … and the role of those departments is to support the guests … so the guests are actually at the top of the heap … and the whole lot sits firmly on the shoulders of God. So it sounds like a pretty solid foundation to me.

Claims about inverted hierarchy aside, to the extent that bureaucracy can be reduced to *process*, the organizational structure at Findhorn is therefore bureaucratic. In this sense, the fact that the structure is ostensibly inverted is of less significance—the salient point is that there *is* a hierarchical structure. As I discovered, offices at Findhorn are delineated both by function (work departments) and level (guests-staff-focalisers-managers), and roles are assigned (via a process known as 'attunement') in the spirit of bureaucratic administration. Moreover, one might plausibly argue that the servant leadership structure Alfie describes is bureaucracy *par excellence*, since occupiers of the bureau, are—or at least ought to be—regarded as ('public' or 'civil,' for example) 'servants.' Indeed, this resonates specifically with Weber's discussion of bureaucratic rulers, for whom he describes as 'the first servants' of the state (Weber, 1968 [1922]: 957).

Over the course of my research, I met—and in some cases got to know very well—many different people. As my relationship with participants grew stronger, and where circumstances permitted, I oriented our conversations to get a feel for their lives prior to and beyond Findhorn. I collected life historical data for 31 subjects in total. This data suggested that the perennial appeal of Findhorn lies not in its exotic presentation, but in its ability to offer participants an experience which is familiar, conventional, and *bureaucratic*. So why exactly is Findhorn so desirable? Well, it seems the people it attracts are those for whom such conventional organizational experiences are now out of reach. In profiling the participants, I noted that they are typically unemployed, precariously employed or retired. Clearly, we must be wary of conflating correlation with causation which is why the qualitative flavour of the research was so important; however, *all* participants reported on feelings of anomie, which were attributed directly to the neoliberal agenda (see chapters 2 and 3). Initially, at least, participants typically described the appeal of Findhorn in terms of either its spiritual or ecological credentials, but deeper analysis revealed that it was the appeal was far more prosaic: it was the sense of togetherness, camaraderie, routine, and formality that constituted the enduring attraction.

## VineLogistics (2007–2014)

While studying for my PhD, I decided to start a business so as to maintain an income to supplement my grant. The horror stories of red tape encountered when seeking to establish a small business simply didn't apply in my case. I continued to use my own bank account and I completed a tax return each year. I adjusted the insurance on my own vehicle to cover business use. I had a basic website. I tapped into my existing network of organizational contacts. I could pick and choose the jobs I fancied to work around my academic commitments. However, to begin with I lived in constant fear of the tax return process. Not because I was fearful of getting something wrong, but I kept thinking how easy it would be to lie about my income (or, more plausibly, overstate my expenses). Who on earth would actually bother checking? Her Majesty's Revenue and Customs presumably have bigger fish to fry. A decimal place in the wrong place could save me £3,000. I could pretend it was a mistake if they ever chased me. I could keep records to show how the mistake was due to an oblique photocopy or whatever. I would fantasise about ever more complex scenarios in which I'd manage to fleece the government. Ultimately, I was always entirely honest in my returns and continue to be today. The question is: why are we so honest if it is so easy to fleece the system? The answer, I think, is that the bureaucratic process is all-encompassing. A rogue record will *always* exist. It will niggle away. It's there in black and white in a lever arch file on a shelf in the basement of the Income Revenue offices (think closing scene of *Raiders of the Lost Ark*) or, more likely, tucked away in an electronic database somewhere. And even if no-one ever finds out, the paperwork knows; the bureau knows. And that is what counts. The bureau is unseen but all-knowing.

## The London School of Management and Science (now defunct)[1]

Christ on a bike. This was an interesting experience. I was fresh out of my PhD. Within seven weeks I was leading the MBA programme at the now defunct London School of Management and Science (LSMS). This is not to imply that I was some sort of whiz kid. No. It was fortuitous. Or not. This was a business school located on the 7th Floor of a grubby office block in a deprived part of London. The enrolled students were all international, and recruited predominantly from a specific region in India. Several studied dutifully, but of others suspicions circulated regarding the visa game. Everything was in a state of flux and confusion. I went three months without pay. I did eventually receive my pay, but only when I threatened legal action. There was no contract, no role description, no paperwork, no office, no permanent staff. In fact, I could reel off each of Weber's characteristics of bureaucracy (security, hierarchy, monocracy, linearity, departmentalisation, impersonality, certification, stability, efficiency, classlessness, secrecy, and ubiquity) one by one and note that *none* of them applied at LSMS.

So, what's the point? Well, I have never been less happy in a place of work. This should not negatively reflect on the shortcomings of LSMS. Its staff were doing their best. The problem came down to the fact that the organization had grown too quickly and was completely devoid of structure. To work there was to feel completely and utterly alienated, and this of course meant that the quality of education students received was severely compromised. I couldn't help but conclude that alienation comes not from the economic superstructure as Marx suggested, but from its complete absence.

## *The University of Suffolk*

Graeber (2016: 53–4) notes that the underrepresentation of ethnographic work in the study of bureaucracy is rather odd because:

> you would think academics are personally positioned to speak of the absurdities of bureaucratic life. Of course, this is in part because they *are* bureaucrats—increasingly so. 'Administrative responsibilities,' going to committee meetings, filling out forms, reading and writing letters of support, placating the whims of minor deans—all this takes up an ever-expanding portion of the average academic's time. But academics are also reluctant bureaucrats, in the sense that even when 'admin,' as it's called, ends up becoming most of what a professor actually does, it is always treated as something tacked on—not what they are really qualified for, certainly, and not the work that defines who they really are. They are scholars—people who research, analyse, and interpret things—even if increasingly, they're really scholarly souls trapped in a bureaucrat's body. You might think that an academic's reaction would be to research, analyse and interpret this very phenomenon … [y]et for some reason, this never happens.

I hope to address the deficiency Graber describes. Suffolk is my current employer and so my experience of bureaucracy here is freshest. That is not to say it is more or less bureaucratic than any of the other organizations I have been a member of (apart, of course, from LSMS). There is one episode, in particular, on which I would like to reflect.

I began at Suffolk in January 2012. Later that year, I was appointed programme leader for the MBA programme. For the first couple of years, I enjoyed this role. Eventually, however, Registry decided that all decisions regarding extenuating circumstances would be centralised. This struck me as absurd. Those furthest away from the students and hence least familiar with them, their intentions, attendance, and personal circumstances would be making decisions about their future. What was *my* role, I asked? I started to avoid speaking to my students fearful that anything I did say would prejudice their particular case. Ultimately, I used my biannual board report to outline my concerns. I present the relevant section from this report, below.

I have concerns about the future of the MBA programme. Upon my appointment in 2012, it was explained to me that my programme leadership responsibilities were fourfold: 1. to make admissions decisions; 2. to improve quality; 3. to get the very best out of each student; and 4. to provide strategic direction. With the exception of admissions decisions where—thankfully—I continue to receive full support from the University, I am now unable to realise any one of the other three objectives.

As academic leaders, any scope we had to exercise professional judgement has been systematically removed over the intervening 5 years. This includes advice regarding mitigating circumstances, extensions, deferrals, and intercalation. And this is pertinent on a degree such as the MBA where almost all students are juggling a combination of professional, entrepreneurial, family and academic commitments. My students visit me weekly during my office hours for advice and support but I am now, of course, unable to offer this. Indeed, I now deliberately distance myself from them, concerned that anything I do say will likely prejudice their formal correspondence with the university.

This centralisation of decision-making has also, in effect, eroded the one clear advantage Suffolk had over its competitors: the much coveted close and supportive relationship between its academic staff and their students. What has the potential to be a customer-focused HE provider operating within sensible administrative parameters, has instead resigned itself to bureaucratic obstinacy. We are now in the position where those furthest removed from the students and their circumstances are making decisions about their future. Notably, the MBA attracts large international cohorts. Where once word of mouth could be relied upon as an effective means of marketing our programmes overseas, our students are now flummoxed by the ethnocentric and impersonal manner in which they are treated by the university. Upon graduation they are returning to their home countries where, inevitably, they report these negative experiences. Commercially, this centralisation of decision-making is akin to shooting ourselves in the foot.

Unless we, as an institution, are able to address these shortcomings, I fear the future of this programme—and probably many others—is at risk.

Reflecting on this, I note that the centralising changes that the University was implementing ultimately meant that a large proportion of what was previously considered part of my role was now being done for me. I realise now that it wasn't the bureaucracy I objected to, but my inability to deal with the change. Since this time, not only I have fully accepted the change, I now routinely explain to students that my role is to provide academic direction; administrative questions must be addressed to other personnel. In fact, not only have I accepted the change but I think I appreciate it. I now enjoy a considerably reduced administrative workload, and have welcomed the opportunity to dedicate more of my working week to research, thus enabling me to craft an academic identity more in line with what I originally expected when I took the first tentative steps towards an academic career. Equally, the ramifications of centralisation I outlined in this report were premature. While centralisation did, initially at least, unsettle the student body, ultimately the students developed supportive dialogues with administrative staff, in addition to me as their programme leader. Ultimately, I think they now value the broader range of support offered. At the time—like me—they reacted to the centralising shift negatively. But—and like me—their frustrations were misattributed; it was most likely the difficulties processing the change that was the source of this frustration. This anecdote helps illustrate a fundamental part of my broader thesis: we routinely assume that bureaucracy is our enemy when, in actual fact, it usually resistance to change that we are experiencing.

## Births, marriages and deaths

Clearly, I can't reflect on the bureaucratic nature of my own death. However, my mum died in 2012 at the age of 63. Probate was an unpleasant experience. In her infinite wisdom, my mum had left unopened mail dating back three years. Half a cubic metre or so. My family and I slowly began the task of going through the letters. In doing so it became more apparent why she had left it unopened. Most letters related to unpaid bills or, worse, unwise financial investments. My mum had developed a rather unhealthy addiction to teleshopping, and it transpired that she had bought a flat in Scotland way back in 2007. This was probably intended to be *the* investment to help her out of her financial hole. And then, of course, came the financial crash. At the time of her death in 2012, the flat was worth half what she had paid for it. The mail constituted bureaucratic-authoritarian evidence which is probably why she didn't destroy it. But, unopened, it was in effect 'out of sight, out of mind.' Having said that, the pile in her spare bedroom must have served as a perpetual reminder that she was in debt. It must have been heart-breaking. It did, of course, make the whole probate business unpalatable, too. I suffered from severe anxiety and depression. Why do creditors hide behind black and white bureaucratic documents? We're taught that the pen is mightier than the sword, but—typically—this is meant to imply that reasoned debate is more effective than violence. In my mind, it has another—unseen—meaning: the pen is more terrifying than the sword, because the pen more clearly represents the bureau.

Just over a year after my mum passed, I met Becky. We married in 2015. We decided to have two ceremonies. One at the Register Office with close family (which I enjoyed). A second, two days later, at our Local Village Hall where we were tasked with entertaining 160 guests (which was immensely stressful). The ceremony at the Register Office is the one that 'counts,' and yet I felt obliged to speak most fondly of the second 'more personal' ceremony. For me, however, it is the other way round. I liked the officialdom of the original ceremony. I liked the bureaucracy of it. Interestingly, my wife has commented that it was also the more emotionally meaningful. Suffice to say, we each feel a nagging sense of guilt about these memories.

In early 2018, we discovered that Becky was pregnant. Both pregnancy and birth are, as Etzioni (quoted at the beginning of this chapter) implies, loaded with bureaucratic meaning. Prenatal form filling, for example. During our first meeting with the midwife, Becky was given a pack which we were instructed to bring with us to each of the subsequent visits to the midwife. And—notably—'the midwife' presents as a bureaucratic role rather than a clinical one; it is one which is descriptive of an office rather than a single person since 'the midwife' role transitions between multiple persons throughout her pregnancy in accordance with duty and roster. As the pregnancy developed and more and more sections in the pack were completed, it became clear that the baby was being keyed onto the bureaucratic apparatus before even being born. Becky gave birth to our daughter, Sophie, in October 2018. The birth itself was, of course, an incredibly moving and special moment, and one I will never forget. But it is worth noting that I doubt I will ever forget the moment I went to the local town hall to obtain Sophie's birth certificate, either. The sense of joy—and relief—was overwhelming. For Graeber (2016: 22):

> There is a rich anthropological literature … on the cult of certificates, licenses and diplomas in the former colonial world. Often the argument is that in countries like Bangladesh, Trinidad, or Cameroon, which hover between the stifling legacy of colonial domination and their own magical traditions, official credentials are seen as a kind of material fetish—magical objects conveying power in their own right, entirely apart from the real knowledge, experience, or training they're supposed to represent.

What Graeber notes in respect of former colonies, I see more generally. There *is* something festishistic about official documentation. By way of further illustration, consider the mail we received following Sophie's birth. There were, of course, dozens of beautifully handwritten cards with heartfelt messages from family, friends and people further afield. Ironically, however, it was the typed letter from the doctor's surgery, addressed to Sophie Vine, which moved me most. Why? Perhaps it was due to the fact that not only was the letter a bureaucratic artefact (like the birth certificate), but it had been delivered via a formal—and bureaucratic—postal system, the Royal Mail. This had lent it an even greater degree of officialdom. Sophie was finally a real person. Sophie was finally official. She *mattered*.

## Note

1 The organisation referred to is no longer trading. Any similarity with new organisations operating under the same (or similar) name is purely coincidental.

# 7

# WORKING *WITH* BUREAUCRACY

Is bureaucracy desirable or undesirable? This is not really a question that can be answered, at least not in a meaningful sense. Bureaucracy simply *is*. In this chapter, I argue that it is how we *interact* with bureaucracy that is most pertinent. To this end, I suggest that bureaucracy is, invariably, co-constructed. It is something in which each of us is implicated. I dedicate the latter part of the chapter to speculating on how a fresh education in respect of bureaucracy might look.

Is there any sense distinguishing good bureaucracy from bad? '[A]s Weber indicated long ago, an abstract celebration or denunciation of 'bureaucracy' makes little sense' (du Gay, 2005: 5). Reflecting on the research presented in this book, it is tempting to distinguish 'good' bureaucracy from 'bad.' Certainly, we could tentatively speculate on what 'good' bureaucracy might look like. For example, I could convincingly distinguish those experiences of bureaucracy we typically describe in positive terms from those which we typically describe in negative terms, and catalogue these for posterity. To this end, I could distinguish *bureaucratic fundamentals* (security, impartiality, equity, and so on) from *bureau-pathology* (institutionalisation, total institutions, jobsworthiness, and so on). Or, perhaps, I could distinguish 'constructive' forms of bureaucracy from 'sterile' forms of bureaucracy. Or, as Gouldner (1954) did, distinguish between 'punishment-centred bureaucracy' and 'representative bureaucracy.' But to demarcate in this sort of manner would, I think, compromise the pedagogical value of this book. It would be a mistake to identify and isolate the desirable manifestations of bureaucracy (as distinguished from the undesirable ones) and expect organizational life to neatly fall into place. No, if our thesis is to have a fruitful bearing on the field, it must explore ways in which we might *interact* with bureaucracy more effectively; it must explicate desirable behaviours, rather than specific (and so-called 'desirable') ends. Besides, a focus on *interaction* more accurately reflects the broader ontology on which I have relied throughout: we inhabit a world which we co-construct.

Another question we might ask (and one I've explored implicitly throughout this book), is in which *circumstances* do we regard bureaucracy positively and in which do we regard it negatively? In my mind this is a question with greater value. What the answer demonstrates is that positive accounts of bureaucracy require much greater explication than do the negative ones. This is because many of us struggle to recognise positive experiences of bureaucracy as in any way related to bureaucracy (despite the fact that the experiences in question qualify as bureaucratic in accordance with Weber's well known typology). For example, it is bureaucracy that facilitates a sense of both professionalism and identity; but we frequently forget this. How would we feel, for example, if upon graduation at a newly configured 'post-bureaucratic' University we were heartily congratulated in person by the University's vice-chancellor, but received no certificate? And this is where it gets interesting. One implication is that bureaucracy is in dire need of an image overhaul. If we are to cultivate a better, fairer understanding of bureaucracy in the public psyche, then perhaps we stand a good chance of improving our lived experience of organizational life. So how might we go about improving the image of bureaucracy? How—and why—do the media and writers of fiction continue to engage in bureaucracy-bashing? I very much hope that my modest contributions in respect of the pertinence of both fiction and filmmaking are taken seriously. While most of us are familiar with the suggestion that art both reflects and constructs life, in the case of bureaucracy it is difficult to discern much in the way of reflection. To address this imbalance, perhaps writers and filmmakers will begin to feel inspired to explore the existential vacuum we are presented with in times (or *periods*, if we accept the cyclical argument outlined in chapter 3) of *post*-bureaucracy.

My approach to working with bureaucracy is sensitive to phenomenology and social construction. Notably, I am not suggesting that organizations (or individuals within those same organizations) should develop more effective means of *wielding* bureaucracy. No, 'good bureaucracy,' if this is not too glib a term, involves the manner in which each of us *consume* and *craft* bureaucracy. To this end, universities need to think seriously about how to equip their students with the life skills necessary to *navigate* bureaucracy: as a civil subject, as an end user, and as an employee within an organization or indeed across organizations in respect of business conducted with other organizations (as suppliers, collaborators, competitors, and so on).

Of my own life experiences of various bureaucratic environments (see chapter 6), with the exception of LSMS where we faced far greater concerns, I have not worked—or participated more generally—in an organization in which people do not complain about paperwork, or indeed the relative power of the 'bureaucrats' vis-à-vis the service providers themselves. Allow me indulge myself a little and repeat that: I have not worked for an organization where my colleagues do not consider that organization overly bureaucratic or overly dependent on paperwork or, indeed, 'run by the administrators.' Every organization, it seems, is like this. Such dissatisfaction seems inevitable. Better surely to learn how to *process* these environments effectively. To this end, I'm referring to a fundamental shift in business education (currently it is either *how to do* [the functionalist approach] or *how to critique* [the critical approach]). The problem with both is that they each assume—unreflexively—that there is a desirable way to manage. In my mind, there is room for a third approach: *navigating organizational life effectively*. To this end, we may be better off equipping our students not with functionalist or indeed critical skills, but with the skills necessary to interact with bureaucracy effectively. It is here that I draw inspiration from family therapy. Family therapists often argue that rather than try to identify a fault line in family relations or indeed a culprit, we are better off equipping family members with effective responses when crises emerge (see, for example, Minuchin, 1974). Try as we might, we cannot rid organizations of bureaucracy or indeed the frustrations that are bundled with it. The 'non-bureaucratic,' perfectly functioning organization will forever remain out of reach. To some degree at least, it is pointless to identify fault lines or guilty parties. We are better off learning how best to deal with the inevitabilities of organizational life.

This necessitates the cultivation of organizational life skills. We need to bring the study of bureaucracy back into business schools—and university programmes more generally—not simply to explore its history and acknowledge its shortcomings but to actively acknowledge that organization *is* bureaucracy. Once we've accepted this, it will become obvious why we need to learn how to live with it and what its associated pedagogy would involve.

## Bureaucracy: towards a new education

In chapter 4, we noted the typical student's reticence to acknowledge—let alone explore—the benefits of bureaucracy, even when primed to do so. Bureaucracy remains a pariah. What, then, is to be done? The literature specifically related to education and bureaucracy has not exactly helped. In 2006, for example, the respected journal *Management Learning* published an article by John Hendry called 'Educating Managers for Post-bureaucracy: The Role of the Humanities.' While I applaud the attempt to engage with the humanities in respect of management education, I think we are barking up the wrong tree by fixating on post-bureaucracy. Better, perhaps, to begin a class on bureaucracy by quoting Harvey (1988: 80), who, in turn, presents an excellent summary of the work of Jacques (1976):

> [F]ormal organization does not imply that collusion in atrocities is inevitable. Bureaucracy … sometimes produces trust, confidence and love. At other times it produces distrust, alienation, and paranoia. Which it produces depends on how we construct it and the consequent actions we take, day by day, as we work within it.
>
> *(Harvey, 1988: 80)*

This observation from a generation ago has been all but overlooked in the 'serious' scholarship of bureaucracy. Bureaucracy isn't good or bad. It just is. Our experience and attitude towards bureaucracy will most likely depend on how we choose to interact with it; whether we choose to accommodate it, or to resist it. On a personal level, I have slowly learned to accept it and work with it. My experience at Electoral Reform Services (see chapters 4 and 6) for example is not, I suspect atypical of post-industrial workplace experiences.

If bureaucracy simply *is*, we need to re-establish it as a principal aspect of education. But this is not going to be straightforward. As Albrow (1970: 14, cited in Styhre 2007: 11–12) implies, there are inherent challenges to teaching bureaucracy:

> The student coming to the field can be excused bewilderment. Sometimes bureaucracy seems to mean administrative efficiency, at other times the opposite. It may appear simply as a synonym for civil service, or it may be as complex as an idea summing up the specific features of modern organizational structure. It may refer to a body of officials, or to the routines of office administration.

And that was in the 1970s. The field is even more akin to a minefield now. Furthermore, in my experience the best analysis of bureaucracy in any textbook in the field of management and organization is Watson's 2002 edition of *Organising and Managing Work*, but tellingly this section was removed in subsequent editions of the textbook. This is regrettable as this was one of the sections that marked out the earlier edition as notably different from other generic business and management textbooks. I fear Watson's second edition has fallen victim to a form of institutional isomorphism, in which all textbooks become largely indistinguishable from one another. If this is indicative of the direction in which we are headed, this is worrying. Our business and management students need to *understand* bureaucracy. They need to recognise that it is an emergent phenomenon; it is *not* something that mean-spirited people or 'jobsworths' put into practice to exasperate 'reasonable' organizational men and women. Weber (1968 [1922]: 987, original emphasis) himself noted that '[b]ureaucracy is *the* means of transforming social action into rationally organized action.' Our students must recognise that bureaucracy represents what it means to desire some semblance of order in a chaotic world. They need to recognise that bureaucracy has had a bad press and so our perception of it is significantly at odds with what we see when we level more nuanced analysis. Our students need to recognise that a world without bureaucracy is probably one in which we would not wish to live. Our students might also be encouraged to reflect on the fact that *all* academic modules on their programmes are underpinned by what are, essentially, bureaucratic artefacts: accounting ledgers, marketing plans, sales forecasts, personnel contracts, project budgets, memoranda of understanding, and even green audits. For better or worse (and I firmly believe it is for better) we live in a world in which bureaucracy represents the genetic matter of organization.

These, I hope, are compelling arguments for incorporating the study of bureaucracy. But, how—precisely—might this be achieved? I think part of the reason management students might be persuaded to study bureaucracy is to get to grips with contemporary organizational frustrations. Gone are the days in which Trade Unions represented the manager's nemesis. (And in some respects, those days were more straightforward for the manager; there was a clearly defined opponent.) Now the nemesis is bureaucracy but the problem here is that any managerial initiative to tackle bureaucracy itself involves a new regime of bureaucracy. New systems to eliminate paperwork, layers, committees and so on all invariably involve paperwork themselves. We have the old problem of creating a committee to establish why it is that we have so many committees. And, in any event, it is often more about identity than efficacy. One is here reminded of the infamous sketch in Monty Python's *Life of Brian*, in which the People's Front of Judea oppose the Judean People's Front with extraordinary gusto:

BRIAN: Are you the Judean People's Front?
REG: Fuck off!
BRIAN: What?
REG: Judean People's Front. We're the People's Front of Judea! Judean People's Front. Cawk.

A few years ago, there was a running joke at Suffolk about the preponderance of paperwork. It was my then boss (who shall remain nameless) who started it. It involved somebody, usually my boss, interjecting at the appropriate point in a meeting or departmental discussion with the following quip: 'Welcome to the University of Suffolk; we have a form for that!' As part of the research for this book, I have heard the same—or very similar—quips used in other organizations, in a variety of industries. Suffolk is by no means special in this respect. Anyway, in seeking to address this much maligned bureaucratic mentality, my boss's solution was to create and circulate a 'master form' from which all relevant information would purportedly cascade. Did this work? No. All it did was reinforce the power of one individual over others: I want it done this way; my form is best. To my boss, it may have saved time (although of this I cannot be certain). To everyone else, however, it created more work. Not only did we have to complete this 'master form,' but ultimately and despite protestations we still ended up completing the paperwork in respect of the pre-existing processes. I relay this anecdote, not to suggest that extant approaches to paperwork are infallible, but to demonstrate how dictates to eliminate paperwork are unlikely to succeed.

It is also worth stressing that bureaucracy has to some extent become a casualty of contemporary epistemological bias. Styhre (2007: 73) comments thus:

> There is a strong orientation in contemporary society towards more fluid and fluxing epistemologies, a variety of perspectives on subjectivity, social institutions, and history as being what is always in a state of becoming, on the move,

in flux. While the worldview of, say, a person in medieval times, was essentially stable and predictable, and captured by the religious scriptures which, in turn, were interpreted on the basis of Aristotelian metaphysics, the contemporary age is an age where continuous change is praised as being responsible for liberating human beings from established structures and institutions. Not only are the contemporary times an age where people tend to perceive the world around them as moving and changing, theories suggesting such views are also fashionable. A variety of natural scientists, social scientists, philosophers and other professional groups subscribe to different theories and epistemologies assuming change over stability, discontinuity over continuity, fluidity over entities. In this episteme, organization forms such as bureaucracy become unfashionable or even illegitimate because they are conceptualised as being opposed to such continuous change and movement.

Our students must recognise, therefore, that although interpretative methods have helped illuminate the world around us in so many new and innovative ways, a discourse saturated by the preferred vocabulary of the interpretivists (fluid, dynamic, subjectivity etc.) can have the effect of undermining the reputation of concepts like bureaucracy. Bureaucracy is a casualty (perhaps *the* casualty) of contemporary epistemologies which typically urge us to think 'out of the box.' And what, exactly, is the 'the box,' if not yet another damning metaphor for the bureau?

## Lessons in bureaucracy

Willmott (2011: 285–6) notes that both Weber and more contemporary contributors assume that

> the principles and ethos inhere in the structure of bureaucratic organization, and do not therefore consider how they are practically constructed and continuously renewed. By default it is assumed that the ethos is well established and/or readily internalized by office-holders.

An education in respect of bureaucracy thus remains absent. I dedicate this subsection to addressing this deficit.

It is worth stressing here, that I am inevitably focussed on how best to re-introduce the study of bureaucracy onto management degree programmes, as these are the programmes with which I am most familiar. However, there is no reason why the recommendations should not apply in the case of degree programmes such as sociology, political science, government studies, and cultural or social anthropology. Reflecting on the research undertaken for this book, any education of bureaucracy ought to recognise the importance of the following: (1) organizations are primarily anthropological phenomena; (2) paperwork has a broader cultural function; (3) inter-organizational tensions can be brought relief through the study of bureaucracy; (4) bureaucracy is culturally contingent; (5) 'administrative gaps' are inevitable but not insurmountable; and (6) bureaucracy outperforms engineered management methodologies. Let's examine each in turn.

## 1 The social anthropology of organization

A nuanced understanding of bureaucracy is inspired by a more general interest in the social anthropology of organization. Contrary to the wishes of critically-minded management academics, what proportion of newly-enrolled students on a business degree are attracted to this field of study because they have a profound interest in organizational anthropology or the sociology of organization? Close to none, I should think. Let's not kid ourselves. The vast majority of those bums on seats are there because they want to be successful in business; by which I mean of course, they want to make large amounts of cash. As scholars of work and organization (who rarely make large amounts of cash), this can be disheartening. One approach, which I fervently oppose, is ideological fiat. I have colleagues who endeavour to 'weed out' this commercial spirit by recourse to an anti-management rhetoric: cue frenzied discussions of Marx, Braverman, Derrida, and Foucault. This is a practice that has been going on for some time. The master's degree I completed while at Warwick University in the 1990s was called Organisation Studies. During the induction session on our first day, one of lecturers commented that it was an 'anti-MBA.' We heard this same claim and similar ones (including the programme was an 'antidote to the MBA'), on multiple occasions throughout the rest of the academic year. What use is this sort of thing? It is only going to create more divisiveness. Furthermore, the formal marketing of such programmes (i.e. those run by critical management academics) rarely ever reveal this ideological bent; to do so would presumably compromise recruitment. As I've argued elsewhere (see Vine, 2011), this amounts to *critical management by stealth*. It is deceptive and I want no part of it. Better, surely, to demonstrate how organization represents a vital social and/or anthropological function. To this end, I typically dedicate the opening session on my MBA Organizational Behaviour module with a back-to-basics assessment of the word organization. This normally involves acknowledging its meaning in three ways: (1) organization a noun, (2) organization as verb, and (3) organization as 'flow of experience.' The first two are straightforward. The third is a little trickier. Here I invoke Weick's wisdom:

> As members [of an organization] enact and punctuate in parallel their individual flows of experience, they develop inferences about their experiences. These inferences are arranged cognitively in causal maps which in turn predispose future behaviour. Individual member's causal maps are altered and developed through experience. This development produces some cognitive and behavioural correspondence which defines, for them, an organization.
>
> *(Weick, 1977: 298)*

A couple of years ago, I read this quote out in front of my MBA students. Feeling rather cocky, one put up his hand and asked, 'What the fuck does that mean?' Well you might ask. And you might even be so bold to ask another question: 'What [the fuck] does this have to do with bureaucracy?' The rationale for citing this third understanding of organization is that it enables us to recognise that organizations are, at heart, social entities. We have developed a tradition of business education that often overlooks this. Organizational behaviour modules, meanwhile, can and should provide an opportunity to think about organizations, businesses, corporations, companies, or whatever synonym you care to utter, not simply in an instrumental sense (i.e. in terms of economics, sales, operations, or accounts), but as assemblies of people. As Wilson (2000: 23) comments: 'To many economists, organizations are … black boxes that convert the will of a single entrepreneur into inputs into outputs.' But this remains a fundamental misreading of the empirical reality. Organizations are social entities *prior to* economic entities. Once students begin to get their heads around this, suddenly any reticence about engaging with research from social scientific disciplines other than business and management evaporates. In my experience, some go on to develop an insatiable appetite for anthropology, sociology, social psychology, and so on. And not because they have become politicised—and hence—*anti*-management, but often because they recognise that an acute understanding of organizational dynamics will make them better managers.

Having explored these three definitions of organization, I then usher in a discussion of bureaucracy. Together, we chart the history of bureaucracy; we recognise the role it has played in the emergence of complex organization, the monetization of trade, the division of labour, technological innovation and—yes—even atrocities such as the Holocaust. Together we try to understand why bureaucracy has become a dirty word, and attempt to disentangle rhetoric from reality. Perhaps the most important exercise of all, however, is when students are urged to think about their own experiences of bureaucracy, catalogue and reflect on them. Invariably, most are heavily-biased towards the negatives, but—with a little guidance—more positive experiences begin to emerge too. By this stage, and with some gentle encouragement, most students realise that bureaucracy—which of course alludes to complex organization going back centuries—has become a straw man, perhaps the definitive straw man in the field of business and management. This class on bureaucracy becomes a pivotal session which we refer back to on multiple occasions throughout their degree programmes; it helps them make sense of abstract ideas encountered later in their studies including social construction, rhetoric, and discourse analysis. Bureaucracy thus becomes an important, familiar, and highly accessible pedagogical device.

## 2 The pro forma and paperwork

Paperwork has a perennial association with bureaucracy. Indeed, despite those championing the onset of the paperless office it seems that paperwork is here to stay. A decade ago e-readers were ubiquitous. If you got on a London Underground carriage in, say, 2009, it would be a safe bet most passengers in that carriage would be nose down in their Kindles. Today, there are virtually none. However, what is particularly interesting is that sales of paperback books have begun to increase again (Wood, 2017). Why is this? Initially, it was assumed by many—including Amazon's Jeff Bezos—to be a question of price. Print edition books were becoming cheaper, in some cases cheaper even than their electronic counterparts. This is, I suspect, an oversimplification (and reveals yet another tendency to prioritise economic metrics ahead of social ones). There is limited research but my suspicion is that at least part of the reason for this resurgence is that paper is more than a functional medium of information: our society has imbued it with symbolism which is not easily shaken off. Paper is an enabler of intellectual intimacy. It serves as a familiar and sacred interface between reader and the world. Reading a book—as opposed to an electronic device—is a sensual experience; the texture of the paper, the smell of the dust jacket, the audible chomp of the turned pages. There is an authenticity to paper. Coincidentally, in that very same year—2009—I was involved in a research project at the British Library which focussed on archival techniques. The librarians were concerned about the digitisation of tangible materials in the British Library archives. The concern was not about how this was to be done, or how much it would cost. No, the concern was more about how digital data would be future-proofed. The fear was that digital data was much more susceptible to being corrupted, erased or in some way lost than was its paper counterpart. One aspect I remember in particular was concern about the shelf life of software. Apparently, huge amounts of digital information were being lost, not because the data itself was missing but because the programmes required to read it had been lost forever. In a fast-moving world such as software development this is a recurrent problem. Paper stocks meanwhile are, apparently, a highly reliable way of retaining information. At the British Library, data on paper can be put in low-oxygen storage areas and will survive relatively intact for thousands of years. Digital data, I was told, doesn't have anything like the same level of resilience.

Reading is one thing, but what about the practice of form-filling? In truth, form-filling is not anything like as arduous as its reputation would suggest. Form-filling is containing; it triages; it officiates. To this end, a module on organizational craft would almost certainly include a study of the pro forma. How and why did the pro forma emerge? Why are we so reliant on them, even in the era of the 'paperless office'? What makes for a good pro forma? Why is it that wet signatures continue to carry greater authenticity than their electronic counterparts? Interestingly, most Business Schools (and most academic departments, I would imagine), routinely provide instruction on the design of pro formas for surveys on research methods modules (in terms of drafting questionnaires, interview question rubics and so on.). So why don't we do something similar on organizational behaviour modules in regards to administrative pro forma design? Graeber (2016: 51) poses a broader question: Why are there not vast ethnographic tomes about American or

British rites of passage, with long chapters about forms and paperwork? He responds to his own question:

> There is an obvious answer. Paperwork is boring. One can describe the ritual surrounding it. One can observe how people talk about or react to it. But when it comes to the paperwork itself, there just aren't that many interesting things one can say about it ... In fact, one could go further. Paperwork is supposed to be boring. And it's getting more so all the time.
>
> *(Ibid.)*

I disagree—and not because I think paperwork is supposed to be interesting. Rather, I think that paperwork serves an important existential-pedagogical purpose. In this sense, we need to move beyond the mind-set that regards paperwork simply as 'necessary'; it is more than that; paperwork is *important*. Completing a form is not just a question of capturing information which enables a functionary somewhere to tick an appropriate box. No. Effective paperwork is containing; it allows us to take stock. Paperwork is reflexive; it allows us to reflect on what we have done. Paperwork also provides direction. We are used to thinking of leadership as embodied i.e. a leader is a *person*. But this is an assumption. Leadership of another kind is conveyed and articulated through paperwork. I can use the example of the pro forma I was required to complete in preparing the proposal for this book. It wasn't just a question of 'filling in a form' to reflect what I already had in mind; no, this book—it's narrative, structure, and—to some extent—its content—only really emerged once I started working through the pro forma in question. One might argue that such an exercise inevitably creates identikit outcomes. Writing a book should not be akin to the proverbial sausage factory. But this misses the point. The book itself is the creative artefact; the pro forma helps channel—and systematise—this creativity. As Law (1994: 4) argues, 'research, too, is a process of ordering.' Now, think about this more broadly. Given the preponderance of paperwork in organizational life, it is extraordinary that—with the exception of questionnaire design—the pro forma is not studied at any point on business and management degree programmes. This needs to change.

It is also worth noting that form-filling is the one thing that has not really been aided by the onset of the electronic age. In fact, arguably, form-filling today is *more difficult* when compared to the pre-computer age. Unlike say, memos (emails), spreadsheets and databases which are vastly improved in the electronic era, pro formas were often easier to complete in the paper age. Think about it. Filling in an electronic form is often plagued with difficulties: masked drop-down boxes, greyed out sections, emboldened fonts, the viability of an electronic signature, and so on. Perhaps the user interface will eventually evolve to improve the experience but—for the time being, at least—it is often easier (and less time-consuming) to print off forms, complete them by hand and then scan them in for circulation. I'm sure most of us have experience of doing precisely this. Aside from anything else, and even if we receive categorical reassurance, there is a nagging doubt that the electronic form carries the same degree of authenticity as its hard copy equivalent.

The pedagogical value of the pro forma is further enhanced by recourse to an anecdote regarding business plans. At a conference held at the Maastricht School of Management in 2018, one of the presenters reported that of the 500 fastest-growing companies in the US, only 28% had a formal business plan. The speaker referred to this as *the sense and silliness of strategy*. The speaker marshalled two points to be gleaned from this. First, it may be that planning is relevant for some people (but not all), or for some initiatives (but not all). Second, for somebody preparing a business plan, they need to justify why *learning before doing* (i.e. preparing a business plan), is better than *learning through doing*. Reflecting on his presentation, I developed a third point: perhaps it is that a business plan is really a type of 'enterprise bureaucracy,' a mechanism through which we prime business people to form-fill, an imperative skill when paying taxes, for example. Perhaps this notion can be used to help justify the inclusion of bureaucracy as a discussion point on business and management programmes in the sense that looked at as a bureaucratic exercise, suddenly the business plan makes sense again. It may be of limited *instrumental* use in respect of enterprise, but it has an important *socialisation* function.

How then would a curriculum including a module on bureaucracy look? First, marketing the module would be challenging. It might be better to call it 'navigating organizational life.' Such a module would be comparable to an organizational behaviour module, but the emphasis would shift away from describing and understanding organizations to experiencing organizations. It would seek to cultivate a sort of *lifecraft*. Or, more specifically, *organizational craft*. We might begin such a module by asking our students who they admire most in organizations, irrespective of rank. I would imagine that most would think about people who are—intuitively—good at what I am describing here as organizational craft. They are the people that are capable and willing to see things from other people's and departments' perspectives (interestingly, Graeber hints at this when he uses the term: *interpretive labor*). We tend to admire those who have honed effective skills of diplomacy. We tend to admire those who understand context. We tend to admire those whose immediate response upon being asked to complete a pro forma is not *why the fuck have I got to do this—again?* but *I wonder why I am being asked to do this again; perhaps it will make somebody else's life easier?* Such concerns may appear trivial at first glance, but upon closer inspection they hint at a broader ability to navigate organizational life effectively.

Skilled organizational men and women recognise the purpose of the bureau. Rather than moan about paperwork, they develop their own efficient ways of dealing with it. So, for example, they might retain master documents locally from which key information can be gleaned easily and efficiently. It is no use saying, 'another part of the organization has this information so why can't you get it from them?' Believe me, more often than not, if the information can be gleaned more easily from elsewhere, it will be. There is usually a compelling reason as to why it can't be sourced from there. And—more pertinently—there is a behavioural aspect to form-filling. It serves an important purpose: it is a reflexive practice. For example, when asked to supply publication details (yet again), rather than direct the requestor to the relevant page of the University's website (my usual response in years gone by), in copying and pasting the relevant parts from a locally-held copy of my CV, I am reminded that it is out of date and my latest publication is missing. I therefore use the practice of form-filling to benefit not just the recipient but myself and the University as well. Finally, there are discernible therapeutic advantages to form-filling: for better or worse, forms have become our society's way of containing ourselves; they facilitate reflection on our career, our identity, our professional and existential aspirations.

Now, it is I think important at this point to engage with one of Graeber's (2016: 23) astute observations, in this case in respect of equity and paperwork:

> While measures are touted—as are all bureaucratic measures—as a way of creating fair, impersonal mechanisms in fields previously dominated by insider knowledge and social connections, the effect is often the opposite. As anyone who has been to graduate school knows, it's precisely the children of the professional-managerial classes, those whose family resources make them the least in need of financial support, who best know how to navigate the world of paperwork that enables them to get said support.

This is an important point, and one that strengthens my resolve. If it is the privileged that know best how to navigate the world of paperwork (in one sense this is precisely what the professions of law and accountancy, for example, are dedicated), there is an argument here for introducing the study of paperwork—and organizational craft more generally—among school age students, making it more broadly accessible.

## 3 Intra-organizational relations

In many organizations, including universities, administration is regarded as a rather lowly profession. It is rarely paid well and those who occupy administrative roles seldom command much respect. And yet talented administrators (or bureaucrats *par excellence*) make a huge amount of difference. I regularly hear people comment, sometimes patronisingly, that good administrators as 'worth their weight in gold.' As du Gay (2011: 24) notes,

> while it may never be possible to rid the term 'bureaucrat' of negative connotations, it is nonetheless the case that the disappearance of such a category of person would have profound and far from positive effects on many aspects of existence that we tend to take for granted.

Ironically, effective managers need to look not up the chain of command but down if they are to develop their craft. Whether or not they are billed as such, the vast majority of jobs in organizations are administrative in the sense they involve communicating information effectively between two or more groups of stakeholders. So why do we not include the specific study of administration on our management degree programmes? In an interview for McGill University, management theorist Henri Mintzberg commented that in the 1960s when he was studying for his PhD, people weren't even interested in management and that there wasn't even a course with the word management in it (Mintzberg, 2010). Clearly, things have changed: Business School courses today almost always include the word management: supply chain *management*, logistics *management*, human resource *management*, marketing *management*, and so on. But do we ever see courses with the word administration? Rarely ever. And how often do we see the full title of the MBA presented: Management of Business *Administration*; rarely ever—it is almost always acronymised. Now, I suspect the reason for this is because—like the word bureaucracy—the word administration does not sound sexy enough. Our discipline has become the victim of a sort of self-imposed vocabulary Fascism. We avoid these terms because they are unfashionable but in so doing we effectively disengage with their associated patterns of behaviour. Let us not forget that we co-construct our world. If we ignore these terms, we ignore what they refer to. It is time to address this deficit. In this vein, and as readers of earlier chapters will have no doubt noticed, the other words I am concerned about are institution, institutionalisation and—to some degree—jobsworth. These are unfashionable but describe vital social phenomena. A module called organizational craft (or something similar) would help resurrect these concepts and allow students to understand the processes in question. What will, I suspect, become patently obvious at this point is how important it is to reflect on organizational experience. Notably, this will—by implication—bolster the rationale for postponing MBA study until such time applicants have garnered valuable organizational experience. By way of illustration, in this case with respect to mathematics, Nietzsche notes the following:

> Think of that period of our lives when we had mathematics and physics forced down our throats, instead of being first of all made acquainted with the despair of ignorance, and everything occurring in our houses, our workshops, in the sky, and in nature, split up into thousands of problems—and thus having our curiosity made acquainted with the fact that we first of all require a mathematical and mechanical knowledge before we can be allowed to rejoice in the absolute logic of this knowledge!
>
> *(Nietzsche 2007 [1881]: 195)*

An MBA is better undertaken mid-career (as opposed to pre-career). At this later stage, candidates can reflect upon a greater depth—and breadth—of experience in respect of bureaucracy.

And let us not forget that for many of us today our employer is our default community; our default kin. With this realisation, perhaps the binding forces of bureaucracy begin to make a bit more sense. Not all organizational actors are the same. Many—perhaps most—students enrolled on business and management degree programmes might be expected to be dynamic and entrepreneurial individuals. But this should not imply that all employees of a given organization have those same character traits; they don't. As the saying goes, we need the 'details people.' Some people are simply happier working in formal, bureaucratic environments. We shouldn't chastise these people for doing so. And nor should we avoid employing them. To do so would not eliminate the bureaucracy; it will simply mean that its responsibility ends up falling to those who do not want to do it.

## 4 Bureaucracy and cultural contingency

Bureaucracy manifests itself differently in distinct administrative traditions. And these distinctions become even more pronounced when we consider different cultural traditions. Over the course of my studies in the field of international business, I have come across countless examples of business deals failing because of cross-cultural misunderstanding. So, for example, some time ago, I was made aware of a business deal (which was all but complete) between a US firm and a Saudi firm which fell apart at the last minute. The reason? Apparently, while the US side was insisting on a written contract to reflect what had been agreed, the Saudi party was insulted at this request as it implied that their word was not good enough. In many cultures, trust is considered an imperative component of business; if you can't trust me, what's the point in us doing business? As has become customary in the West, the Americans required what is essentially a bureaucratic artefact to galvanise—and make 'sacred'—their agreement. They wanted the agreement to be bureaucratised. The Saudis, meanwhile, who observe different customs, felt this was insulting. The point is not that Americans are bureaucratic and Saudis are not. No, the point is that bureaucracy is a culturally contingent; in manifests itself in different ways in different cultures.

I travel to Indonesia regularly for work and while I'm there my routine involves getting up early whereupon I head to the hotel's outdoor pool to swim fifty lengths before breakfast. Most mornings, a guard jots down my room number as I arrive at the pool. To the best of my knowledge, it serves no obvious instrumental function. Every guest is entitled to use the pool, and the pool is inaccessible to the public. Nonetheless, this chap sits there and duly records room numbers as they are presented to him. Why, I wonder. Well, although it does not serve a specific instrumental function, what it does do is create a sense of legitimacy and officialdom. This hotel is *organized*. It isn't some shack on the edge of a highway. It is unlikely that this particular manifestation of bureaucracy would be found in the West. However, there are aspects of Western bureaucracy that are rarely found in Indonesia. So, for example, early on in my travels in Indonesia, I encountered *Jam Karet*, or, in English, 'rubber time.' *Jam Karet* has important implications. Suppose you arrange a meeting in Jakarta for, say 3pm, it is unlikely that all parties will be present until, say 3.30pm. The emergence of rubber time is usually attributed to the fact that travel times in Indonesia are so unpredictable (readers who have spent time sat in Jakarta's notorious traffic jams will know exactly what I mean). However, it was recently explained to me as part of a project I have been collaborating on with Binus University that rubber time is really about *respect*. Rather than tut (the British response), get frustrated (the American response), or express disbelief (the German response), in Indonesia it is assumed that if you are late for an appointment there is a very good reason for this and so accommodating it is expected. The time of a meeting is not ensconced in a bureaucratic artefact. Once again, the point is not that Westerners are bureaucratic, and Easterners are not (notably, the Japanese—for example—are routinely regarded as the most punctual of all nationalities), but that bureaucracy manifests itself differently in different cultural contexts. Recognising this will, I think, constitute an important part of an improved education in respect of bureaucracy.

## 5 Coping with 'bureaucratic gaps'

In *Economy & Society*, Weber (1968 [1922]: 979) notes that

> [t]he idea of 'law without gaps' is, of course, under vigorous attack. The conception of the modern judge as an automaton into which legal documents and fees are stuffed at the top in order that it may spill forth the verdict at the bottom along with the reasons, read mechanically from codified paragraphs—this conception is angrily rejected, perhaps because a certain approximation to this type would precisely be implied by a consistent bureaucratization of justice. Thus even in the field of law-finding there are areas in which the bureaucratic judge is directly held to 'individualizing' procedures by the legislator.

The point here is that we can never *totally* bureaucratise everything. There is always room for agency. Without this, and as I have argued elsewhere (see, for example, Vine 2018c) we wouldn't be human. It is, of course, how we mobilise this agency that matters. It is how *discretion* is exercised that distinguishes good organizations from bad, good people from bad. An effective administrator will not panic when presented with these bureaucratic 'gaps,' but exercise selfless sound judgement. This begs a final point. We need to invite students to ask themselves the following question: How exactly should we *perform* bureaucracy? A focus on performativity will hopefully enable students to think less in terms of whether bureaucracy is good or bad (which is unhelpful), but how their own approach to bureaucracy has discernible influence on its overall guise within that same organization.

## 6 Bureaucracy outperforms engineered management methodologies

Scholars of management and organization almost always advise their students to avoid management guru literature. It is there to make money, pure and simple.

Does it rely on solid empirics and/or robust argumentation? Rarely ever. Instead, it is written in a compelling fashion; to flatter egos and reinforce the idea that management agency is a thing. It isn't. So why do we not do the same in respect of management methodologies? Prior to my academic career, I worked as a project manager. I subsequently taught project management at both undergraduate and postgraduate levels. One of the biggest challenges I faced was trying to get students to recognise that project management methodologies were there to make money, not to improve the journey of a project. What, I think, is interesting about bureaucracy is that unlike, say, LEAN, Six Sigma, or even TQM, bureaucracy has at no point been *engineered*. It is, in this respect, a candidate for a naturally emerging management methodology. Although it manifests itself differently in different contexts, it transcends culture, time, and industry. It is, as we've observed throughout this book, immanent, emergent, and resilient. It is a management methodology *par excellence*. When educating managers of the future, we have a choice: we can either equip them with the skillset required for one or more engineered methodologies or we can equip them to *perform* bureaucracy effectively. My inclination is that the latter approach is likely to be most desirable. I say this because engineered methodologies require tailored training and specific software; rarely tap in to a natural inclination; inevitably have a shelf-life, such is the fickle nature of the management *zeitgeist*; are unlikely to export beyond specific sectors without resistance; and rarely ever yield the promised commercial advantages.

But: do we *consciously* embrace bureaucracy? Consciously? No. I don't think so. It's not like—say—a conscious embrace of LEAN. No, instead bureaucracy appears to be *immanent*. Of course, this in and of itself doesn't necessarily mean it is desirable. It just *is*. However, it does demonstrate a virtue of bureaucracy. If a firm wants to be LEAN, it has to consciously initiate this and perpetually reinforce it. If it wants to be bureaucratic, this will happen naturally. It is also worth commenting on leadership at this point. Despite reams of coverage, the concept of leadership—as Meindl et al. (1985) remind us—remains elusive. Have we for too long regarded good leaders as those who shout loudest in defiance of bureaucracy? Perhaps—and as my exercise about who we admire most in organizations irrespective of rank demonstrates—the key to good leadership has been staring us in the face for generations; perhaps it's as simple as demonstrating a good understanding of bureaucracy, its mechanics, subtleties, and existential purpose. Perhaps this is what makes a good leader. A systematic study of bureaucracy which recognises both the seductiveness and inevitable fallacies of bureau-phobia, then, may well reveal a solid foundation for developing leadership skills.

Finally, let's briefly consider the evidence for the claim that (immanent) bureaucracy outperforms other (engineered) management methodologies. Although it is not presented as such, we can glean several examples of precisely this from the more recent literature. Robertson and Swan (2004, cited in Styhre 2007: 106), for example, show that a UK-based consulting firm changed its organization structure and its management control systems from a flexible adhocracy structure and entrepreneurial governance in the mid-1980s to what the pair call a 'soft bureaucracy' and tighter forms of formal and professional control at the beginning of the new millennium to cope more effectively with changes in the market. And, perhaps most pertinent and unexpected of all, is Kallinikos's account (in du Gay, 2004) of the British Car Industry. What he argues is remarkable—it is surprising that it hasn't been acknowledged more broadly. He argues—lucidly I might add—that the decline of the British Car Industry can be attributed to the fact that it wasn't bureaucratic enough. This, perhaps more so than anything else, will persuade students to look beyond the dilettantish musings of self-styled management gurus.

# 8

# CONCLUDING THOUGHTS

In this concluding chapter, we revisit the questions posed at the very beginning of the book. Does it make any sense to speak of organization *without* bureaucracy? Is bureaucracy an organizational universal? And this latter question invites supplementary ones: To what degree is bureaucracy—like organization more generally—an emergent logic that 'patterns' our institutional existence irrespective of whether or not it is willed? Is bureaucracy self-replicating? Is bureaucracy self-sustaining? Provisional responses to these questions are drawn together into a framework which I tentatively describe as *The Quantity Theory of Organizational Participation*. By recourse to the concepts of pattern, paradox, balance, and sensemaking, the latter part of the chapter reflects on some practical implications for living with bureaucracy.

## Is non-bureaucratic organization possible?

Willmott (2011) reveals some uncharacteristic ambiguity when flirting, if only briefly, with this question. Clegg et al. (2016: 172), meanwhile, conclude their study of ostensibly Kafkaesque organizations thus: *No organization is born Kafkaesque.* Thankfully not. But I'd like to suggest that all organizations *are* born bureaucratic. What's more, if they are to succeed, they must retain some semblance of that bureaucratic identity. If they don't, they will cease to be organizations and the bureaucracy that they once hosted (and this, I believe, is the appropriate verb) will manifest itself elsewhere. Convinced? If not, permit me to remind you of the following. First: the extraordinary experience described at Findhorn (see chapter 6). A self-declared New Age community, Findhorn is perhaps what one might imagine when tasked with hypothesising a non-bureaucratic organization. But what did we see here? First, we saw that the commune was organized along remarkably conventional—prosaic, even—lines. And, notably, unlike the vast majority of communes that sprang up in the 1960s and 1970s it *has* survived. It has survived precisely because it is bureaucratic. What's more, for those who live in, work for, or regularly visit the commune, the data show that the appeal lies in its very bureaucratic nature. Without exception, the profiled participants all reported institutional voids in their lives which Findhorn was able to fill. If we are unable to discern a sense of non-bureaucratic organization at Findhorn, then it is unlikely to exist elsewhere. Well, hypothetically it could exist, but it would not survive. Schumacher's infamous *Small Is Beautiful* thesis was presented in 1973. Though compelling in so many ways, it failed to reflect certain specifics of our world. Why? It has nothing to do with what you might imagine. It has nothing to do with the supposed greed of large multi-national organizations, or totalitarian governments. It fails to recognise that each one of us is predisposed to be a part of something much larger; and more often than not this takes the form of a bureaucracy, be this at our place of work, our place of worship, a sports club, or some other shared interest group. Finally, recall the data that underpinned the development of the pan-organizational association (see chapter 3). This, more so than anything else, illustrates how bureaucracy has an extraordinary protean ability to emerge, adapt, and propagate in the most unlikely of circumstances.

## Is bureaucracy an organizational universal?

Anthropological universals are well established motifs in academic enquiry. These universals are generally explored in respect of behavioural modernity, that is, the traits that distinguish *Homo sapiens* from prior hominins and primates; the human condition (Korisettar and Petraglia, 1998). The work of Lévi-Strauss (1966) in respect of these anthropological universals is, perhaps, the most celebrated. But what of organizational universals? I have argued in this book that bureaucracy is an example *par excellence* of an organizational universal. It also seems that bureaucracy is in some significant sense related to anthropological universals. There are at least two emergent anthropological universals that can be understood as precursors to bureaucracy: agriculture and technology. Agriculture emerged independently in multiple regions across the planet, and in each case became a precursor to the development of complex social organization and a formal division of labour (see, for example, Violatti, 2018). This historical precedent enables us to understand bureaucracy as a direct descendent of the Neolithic Revolution. It is, however, bureaucracy's relationship with technology that is most illuminating. If we accept that technology is an anthropological universal and that there is a logic of some sort inherent to humankind to continually advance technology (and there is compelling evidence to support both), then complex organization—and the bureaucracy it necessitates—is inevitable. Bureaucracy is both ramification and enabler of technology. So, and as DeGregori and Thompson (1993: 90, 92) note:

> As technology … becomes more complex, coordination becomes necessary. The role of organizations in human society is to facilitate this coordination of

knowledge, skills and materials ... Complex organizations, in turn, encouraged the development of ever more sophisticated technologies. Organizational characteristics, such as the chain of command, space of control for management, specialization by expertise, and the routinization of tasks, are themselves a form of technology ... Bureaucratic organizations are by design self-sustaining replicative systems. They are structured so that individual members can be replaced without the system being impaired, so that the organization can theoretically exist and function in perpetuity. The impersonal nature of bureaucratic relations, about which many people complain, is an essential characteristic. If not taken to extreme, impersonal behaviour both in internal and external relations is necessary in order for various functions to be carried on with fairness and impartiality.

Although I agree with the broader argument here (i.e. that bureaucracies are self-sustaining replicative systems), I am far from convinced that this is by design. On the contrary, I see bureaucracy as both emergent and inevitable. It is hoped that this book has been able to demonstrate this. Are organizations ever designed, apart from in an extremely limited sense? According to Institutional Theory, for example, organizations are at the mercy of external forces; they are 'other directed' and—inevitably—succumb to isomorphic pressures. And if we accept that organizations are bureaucracies, then bureaucracies too are emergent and other-directed. Organization is, at its heart, a division of labour. To the extent that bureaucracy is coterminous with the division of labour, bureaucracy is indeed as old as civilisation itself. For Kallinikos (2006: 612): 'romantic humanism has managed to sculpt an image of bureaucracy that has substantially obscured the fundamental fact that modern life would have been impossible, indeed unbearable, without the social and organizational order bureaucracy is associated with and helps sustain.' Thompson (1993: 193) echoes this broader sentiment:

> Institutionalists hold a variety of views with respect to why certain organizational forms such as bureaucracy emerge. A number of institutionalists, especially in the area of organizational studies, argue that an overarching institutionalist theory of organizational origins is required ... bureaucracy is both a technology and an institution innate to humankind's attempts to organize, regulate and disseminate complex technology in a social system where behaviour must be controlled for the common good.

Despite the preponderance of negative rhetoric, bureaucracy *survives*. And this relationship with technology is an exemplar of this. Even more interesting is that despite claims to the contrary, technological advance hasn't rendered bureaucracy obsolete.

> New technologies are often seen as foreshadowing wonderful things. Even old technologies were once new. In the nineteenth century, the typewriter was a

> profound mechanical invention. It speeded up clerical and recording systems that had been based on hand-writing. In Weber's view, the typewriter directly contributed to the creation of modern managerial bureaucracies.
>
> *(Clegg, 2011: 211)*

The typewriter may well have been instrumental in the emergence of modern managerial bureaucracies, but this should not suggest that it is one of just a small handful of technologies that are related to bureaucracy. Indeed, there is a temptation (not just in the public imagination, but in the academy, too) to associate bureaucracy with specifically Victorian—i.e. mechanical—technologies. This is little more than cliché. Nonetheless, there is some sense in which that most traditional medium of information—paper—is deeply rooted in bureaucratic norms. As noted in the previous chapter, the much coveted 'paperless' office has yet to emerge and, for the first time in many years, sales of hard copy books and magazines are once again increasing. Technologies are themselves acutely bureaucratic in either guise or association, and many recapitulate bureaucracy in new ways. The example of personal computers and the development of popular software presents a striking illustration. Computer software has actively embraced the iconography and labelling conventions of the traditional bureaucratic office (in-trays, out-trays, envelopes, wastepaper baskets, and so on) and re-appropriated them in the electronic ether. This is reminiscent of Garston's (1993b: 17) commentary in respect of how technology advances: 'what [was] functional once may become ceremonial when methods of production change.' Could it be, then, that the use of the wastepaper basket icon in MS Windows is a *ritualised* aspect of bureaucracy? Think also about how you manage your inboxes. Most of us do so by filing neatly, logically and—indeed—bureaucratically. Functional or ceremonial, bureaucracy is a deeply cultural phenomenon.

## A quantity theory of organizational participation

What this book has really hinted at—and one of the central ramifications of considering bureaucracy in the manner in which we have done so here—is what I tentatively refer to as a *quantity theory of organizational participation*. In terms of semantics, at least, I attribute the theory to Will Self's (1991) fictional 'Quantity Theory of Insanity,' a short story in a collection of the same name. Self implies a fictitious law: this law states that if the mental well-being of one section of society is improved, then a proportional decline must occur elsewhere. This is not precisely what I am arguing in respect of organizational participation, but it is not far off. Experience demonstrates, time and again, that each of us desires organizational participation in some form or other. This is manifestly clear in respect of several distinct arguments presented throughout this book. Furthermore, the quantity theory of organizational participation appears to hold both spatially and temporally. Each of us demands several organizations in which we can participate at any stage in our lives (an employer, a place of worship, a sports club, a shared interest group,

Concluding thoughts 137

and so on), and over time, we are compelled to substitute new forms of organizational participation for old. The quantity theory of organizational participation helps make sense of the various institutional holding environments we pass through over the course of our lives (as discussed in chapters 2, 3, and 6). We are typically born in hospitals then primed through a series of educational institutions, before graduating. We then pass through a series of workplaces, before retiring. Upon retirement, we typically join clubs, volunteer for charitable initiatives, and engage in various organized recreational initiatives. We then die, usually in a hospital. Interestingly, noted management theorist Charles Handy provides an instructive example of how this substitutive tendency takes place both temporally and spatially:

> [Towards the end of his career] my brother-in-law left his full time job [and] looked for part-time work for some four days a week. Four years later he thinks that he might manage to fit in an occasional day. He is far too busy to do more. He is a local magistrate, a governor of a local school, and a member of the parish council; he sits on various committees of the local judiciary and the police authority, runs the local gymkhana ... In place of one rather monotone business organization, he now belongs to a variety of groupings.
> 
> *(Handy, 1994: 258)*

Of the typical post-industrial life narrative there are two key transitional stages. The first is when places of learning are substituted by places of work (typically in our early 20s); and the second is when places of work are substituted by social clubs and other associations borne of retirement (typically in our late 60s). What is, perhaps, most interesting about these two transitional periods is that they are considered high risk stages in life in respect of mental illness, especially anxiety and depression (see, for example, Kets de Vries, 1980). These are the two stages in life in which we are least rooted in organization. We experience displacement as we weather the transitions between organizational holding environments (or, as Petriglieri and Petriglieri, 2010, refer to them: 'identity workspaces'). Uncertainty during these transitional stages is rampant. We crave the certainty and protection that the bureau affords.

The model of the pan-organizational association (presented in chapter 3) is relevant here, too. One of the extraordinary challenges of our era has been the disorienting effects of neoliberalism. As fewer of us is able to lay claim to permanent, secure work, we have witnessed the emergence of surrogate forms of organization. These, in effect, transcend multiple organizations, often along professional rather than company lines. Where once an individual could lay claim to a relatively stable sense of identity, belonging and existential security from their employer, the nature of changing employment (towards part time, temporary, contracted, or project-oriented work), has meant that more and more of us has had to search harder to find it. In response, that sense of identity is now emerging in cross-organizational professional groups as well as in informal networks. A cursory glance at the evolving make-up of the British high street illustrates this amply: retail outlets are increasingly giving way to coffee shops. This is not due to a growing caffeine-addition problem, but because the coffee shop space is ideal for rekindling a sense of workplace identity. What proportion of coffee shop customers is there purely for the coffee? Close to none, I should think. Coffee shops are social spaces perfect as surrogate workplaces for today's telecommuters. My own experience is illustrative here, too. I regularly work from home, but on those days I do, each morning I habitually get in my car, drive six miles to the town closest to where I live (Diss), and then walk along the high street to Costa to coincide with its opening time (7.30am). I order a medium-sized Americano, and then sit in the same seat each time. I briefly chat to the other regulars (many of whom are telecommuting, too), before taking a deep breath and cracking open my inbox. For me, I can channel the bureaucratic warmth of the organization more readily in a co-working space such as a coffee shop than I can at home. Take a look around next time you are in your local coffee shop. What proportion of customers is merrily plugging away on their laptop while sipping their flat white? It's quite substantial, I would think. I do not wish to suggest that this is a sorry state of affairs (as those determined to apply an ideological critical management agenda might seek to do so). No, my point is different: what this reveals is that there is something inherently compelling about the collective. And, contrary to received wisdom, it is not only the sense of camaraderie and emotional support that we crave. Whilst a collective will elicit a sense of camaraderie, only a bureaucracy (traditional, surrogate, distributed or otherwise) provides the sense of existential security we crave. The data from Findhorn is testament to this. To think about bureaucracy in this manner (i.e. beyond traditional, discrete delineations) necessitates a fresh approach inspired, perhaps, by our extant understanding of the word organization; not just as a noun but also as a verb and flow of experience (see chapter 7).

And, finally, it is relevant in terms of institutionalisation (as explored in chapter 4). Most of us—and not just those schooled in critical thinking—regard institutionalisation negatively. We tend to overlook the fact that, at its heart, institutionalisation describes the process by which we gradually assume the culture and characteristics of the organization in which we are immersed; this is something seemingly intrinsic to the human condition. We have a will to participate in organizational life and—by implication—we need bureaucratic security, in one form or another.

Ultimately, then, it seems we have an innate will to order, a will to organize, a will—perhaps—to bureaucratise. Think about the perverse sense of satisfaction gleaned from re-ordering a pencil case, a toolbox, a sewing box, or a spice rack. Freud focussed on sexual pleasure, but we might legitimately ask ourselves whether there is a pleasure in re-ordering our stuff. Is there some sort of sexual overtone? Is this behaviour, at its crux, the source and reason for our pervasive bureaucracy? A convincing response to this question will, I suspect, require the coordinated efforts of anthropologists, ethnographers, sociologists, psychologists, and so on. In the meantime, let's not ignore bureaucracy on our degree programmes and in our research. Let's embrace it.

## Bureaucracy and pattern

> There is ground for expecting that bureaucracies generate an intricately ramified network of consequences, many of which are below the waterline of public visibility. Though not easily accessible to view, these consequences can, nevertheless, contribute considerably to bureaucratic survival and development. It would be entirely premature, then, to assume that bureaucracies maintain themselves solely because of their efficiency.
> 
> *(Gouldner, 1954: 27)*

This overlooked comment of Gouldner's is vital. Yes, bureaucracy is frequently described in terms of its efficiency (or, more recently, its inefficiency). But it is important for other reasons: its existential currency, its resilience, and its pervasiveness. Bureaucracy patterns our lives in three distinct but related sociographical senses: in terms of an epochal dialectic; in terms of Deleuzian difference/repetition; and in terms of hierarchy.

### *The epochal dialectic*

In chapter 2, we noted how historical attitudes towards bureaucracy are cyclical. Beginning with Wilson's study of administration in 1887, our analysis in that chapter extended approximately 140 years into the past. Over this period we saw how scholarly attitudes towards bureaucracy have come full circle: from pro-bureaucracy, to anti-bureaucracy, and back to pro-bureaucracy. We also recognised that since bureaucracy can be presented as a counterpoint to freedom, at least in its negative guise, our changing attitudes towards freedom (which appear also to be cyclical) are similarly illuminating. To this end, we explored the pertinence of Erich Fromm's work from the 1940s, and noted here that the discernible fear of freedom found in Fromm was lent important context by Karl Mannheim (1936), writing a few years earlier:

> The utopia of the ascendant bourgeoisie was the idea of 'freedom.' ... it contained elements oriented towards the realization of a new social order which were instrumental in disintegrating the previously existing order and which, after their realization, did in part become translated into reality. Freedom in the sense of bursting asunder the bonds of the static, guild, and caste order, in the sense of freedom of thought and opinion, in the sense of political freedom and freedom of the unhampered development of the personality

become to a large extent, or at least to a greater extent than in the preceding status-bound, feudal society, a realizable possibility.

*(Mannheim, 1955 [1936]: 203–04)*

The aspirations for 'freedom' Mannheim describes were therefore themselves part of a rejection of a previous—feudalistic—order. This of course lends further weight to the cyclical nature of our collective attitudes to bureaucracy (as a corollary to freedom) in the modern era. In all probability, the pattern described is one that echoes a much longer, more fundamental, and all-too-human toing and froing.

## *Deleuzian difference/repetition*

In chapter 3, we saw how bureaucracy is (re-)manifesting in new pan-organizational forms. In so doing it resonates with Deleuze's (2004 [1968]) motif of *Difference and Repetition*. At the risk of over-simplifying what amounts to something significantly more complex and nuanced, to the extent that a Deleuzian reading of difference and repetition emphases their inextricable relatedness, bureaucracy as presented here can be interpreted as Deleuzian. It is a form of what Marsden (2002: 20) describes as Deleuze's *derivative transcendental*. Bureaucratic characteristics gradually re-manifest, but in subtly altered appearance. It is—as we noted—a patterning that evokes certain of pianist Philip Glass's musical compositions which, despite evolving all the time, retain a signature rhythm throughout. The empirics presented demonstrated how each response to the anxiety experienced as a result of the post-bureaucratic identity crisis could be illustrated by recourse of the pan-organizational structure (or, more accurately, pan-organizational association) depicted in Figure 3.1. This, we noted, enabled us to represent traditional micro-organizational organograms as part of a broader macro-sociological context. Ultimately, this was presented as a refined reflection of the contemporary organizational landscape.

## *Hierarchy*

It was of course Erich Fromm's *The Fear of Freedom* which ushered in a fresh understanding of the ostensibly dysfunctional behaviour associated with submission, particularly in respect of totalitarian politics. So tainted are our thought processes by a semantics of freedom we struggled to get our heads around this apparent submission to authoritarian ideologies. But hierarchy provides a sense of existential security; it is a means of anchoring us in an uncertain world. Whether hierarchy represents the traditional pyramid (in the case of most military organizations), or whether it is subject to rhetorical attempts to invert it in pursuance of a servant leadership model (say in the case of Findhorn) hardly matters. As Agre (2003: 416) stresses, 'hierarchy need not imply top-down relations.' What is important is that there is some sense of continuity to the relations. This of course ushers in a new understanding of leadership, as noted in chapter 7. Leadership is routinely touted as instrumental in terms of strategy. In reality, and as Mintzberg (2010) reminds us, strategy rarely ever emerges 'Moses-style' out of the desert, but arises at grass roots level. For Pfeffer and Salancik (1978: 31): 'Leadership is the outcome of an attribution process in which observers ... tend to attribute outcomes to persons rather than context.' Additionally, according to Grint (1997: 228) 'Since we cannot know what will happen next, and since there is no one to blame for what happens next, we prefer to concentrate responsibility on one person.' So does this mean we must dispense with leadership? No! Even if we routinely misattribute organizational outcomes to the action (or inaction) of a leader, the *perception* of control is important. Followers place their faith in leaders. With this in mind, it is extraordinary that while leadership is one of if not the most popular subjects in the study of business and management, the subject of followership remains one of the least popular. And yet you cannot have one without the other. The concepts are united in the study of structure (specifically) and bureaucracy (more generally). With all this in mind, and as argued earlier in this book, our approach to management education is in need of overhaul. Hierarchy is considered an immanent part of the natural world; for complex life forms to evolve from simple ones, hierarchical processes are considered essential. This is what became known as Herbert Simon's 'hierarchical principle,' following the publication of his paper *The Architecture of Complexity* in 1962. Arguably, organizational life (which involves a comparable shift from simplicity to complexity) necessitates hierarchical patterning in the same way. We saw precisely this in our depiction of bureaucracy as an organizational universal.

## Bureaucracy and paradox

In chapter 5, we noted that writers of dystopian fiction and makers of dystopian films have failed to recognise the nuance associated with bureaucracy. Ironically, it is perhaps in acknowledging the peculiar dynamic between utopia and dystopia themselves that we might persuade writers of fiction and filmmakers to interpret and present bureaucracy with more refinement. We realised, for example, that utopia is in a perpetual state of paradox: the more utopian one's aspirations, the more dystopian the probable outcomes. Bureaucracy reveals a plethora of paradoxes that go to the heart of the human condition. It is therefore fundamentally misguided to represent bureaucracy as the marker of all things dystopian (and hence, undesirable). Bureaucracy is, inevitably, much more complex; and recognition of this complexity dates back at least to Weber. Most of us tend to think of Weber as a proponent of bureaucracy. In fact, his intellectual deliberation is subtler. I avoided beginning this book with a systematic distillation of Weber's works as I didn't want to prime myself in respect of his precedent. And I very much hope that this has enabled me to generate a fresh contribution. But I do wish to conclude this book by drawing on key—but often overlooked—aspects of his canon. I am guided here by an excellent paper published in 2008.

> [T]here is a highly distinctive form of paradox that Weber uses extensively throughout his writings. Weber deploys this term in two main senses: as a universal condition of human action; and as a specific way of understanding the logic of western modernity ... For Weber, bureaucracy is the extreme culmination of paradox in western modernity ... In fact, the rise of bureaucracy might be seen, on one level, as the final phase of the paradoxical logic of western religious rationalization.
>
> *(Symonds and Pudsey, 2008: 223, 236)*

Despite this, Symonds and Pudsey suggest that '[t]he specific nature of "paradox" in Weber's work has been neglected or under-theorised in the secondary literature' (ibid. 236). They dedicate their paper to redressing this. To this end, the authors discern multiple themes, several of which warrant discussion here: (1) *The relationship between paradox, fate, and agency*; (2) *The paradox of unintended consequences*; and (3) *The paradox of routine and charisma*. I unpack each below, and add one of my own: (4) *The paradox of bureaucratic flexibility*.

## (1) The relationship between paradox, fate, and agency

Symonds and Pudsey are unequivocal in their claim that 'paradox offers an understanding of how fate and agency work in modernity for Weber' (ibid. 224). More specifically, they argue that paradox is an important *ramification* of fate and agency working together. They begin by noting that 'Weber's famous understanding of western disenchantment (*Entzauberung*), or de-magicalisation, of the world provides a rich source of the paradoxical.' 'In fact,' they continue, 'Weber's use of paradox in this sense seems to imply that paradox is the defining characteristic of modern life; that it is the inevitable consequence of all social action in modernity' (ibid. 229). However, its relevance is not restricted to modernity. To this end, they argue that Weber regards paradox as an integral aspect of human action:

> Weber's favoured use of the term paradox, throughout his works, seems to refer to a universal human experience whereby intentions are betrayed by actual events, or to put it slightly differently, where the means to achieve a particular end undermines that intended end, often by becoming an end in itself. The workings and universal nature of such paradoxical experience are most prominently revealed in Weber's extensive works on the world religions. These works are studded with references to means undermining intended ends. For example, in his discussion of the religious intentions of monks, Weber notes that: 'The *paradox* of *all* rational asceticism, which in an identical manner has made monks of *all* ages stumble, is that rational asceticism itself has created the very wealth it rejected' (*Remarks*, 1948b; also *Economy/Society*, 1978: 586, emphases added).
>
> *(Ibid. 226)*

But what has any of this got to do with bureaucracy? On the face of it not much. However, what it does demonstrate is that as a thinker Weber had successfully transcended the seductive allure of linear logic; he was prepared to acknowledge that the world is far more complex than straightforward cause-and-effect logic implies. From what might be considered fairly esoteric comments about Monks, Weber became interested in what has variously been referred to as the historical paradox, the fatefulness of human intentionality, or—most accurately—the paradox of unintended consequences.

## (2) The paradox of unintended consequences

Symonds and Pudsey draw upon the work of various contributors to demonstrate that Weber was both interested in—and persuaded by—the idea of a paradox of unintended consequences. For example, they draw a comparison between Weber's analysis and the paradoxes of both Adam Smith (individual self-interest produces social virtue) and Edmond Burke (radical social action yields results far worse than intended). It is, perhaps, this idea of the paradox of unintended consequences which is of most relevance to the broader argumentation in the book you are reading. Bureaucracy manifests itself irrespective of whether or not it is willed. As we have seen, attempts to eliminate bureaucracy are themselves acutely bureaucratic in guise. Indeed, the paradox of unintended consequences is perhaps understood best through an examination of bureaucracy.

> A final example of the self-defeating nature of agency in modernity is found in the paradox of modernity ... this paradox emerges via the contradiction of how a large and powerful bureaucracy, a necessary component of the administrative means of the nation-state or any organization, will itself become a force of such dominance that it threatens the very aim of that state or organization. For Weber, this occurs in two ways. Firstly, when the state aims for democracy, bureaucratic power will ensure that all are democratically levelled before the democratic state. Providing power and resources to bureaucracy to achieve this end raises it to new levels of authority and social control. Democracy is dependent on a means that is in contradiction to its egalitarian ends. Secondly, and more generally, the power and position of the bureaucracy entails that the ends of government (or any large organization) will be doubtfully realized because the ends of the bureaucracy itself will become pre-eminent.
>
> *(Ibid. 235)*

The paradoxical character of bureaucracy helps explain how generations of scholars have noted Weber's ambiguous attitude towards (and relationship with) bureaucracy. Does Weber endorse bureaucracy? Or, does he damn it? The truth is he does neither. And this is what makes him such an excellent scholar; he refuses to succumb to ideological conviction. And there are other, more recent, examples of this paradox in respect of bureaucracy. Clegg et al. (2016: 172), for instance, consider 'how [we can] restructure unwieldy organizations without succumbing to the bureaucratic temptations of the audit society.' The authors are unable to present a clear response to this question because such an end can only exist in hypothesis. I have also published elsewhere on this idea, developing what I have called, quite simply: the paradox of bureaucracy (see Vine, 2018c). In that publication, I suggested that organizational problems are both created and purportedly solved by an appeal to greater proceduralisation. I was brought to this conclusion by a combination of events, notably the reading of March and Simon's (1984) 'The Dysfunctions of Bureaucracy,' and then my own organizational experience at Electoral Reform Services and elsewhere. I use a diagram to help illustrate this paradox (Figure 8.1).

Supposing rectangle 'A' represents the scale of your operational system. All is going well. And then one day, one of your clients discovers a problem. The problem is one that you've yet to encounter, and your system is not set up to detect it. The solution? You incorporate a check in to your system so as to detect this problem, should it arise again in the future. Your system expands accordingly, and is now represented by 'B.' All goes well from here for a few weeks. And then another client reports a problem. Again, it was unanticipated and your system is

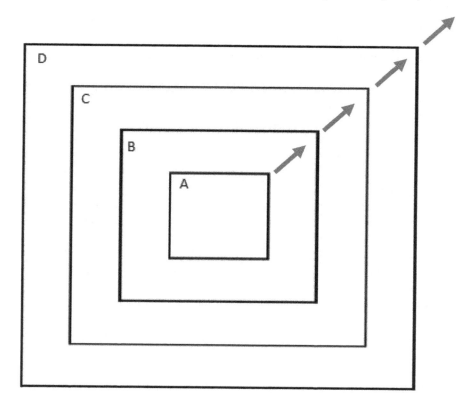

**FIGURE 8.1** The paradox of bureaucracy

not set up to detect it. The solution? Once again, you incorporate a check into your system so as to detect this problem, should it arise again in future. Your system expands accordingly, and is now represented by 'C.' All goes well again, for another few weeks. But then, yet another problem! And so the cycle continues. I would bet what little hair I have left that we are all familiar with exactly this. Over time, our bureaucracies slowly expand to incorporate additional checks to remedy unanticipated problems. The unforeseen difficulty, however, is twofold. First, despite what we might like to think, this expansion will continue perpetually; we will never create a perfect, full proof system. This, of course, is because we inhabit a world characterised by change. Second, the expansion of the system (or bureaucracy) compounds the problem. This is because as it gets larger and larger we place more and more faith in it to deliver in the face of uncertainty. We become *reliant* on the system to such an extent that we each become complacent. Indeed, if we genuinely want to minimise the chances of our clients experiencing problems we are—arguably—better off dispensing with the system completely and addressing their specific needs on an *ad hoc* basis. Of course, in reality, this approach would fail to gain commercial traction because we'd be unable to secure economies of scale. We are therefore compelled to engage in an ever-expanding system, or bureaucracy. Hence, the paradox of bureaucracy.

In *Gödel, Escher, Bach: An Eternal Golden Braid*, mathematician Hofstadter (1980) suggests that reasoning is a patterned process, not a linear one. Hofstadter, refers to what he regards as Strange Loops. 'The "Strange Loop" phenomenon occurs whenever, by moving upwards (or downwards) through the levels of some hierarchical system, we unexpectedly find ourselves right back where we started' (ibid. 10).

Implicit to Strange Loops is the concept of infinity, since—for Hofstadter—what else is a loop but a way of representing an endless process in a finite way? What Hofstadter implies is that hierarchy (thought of in very general terms) has emerged to help address paradoxes (in the form of strange loops). It helps render linear a nonlinear world. Bureaucracy is therefore an emergent means of mitigating the fact that the social world is tainted by paradox; on the one hand, we seek out individuality, on the other we are social creatures. In truth, the two are not in opposition, but are intricately—if complexly—related. Bureaucracy assists to this end. We live in a world awash with paradox, contradiction, complexity, and uncertainty. Bureaucracy is philosophically-incorrect, but it does serve a means of helping us weather this world. This I'm sure is why so many of us have struggled to get our head around the concept of bureaucracy. It is a double-edged sword, a necessary evil. We can't live with it; we can't live without it. Notably, we have only been able to reveal this sort of complexity by adopting the controversial methodological approaches outlined at the outset of this book. Such insight is forever obscured from us where we limit our scholarship to empirco-theoretical approaches since they too are premised on a linear mode of thought. Bureaucracy is emergent precisely because we live in a paradox-riddled, contradictory, complex, and uncertain world.

Such a rendering of bureaucracy has been hinted in other research, too. For Merton (1940: 563), for example, there is paradox associated with bureaucracy in respect of efficiency. Trained incapacity derives from structure, as Merton's four-stage process illustrates: (1) An effective bureaucracy demands reliability of response and devotion to regulations. (2) Such devotion to the rules leads to their transformation into absolutes; they are no longer conceived as relative to a given set of purposes. (3) This interferes with a ready adaptation under special conditions not clearly envisaged by those who drew up the general rules. (4) Thus, the very elements which conduce toward efficiency in general produce inefficiency in specific instances. du Gay (2004: 53) notes another tension, in this case that post-bureaucracy creates new forms of bureaucracy:

> [E]ntrepreneurial governance combines 'loose' and 'tight' forms of organizational control in a distinctive manner: MTMs [market-type mechanisms] for instance, enable direct commands to run alongside markets and thus for the non-market language of 'quality control' to be part and parcel of the functioning of entrepreneurial governance. 'Enterprise' may well disaggregate and undermine established forms of bureaucratic conduct—as with the Next Steps agencies programme—but it relies for its effects on new kinds and levels of bureaucratization.

Similarly, in the introduction to their edited collection on *Managing Modernity: Beyond Bureaucracy*, Clegg et al. (2011: 2) note the following: 'The overall picture is one of paradox and contradiction: new hybrid forms promise new forms of social action and new conceptualisations of control, but these new forms may also create new forms of "centralized decentralization".' More recently, still, Graeber (2016: 17) sees paradox in respect of regulations. He writes:

> Simply by labelling a new regulatory measure 'deregulation,' you can frame it in the public mind as a way to reduce bureaucracy and set individual initiative free, even if the result is a fivefold increase in the actual number of forms to be filed, rules and regulations for lawyers to interpret, and officious people in offices whose entire jobs seems to be to provide convoluted explanations for why you're not allowed to do things.

From Weber through to Graeber, then, it seems there is an inherent recognition of the contradictory nature of bureaucracy, even if it is not expressed as such. What seems so puzzling is how this contradictory nature of bureaucracy is largely ignored by those who critique bureaucracy. It is, I suspect, because conventional analyses hastily sweep paradox or contradiction under the carpet. This is a mistake. We need embrace these ugly contradictions! We need to bring them to the analytical fore and dissect them publicly.

## (3) The paradox of charisma and routine

For Symonds and Pudsey, many of the examples of the paradox of means and ends found in Weber's writing on religion relate to the dialectic between charisma and routinization. Charismatic attempts to destroy mundane structures of this world (normally by spiritual leaders) are usually superseded by the need to organize and 'protect' the original charismatic inclination. An organization characterised by routine and predictable structures typically follows; we've thus come full circle! Weber provides an example of just such a process in his analysis of Ancient Buddhism's attempt to avoid organized hierarchy.

> All in all, in consequence of this intentional and consistent minimization of ties and regulation, Buddhism persisted in an unstructured state which from the beginning was dangerous to the uniformity of the community and which actually soon led to heresies and sect formation ... Hence the establishment of an order and likewise the fixing of the teaching, occurred only after the death of the founder and against his own intentions.
> 
> *(Weber, 1958: 223)*

In this way, Symonds and Pudsey explain that the challenge to societal order contained within the original charismatic message was in fact lost in the attempt to preserve that message through the inevitability of routinization. What Weber recognised in respect of Buddhism is arguably also apparent in respect of Islam. Islam is not generally considered a hierarchical religion (unlike, say, Catholicism). As a result sects inevitably develop and these appear to be eminently more dangerous, at least in current times. I recall a conversation by a coffee machine at the Electoral Reform Services shortly after the first anniversary of 9/11. A softly spoken chap close to retirement knew I had just graduated with a master's degree in organization studies and he was keen to discuss what he proposed as the institutional causes of the terror attacks. He noted something interesting. He noted that had the Twin Towers been toppled by Catholic fundamentalists, the Pope would be expected to speak out and bring splinter factions under control. There was, he implied, a sense of collective responsibility. Why, he pondered, did Muslim leaders not do likewise? The answer, of course, is that they are characterised by different structures. Islam is not hierarchical in the same way the Catholic Church is. Now, this isn't a wholesale defence of hierarchy; far from it. But what it does reveal, I think, is that a sense of formality and organization can have a mediating influence. Controversial as this may sound—and if what I am arguing more broadly has credence—Islam may eventually be compelled to succumb to the pressures of formal organization

It seems charisma is of principal import only at the point of an organization's inception.

*It is only in the initial stages* and so long as the charismatic leader acts in a way which is completely outside everyday social organization, that it is possible for his followers to live in a community of faith and enthusiasm.

(Economy/Society, 1978: 249, as cited in Symonds and Pudsey, 2008: 228, emphasis added)

Following this initial period of charismatic leadership, an organization typically yields to the pressures of routine. Once again, this is acutely relevant in respect of Findhorn (see chapter 6). As part of my broader research at Findhorn, I sought to unpack the history of the commune and noted that it was only for the first few years that charisma 'carried' the commune; thereafter Findhorn had to organize—and indeed bureaucratize—if it was to survive. Other communes of the 1960s and 1970s vociferously resisted conventional organising principles and floundered as a result.

## *(4) The paradox of bureaucratic flexibility*

To Symonds and Pudsey's Weberian paradoxes I add a fourth: the paradox of bureaucratic flexibility. Paradoxically, bureaucracy becomes imperative in the emergent, dynamic world in which we so often claim to reside. Bureaucracy is vital when faced with uncertainty. Karreman et al. (2002: 87–88, cited in Styhre, 2007: 99), argue that since complex environments produce situations wherein ambiguity and uncertainty are endemic, to handle these ambiguities bureaucratic procedures are enacted to achieve a sense of closure, control and predictability in organizations and work relations. We are used to associating non bureaucratic networked management techniques with complex, evolving organizational environments. But it appears to be precisely the opposite that's warranted; bureaucracy is crucial if we are to successfully weather change and maintain a sense of existential stability in a dynamic, fast-changing environment. Consider the words of Gajduschek (2003: 718, emphasis added), too: 'the bureaucratic organization is *the* organizational form which reduces to the greatest possible extent uncertainty both in its internal procedures and in its outputs.' Is it any surprise, then, that ostensibly post-bureaucratic organizational forms, while on the surface appealing to a rhetoric of fluidity actually retain the central practices of the bureaucratic norm? As Willmott (2011: 275) notes 'detailed regulations, record keeping and provision of information in standardized formats are crucial constitutive features of many ostensibly "post-bureaucratic" practices.' Drawing on research by Iedema (2003), Styhre (2007: 97) makes a similar observation: 'many organizations have developed … a post-bureaucratic rhetoric while at the same time, they retain traditional structural hierarchies, expert and specialization boundaries, procedures and processes whose intent is top-down control rather than bottom-up facilitation.'

Finally, it is worth considering the associated—and potentially paradoxical—argument that bureaucracy *is* flexible not in spite of its characteristics, but precisely because of them. As Kallinikos (2004: 23, original emphasis) notes:

Despite its common sense and, to a certain degree, justified associations with rigid and inflexible behaviour, bureaucracy is the first and perhaps *sole organizational form* capable of addressing the demands that incessant social, economic, and technological change induces ... [T]he organizational involvement of individuals qua roles implies the dissociation of the process of organising from the emotional and cognitive complexity of agent qua persons. By contrast to persons, roles can be adapted, modified, redesigned, abandoned or reshuffled to address the emerging technical, social and economic demands the organization is facing.

For Styhre (2007: 168), large organizations are frequently assumed to adapt poorly to emergent conditions and new demands imposed by either new forms of competition or regulatory authorities. He suggests that in fact it is quite the opposite. Large organizations have established a series of mechanisms for identifying such external changes and orchestrating responses to them. Of the examples Styhre invokes, there was in no case an intrinsic bureaucratic logic that prevented action from being taken. Instead the companies developed responses to deal with the new challenges. So, while small start-up businesses can capitalise on the *zeitgeist* and hit the ground running with a fresh commercial flavour, a few years on (and when the market changes again) they have no experience of managing change. Compare this to the long-established larger firm. Although it is probably unable to compete with a new start-up in terms of an emergent 'flavour of the month,' it will almost certainly be in a stronger position when the market next changes (since it has experience of multiple changes). Ironically, then, it is the smaller, younger—and supposedly dynamic—firm that has only ever known 'one way of doing things.'

## Why is paradox so important?

You may ask: is any of what is being said here really so revelational? No, not really. The difference, I think, is that I am determined to place paradox at the centre of our analysis. Rather than see it as a logical inconvenience, empirical peculiarity or rogue conclusion, I cast it as a positive facet of bureaucracy; indeed, bureaucracy would not be anything like as resilient or effective without these paradoxical qualities. Paradox is not something that can—or indeed, should—be solved, resolved, or dissolved.

> [F]or Weber, fundamental values or ends are undermined, lost or reversed in the very pursuit of those values or ends; this process is unable to be altered or avoided by human agency—it is, or has been, 'fate' ... The concept of paradox is different to other standard definitions of paradox (e.g. Marx, Smith and Mandeville) in that these non-Weberian paradoxes are open to be overcome, either through resolution or destruction. The contrast with Weber is clear—for Weber there is no going past the paradox of ends/values as a self-

undermining process ... Some choice must be made, but at every turn, at the end of every path in the modern world, lies the final embrace of paradox.

*(Symonds and Pudsey, 2008: 237)*

I'd like to take this argument further and in so doing focus on the supposedly 'mundane routines' (du Gay, 2000) that undergird bureaucracy. du Gay, as already noted, implies that he sees at least some semblance of dignity in mundane routines. Peppered throughout the book you are reading have been examples of routines that elicit more than a semblance of dignity; they are genuine pleasures: form-filling, filing, temping bliss, re-ordering a pencil case, and splitting logs to name just a few. These are, to some degree at least, comparable to what Graeber describes as his *secret joys of bureaucracy*. Guided by the view that bureaucracy is a manifestation of a pervasive paradox, it may be that our damning of bureaucracy as faceless and purposeless misses the point completely: bureaucratic delineations do not alienate (as the cogs in the machine metaphor might imply), but enable each of us to fashion a Husserlian lifeworld in such a way that tasks become genuinely enjoyable on an *individual* basis, as the 'temping bliss' label aptly demonstrates. We've developed these tasks not to keep the amorphous collective happy, but to keep *individuals* happy. Could it be, then, that bureaucracies are ideally configured for enabling a sense of individuality?

More generally, the autoethnographic approach taken in this book has facilitated recognition of the existential importance of means constituting ends themselves. Although others (for example, Watson, 2002) have acknowledged the importance of the cultural aspects of bureaucracy, they have not explored the importance of bureaucratic means as constituting ends themselves. Much of this historical work— even where conducted by scholars who lay claim to critical credentials—has remained firmly subordinate to economic norms. The ethnographical work presented in this book, however, reveals a sense of pleasure in the means themselves. Reflecting on this data, I have thus been able to re-evaluate our broader understanding of organization, not as something of principally economic value, but as something that is inherently cultural. However, I need to tread with caution. In his assessment of the Holocaust, Bauman notes the following: 'Technical responsibility differs from moral responsibility in that it forgets that the action is a means to something other than itself ... *the result is the irrelevance of moral standards for the technical success of the bureaucratic operations*' (Bauman, 1989: 101, original emphasis). My reservations about Bauman's treatment of bureaucracy vis-à-vis the Holocaust notwithstanding (see chapter 4), this is a valid point and it would it be hugely ironic if I ignored this. Too great a focus on means could have catastrophic consequences. Nonetheless, the broader and salient point is that the vast majority of analytical coverage in respect of bureaucracy ignores the importance of means. For du Gay (2011: 21), echoing former British Civil Servant Sir Michael Quinlan:

[A] focus on 'delivery' and 'performance' as part and parcel of a sustained focus on the achievement of practical results can slide into a sense that outcome is the only true reality and that process is flummery. But the two are not antithetical, still less inimical to one another. Process is care and thoroughness; it is consultation, involvement and co-ownership; it is legitimacy and acceptance; it is also record, accountability and clear accountability. It is accordingly a significant component of outcome itself.

## Bureaucracy and balance

For Harris (2006: 80), 'there is a need to go beyond the binary opposition of "bureaucratic" and "post-bureaucratic" forms.' If we accept that at the end of every path lies the final embrace of paradox (and I certainly do), then what more can be said? Well, while authors of *Rescue America*, Morris and Salamone (2011), for example, believe that one way out is to embrace Christian Faith (but presumably any belief system pertaining to absolute certainty would do), I see another approach: I attempt to initiate a *philosophy of balance* and in so doing, invoke a popular idiom:

'He's been here so long, he's part of the furniture'

On the one hand, tenure brings invaluable experience and organizations rely on this, not least in terms of instilling a sense of continuity. On the other, tenure typically brings a lack of new idea generation. It is about balance. But the word 'balance' lacks pertinence and is used glibly. The word has not been subject to anything like the degree of interrogation that it warrants. By contrast, the word 'power,' for example, has attracted reams of coverage. This is a shame. It is not simply a question of weighing up the pros and cons of bureaucratic life and acting accordingly. If we are to develop a truly robust philosophy of balance, we might stand a better chance of navigating effectively between utopia and dystopia, between stasis and existential isolation, and between bureaucracy and adhocracy.

Organizations must endeavour to understand bureaucracy and adhocracy not as ideological convictions but as barometric tools. Just as interest rates are periodically adjusted to help regulate an economy, so too must an organization endeavour to periodically adjust its bureaucratic degree. For example, this might involve adjusting to the particular skill set and predisposition of current staff, the level and nature of competition, and the attitudes of stakeholders. In short, the organization might usefully monitor the degree to which it cultivates or de-cultivates bureaucratic measures in response to the sense of existential angst felt by all involved at any given time. But how might this work in a practical sense? I turn, once again, to my MBA students and their response to another assessment I set: (*'Operational mistakes are simultaneously caused and purportedly solved by an appeal to greater proceduralisation.' Discuss.*) In the formative assignments discussed earlier in this book, I noted that the word 'balance' was used repeatedly, and by most students. This assignment revealed comparable responses, including these:

> 'Although organizations need to maintain a level of control, it is important [that they] remain flexible and fluid in order to meet the ever changing demands in modern day life; therefore a balance between control and flexibility is required.'

> 'In order to minimize the [likelihood of dysfunctional behaviour], organizations must seek a balance between [reinforcing] rules and [cultivating] freedom to think.'

In reminding ourselves that bureaucracy and post-bureaucracy are parameters between which organizational life unfolds, intuiting a sense of balance becomes paramount. Watson (2002: 245) notes that organizations depend on the passive controllability of employees and resources but at the same time require employees willingly to take initiatives and actively commit themselves to organizational tasks. A tension thus exists between pressure to make people controllable and pressure to allow them discretion. Too much control and organizations risk *over*-institutionalisation and the proliferation of the much maligned jobsworth. Too little, and they will not engender a sense of organizational belonging and security.

Though not easy to detect, a desire to establish a philosophy of balance is implied in the literature. For Knights and Willmott (2002: 78), for example, 'the pursuit of autonomy can be as dangerous as its denial'; we need both bureaucracy (as anti-autonomy) and post-bureaucracy (as autonomy) as markers between which organizational life can unfold. For Magee (2000: 113), too, paradox goes much deeper and, inevitably, necessitates a sense of balance: 'The fact that the first step toward civilization is at the same time the first repression of natural feeling, the first repression of instinct, is a matter of profoundest importance in the psychology and life of human beings.'

Permit me for one final time to return to my days as a student at Warwick. Professor Gibson Burrell regaled one of his classes about a little known scholar who one day claimed to have discovered the perfect 'subject-object,' by which he meant—I think—that he had discovered a means of reconciling objectivity and subjectivity in an eminently satisfying way. He noted that this individual committed suicide the very same day. Burrell suggested that the discovery of this point (a point at which life—in an epistemological sense at least—was in harmony) could only be made if we were prepared to pay the final price. Suffice to say, we were all shit-scared, but it had the desired effect. I said to myself that I wanted to find that holy grail and survive. I haven't found it—yet. To be honest, my suspicion is that such a quest will never bear fruit. The reason for this is because it must remain hypothetical; our empirical world is one in which perpetual re-adjustment to maintain a semblance of balance is inevitable; without it, life could be reduced to a pre-determined logic which would completely invalidate human consciousness and any meaningful sense of agency. This sort of detail will, I hope, be fleshed out by establishing a systematic socio-philosophy of balance. In the meantime, let us take inspiration from Nietzsche, Handy (1994) and Standing (2016).

Nietzsche's philosophy has been all but overlooked in the study of bureaucracy. This is unfortunate because his work has much to offer. For example, it can contribute to our understanding of bureaucracy in respect of the dynamic between institutions and individuals (in *Twilight of the Idols*, 93–4); institutions as organizational biographies that bind together sequential generations of inhabitants (ibid.), the argument that effective bureaucracies enable us to endure ineffective leadership (*The Anti-Christ*, 180), as well as the suggestion both that bureaucracy *patterns* our institutional existence, and that attitudes to it are cyclical, by recourse to the familiar Nietzschean idea of *eternal recurrence* (ibid. 110–11). However, although instructive in these various respects, his work is of greatest relevance in developing an approach to balance. In *The Dawn of Day*, Nietzsche (2007 [1881]: 273) notes the following:

> It seems to me that a sick man lives more carelessly when he is under medical observation than when he attends to his own health. In the first case it suffices for him to obey strictly all his Doctor's prescriptions; but in the second case he gives more attention to the ultimate object of these prescriptions, namely, his health; he observes much more, and submits himself to a more severe discipline than the directions of his physician would compel him to do. [...] All rules have this effect: they distract our attention from the fundamental aim of the rule, and make us more thoughtless.

The point here is that too great an emphasis on bureaucracy will inevitably create complacency. However, as we saw in chapters 2 and 3 too great a rejection of the same invokes a sense of insecurity. An effective form of balance is thus warranted, but it must involve more than meagre moderation. Nietzsche (ibid. 278) continues: 'Moderation appears to itself to be quite beautiful: it is unaware of the fact that in the eyes of the immoderate it seems course and insipid, and consequently ugly.' If, as Nietzsche argues, moderation is ugly, are we perhaps better off carving out a more dynamic, pendulous path? This of course is why I am arguing that we are better off positing bureaucracy and post-bureaucracy as *parameters between which live unfolds*. Dynamic—and perpetual—adjustment is the name of the game.

For Handy paradox in organizations is inevitable, endemic and perpetual:

> We used to think we knew how to run organizations. Now we know better. More than ever they need to be global and local at the same time, to be small in some ways but big in others, to be centralised some of the time and decentralised most of it. They expect their workers to be both more autonomous and more of a team, their managers to be more delegating and more controlling.
>
> *(Handy, 1994: 37–8)*

Handy draws upon Stopford and Baden-Fuller's (1990) research. The pair report that successful businesses live with paradox, or what they call dilemmas. Handy's summary:

> They have to be planned and yet be flexible, be differentiated and integrated at the same time, be mass-marketers while catering for many niches, they must introduce new technology but allow their workers to be the masters of their own destiny; they must find ways to get variety and quality and fashion, and all at a low cost; they have, in short, to find a way to reconcile what used to be opposites, instead of choosing between them.
>
> *(Ibid.)*

Balance is critical.

Standing's (2016: 19–20) distinction between the 'salariat' and the 'precariat' is illustrative, too, but in a very different sense:

> In a sense the salariat is drifting into the precariat. The case of Japan's 'salaryman' is illustrative. This twentieth-century worker, with lifetime employment in one enterprise, emerged through a highly paternalistic model of labourism that prevailed until the early 1980s. In Japan (and elsewhere), the gilded cage can easily become the leaden cage, with so much employment security that the outside becomes a zone of fear. This is what happened in Japan and in other East Asian countries that adopted a similar model. [However], the precariat is displacing salaryman, whose pain is revealed by an alarming rise in suicides and social illnesses. The Japanese transformation of salaryman may be an extreme case. But one can see how someone psychologically trapped in long-term employment loses control and drifts closer to a form of precarious dependency. If the 'parent' becomes displeased, or is unable or unwilling to continue the fictive parental role, the person will be plunged into the precariat, without the skills of autonomy and developmental prowess. Long-term employment can *deskill* … this was one of the worst aspects of the era of labourism.

Most pertinent of all, Standing goes on to make the following observation towards the end of his book: 'One can have too much security or too little. If one has too little, irrationality prevails; if one has too much, a lack of care and responsibility prevails' (ibid. 202). Balance is also relevant in terms of education. For Merton (1940: 562, original emphasis),

> actions based upon training and skills which have been successfully applied in the past may result in inappropriate responses *under changed conditions.* An inadequate flexibility in the application of skills will, in a changing milieu, result in more or less serious maladjustments.

Merton adopts Burke's barnyard illustration: chickens may be readily conditioned to interpret the sound of the bell as a signal for food. The same bell may now be used to summon the 'trained chickens' to their doom as they are assembled to suffer decapitation. In general, one adopts measures in keeping with his past training and, under new conditions which are now recognised as significantly different, the very soundness of this training may lead to the adoption of the wrong procedures. In sum: our training may become an incapacity. So, while we certainly need an education *in respect of bureaucracy*, this must remain distinct from an indoctrination *in bureaucracy*. Once again, balance is critical.

In a practicable sense, then, how might these arguments pertaining to bureaucracy and balance be harnessed effectively? In discussions with both the publisher and series editor towards the final stages of this book, we considered the concept of *phronesis*. Dating back to Ancient Greece, it is routinely regarded as a form practical wisdom. More recently, however, and perhaps appealing to a more contemporary vocabulary, McEvilley (2002: 609) has described it as a pertinent form of 'mindfulness.' Interest in ancient Greek philosophy has been on the increase at least since MacIntyre's (1981) *After Virtue*. The concept of phronesis is appropriate for at least two reasons. First, and as Gallagher (1992) notes, it cannot be achieved through formal instruction, but requires experience; it necessitate reflection on our own experiences; and experience is essential if we are to appreciate the role of bureaucracy and its infinitely variable aspects. Second, phronesis encourages us to move away from ideological positions, from 'absolutes,' and instead focus on application. I have argued precisely this in respect of bureaucracy; it's not inherently good or bad, but it must be explicated and applied in varying degrees, in accordance with circumstances. To this end, intuiting a sense of balance becomes imperative, or as, Taylor (1995: 678) notes, developing 'soundness of judgement.' It is at this point that we can rekindle a sense of agency and engage with more familiar ancient Greek philosophy, including Aristotle's *Golden Mean*. For example, Rego et al. (2012) presented a case for reintroducing virtues into leadership, by recourse to the Golden Mean. There is much to be said for incorporating a balanced understanding in respect of bureaucracy as part of such a broader schooling in leadership.

## Bureaucracy and sensemaking

How do we make sense of bureaucracy? In my mind, this is a vital question and one we are compelled to ask of ourselves. Each of us has developed our own techniques, unknowingly. What I have suggested in this book is that we can usefully reflect on these techniques to help refine our organizational craft. In so doing, we must each reflect—critically—on what fashions, moulds and contributes to our understanding of bureaucracy. We are to a large extent conditioned by the arts in this respect. But, as we saw in chapter 5, the arts have yet to evolve to challenge the new and emerging nexuses of power: the post-bureaucratic threat. This is regrettable. There has been some terrific dystopian literature that challenges bureaucracy. Kafka is a case in point. The Kafkaesque literary trope makes for an engaging read; it is controversial, consuming, and foreboding. But, notably, and despite the question presented in chapter 5 about the potential appeal (or 'sexiness') of post-bureaucratic dystopian fiction, I firmly believe that an extreme post-bureaucratic rendering of the world has the potential to be controversial, consuming and foreboding, too. As the manuscript for this book was finalised, I wanted to ensure I was up to date with relevant fiction and films. At the time of publication, the most contemporary dystopian novel was *The Wall* by John Lanchester. I have yet to read it myself, but the BBC's Will Gompertz (2019) notes the following:

> The book has many of the standard tropes of a dystopian novel. There is a totalitarian state operating in a bleak post-industrial landscape caused by a climatic catastrophe, creating the justification for a faceless bureaucracy to suppress and control a cowed population.

Nothing, it seems, has changed. Novelists are still bashing out the same old thing. And this is perpetually reinforcing the way in which we make sense of our bureaucratic existence. It is time for a new myth. The arts aside, we need to completely re-evaluate our approach to educating leaders, managers, and administrators in the spirit of sensemaking. Historically, our approach to management education has been either instructive (endorsed by functionalists) or critical (endorsed by critical theorists). But we can move away from this polarised carving of our pedagogies. There is room for a third approach: *navigating organizational life effectively*. To this end, we must cultivate a sense of organizational craft, enabling us to work with—rather than against—bureaucracy. This will involve instilling in our students a sophisticated, nuanced understanding of the concept. Bureaucracy has been damned, suppressed, or ignored for too long. But these approaches have failed. As we have seen, in the final analysis any and all attempts to eliminate bureaucracy elicits new forms of the same. Bureaucracy is immanent, emergent, and resilient. To properly make sense of bureaucracy (and, by implication, organization) we are obliged to regard it as a manifestation of an underlying existential inertia, a logic which patterns the human condition.

## What now?

Inevitably, there were areas of research that I'd hoped to incorporate in this book that didn't make the final cut. However, these are important and I very much hope future scholars consider them as guiding principles. I see at least three areas of future enquiry. (1) Although I have hinted in this book at the different ways in which bureaucracy manifests itself in disparate international contexts, it is a long way off representing a systematic study. Weber (1968 [1922]: 971) himself notes that 'the direction bureaucratization takes, and the reasons that occasion it, can vary widely' and yet this remains a relatively poorly studied aspect of the field. Ethnographic methods comparable to those presented in this book will, I suspect, enable us to explore the myriad ways in which bureaucracy manifests itself differently, across the world, in diverse cultures. In particular, I am curious to get a feel for the extent to which other languages have a word for 'jobsworth.' Is he [gender bias loosely intended] a creature peculiar to nations unfortunate enough to speak English? And what of different languages more generally? How exactly do semantic devices associated with bureaucracy propagate in different languages; and to what extent does this have a bearing on how bureaucracy is 'consumed' in those cultures? (2) While I explored the relationship between dystopian art forms and bureaucracy, is there more to learn from the relationship between comedy and bureaucracy? Both David Brent's character in *The Office* and the familiar quip, 'computer says no' from *Little Britain* are just two examples. And—once again—are these uniquely British or does the comedy associated with bureaucracy transcend cultural lines? (3) To what extent does bureaucracy break down in periods of liminality and what characterises its (inevitable) re-emergence? Do old ways of bureaucratising yield to new ones?

During the final stages of the research for this book, I happened across a news story on the BBC website: 'How Britain's opium trade impoverished Indians' (Biswas, 2019). The journalist, Soutik Biswas, reported on research conducted by Rolf Bauer, a professor of economic and social history at the University of Vienna. The article explored the relations between oppressor and oppressed and the myriad effects—both good and bad—of the historical trade. What caught my attention, however, was the report's final paragraph:

> By 1915 the opium trade with China, the biggest market, had ended. However, the British Indian monopoly on opium continued until India won independence in 1947. What confounds Dr Bauer is how a few thousand opium clerks controlled millions of peasants, forcing them to produce a crop that actually harms them.

Imperialist factors notwithstanding, I strongly suspect that these farmers were utterly entranced by the bureau. Like so many of us, they will likely have experienced the bureau as a broker of legitimacy, institutional certainty, and existential security, even—as the report notes—in the face of the apparent ill-effects of the work they were undertaking on its behalf. A fuller education in respect of complex organization—and by implication, bureaucracy—will enable us both to make better sense of history, and to intuit some semblance of balance with respect to bureaucracy. And, finally, let us be guided by Hofstadter's (1980: 696) sage words:

> the total picture of 'who I am' is integrated in some enormously complex way … and contains in each one of us a large number of unresolved, possibly unresolvable, inconsistencies. These undoubtedly provide much of the dynamic tension which is so much part of being human.

## Concluding thoughts

Maintaining this dynamic tension is imperative. The all-encompassing bureaucracy of the total institution violates this tension. But so too do vain—and vainglorious—attempts to eradicate the bureau.

# REFERENCES

Adler, S. (1993) 'Time-and-Motion Regained', *Harvard Business Review* 71 (1): 97–108.
Agre, P. (2003) 'Hierarchy and History in Simon's "Architecture of Complexity"', *The Journal of the Learning Sciences*, 12 (3): 413–426.
Arthur, M. & Rousseau, D. (eds) (1996) *The Boundaryless Career: A New Employment Principle for a New Organizational Era*, New York: Oxford University Press.
Ballard, J. G. (1957) 'The Concentration City', *New Worlds*, 19 (55).
Ballard, J. G. (1963) 'Minus One', *Science Fantasy* 20 (59).
Ballard, J. G. (2009 [1963]) 'The Subliminal Man', in *The Complete Stories of J. G. Ballard*, New York: W.W. Norton.
Ballard, J. G. (1970) *The Atrocity Exhibition*, London: Jonathan Cape.
Ballard, J. G. (1975) *High Rise*, London: Jonathan Cape.
Ballard, J. G. (1996) *Cocaine Nights*, London: Flamingo.
Ballard, J. G. (2000) *Super-Cannes*, London: Flamingo.
Barley, S. & Kunda, G. (2004) *Gurus, Hired Guns, and Warm Bodies: Itinerant Experts in a Knowledge Economy*, Princeton, NJ: Princeton University Press.
Bauman, Z. (1989) *Modernity and the Holocaust*, Cambridge: Polity Press.
Bauman, Z. (2017) *Retrotopia*, Cambridge: Polity Press.
BBC FOUR (2019) Indian Hill Railways, episode 1: 'The Darjeeling Himalayan Railway', BBC. https://www.bbc.co.uk/programmes/b00qvk99.
Beirne, M. & Knight, S. (2007) 'From Community Theatre to Critical Management Studies: A Dramatic Contribution to Reflective Learning?', *Management Learning* 38 (5): 591–611.
Bell, E. & Taylor, S. (2004) '"From Outward Bound to Inward Bound": The Prophetic Voices and Discursive Practices of Spiritual Management Development', *Human Relations* 57 (4): 439–466.
Berger, B. (2002) *The Family in the Modern Age: More than a Lifestyle Choice*, London: Routledge.
Berger, P. (ed.) (1999) *The Desecularization of the World: Resurgent Religion and World Politics*, Michigan: Ethics and Public Policy Centre and Wm. B. Eerdmans Publishing Co.
Berger, P., Berger, B. & Kellner, H. (1973) *The Homeless Mind: Modernization and Consciousness*, New York: Random House.

Billing, Y. (1994) 'Gender and Bureaucracies: A Critique of Ferguson's *The Feminist Case Against Bureaucracy*', *Gender, Work and Organization* 1 (4): 179–193.
Billing, Y. (2005) 'Gender Equity: A Bureaucratic Enterprise?', in du Gay, P. (ed.) *The Values of Bureaucracy*, Oxford: Oxford University Press.
Biswas, S. (2019) 'How Britain's Opium Trade Impoverished Indians', 5 September, London: BBC, https://www.bbc.co.uk/news/world-asia-india-49404024.
Boje, D. (2008) *Storytelling Organization*, London: Sage.
Boltanski, L. & Chiapello, É. (2005) *The New Spirit of Capitalism*, London: Verso.
Boncori, I. & Vine, T. (2014) '"Learning Without Thought is Labour Lost; Thought Without Learning is Perilous": The Importance of Pre-departure Training for Expatriates Working in China', *International Journal of Work, Organisation and Emotion* 6 (2): 155–177.
Braverman, H. (1974) *Labor and Monopology Capitalism: The Degradation of Work in the Twentieth Century*, New York: Monthly Review Press.
Brouwer, M. (2002) 'Weber, Schumpeter and Knight on Entrepreneurship and Economic Development', *Journal of Evolutionary Economics* 12: 83–105.
Bryman, A. and Bell, E. (2007) *Business Research Methods*, New York: Oxford University Press.
Budgen, S. (2000) 'Sebastian Budgen on Luc Boltanski and Eve Chiapello', *New Left Review* 1 (January–February).
Burrell, G. (1997) *Pandemonium*, London: Sage.
Carey, J. (1999) *The Faber Book of Utopias*, London: Faber & Faber.
Carrette, J. & King, R. (2005) *Selling Spirituality: The Silent Takeover of Religion*, London: Routledge.
Casey, C. (1995) *Work, Self, and Society: After Industrialism*, London: Routledge.
Casey, C. (2002) *Critical Analysis of Organizations: Theory, Practice, Revitalization*, London: Sage.
Casey, C. (2004) 'Bureaucracy Re-enchanted? Spirit, Experts and Authority in Organizations', *Organization* 11 (1): 59–79.
Chandler, J. (2012) 'Work as Dance', *Organization* 19 (6): 865–878.
Clegg, S. (2011) 'Chapter 9: Under Reconstruction: Modern Bureaucracies', in Clegg, S., Harris, M. and Höpfl, H. (eds) *Managing Modernity: Beyond Bureaucracy*, Oxford: Oxford University Press.
Clegg, S., Courpasson, D. & Phillips, N. (2006) *Power and Organizations*, London: Sage.
Clegg, S., Harris, M. & Höpfl, H. (eds) (2011) *Managing Modernity: Beyond Bureaucracy*, Oxford: Oxford University Press.
Clegg, S., Pina e Cunha, M., Munro, I., Rego, A. & de Sousa, M. O. (2016) 'Kafkaesque Power and Bureaucracy', *Journal of Political Power* 9 (2): 157–181.
Corbett, J. M. (1995) 'Celluloid Projections: Images of Technology and Organizational Futures in Contemporary Science Fiction Film', *Organization* 2 (3–4), 467–488.
Crozier, M. (2017) [1964] *The Bureaucratic Phenomenon*, London: Routledge.
Davie, G. (1994) *Religion in Britain since 1945: Believing Without Belonging*, Oxford: Blackwell.
Dawson, L. (2006) 'Privatisation, Globalisation, and Religion Innovation: Giddens' Theory of Modernity and the Refutation of Secularisation Theory', in *Theorising Religion: Classical and Contemporary Debates*, Aldershot: Ashgate.
DeGregori, T. and Thompson, R. (1993) 'An Institutionalist Theory of Bureaucracy: Organizations and Technology', in Garston, N. (ed.) *Bureaucracy: Three Paradigms*, London: Kluwer.
Dehler, G. & Welsh, M. (1994) 'Spirituality and Organizational Transformation: Implications for the New Management Paradigm', *Journal of Managerial Psychology* 9 (6): 17–26.
Deleuze, G. (2004 [1968]) *Difference and Repetition*, London: Continuum.

Dent, E., Higgins, M. & Wharff, D. (2005) 'Spirituality and Leadership: An Empirical Review of Definitions, Distinctions, and Embedded Assumptions', *The Leadership Quarterly* 16 (5): 625–653.
Deutscher, I. (1969) 'Roots of Bureaucracy', *The Socialist Register* 6: 9–28.
du Gay, P. (2000) *In Praise of Bureaucracy: Weber, Organization, Ethics*, London: Sage.
du Gay, P. (2004) 'Against "Enterprise" (But not Against "Enterprise", for That Would Make no Sense)', *Organization* 11 (1): 37–57.
du Gay, P. (ed.) (2005) *The Values of Bureaucracy*, Oxford: Oxford University Press.
du Gay, P. (2011) 'Chapter 1: "Without Regard to Persons": Problems of Involvement and Attachment in "Post-Bureaucratic" Public Management', in Clegg, S., Harris, M. and Höpfl, H. (eds) *Managing Modernity: Beyond Bureaucracy*, Oxford: Oxford University Press.
du Gay, P. & Morgan, G. (2013) *New Spirit of Capitalism: Crises, Justifications and Dynamics*, Oxford: Oxford University Press.
Ehrenreich, B. (2005) *Bait and Switch: The Futile Pursuit of the Corporate Dream*, New York: Henry Holt and Company.
Etzioni, A. (1964) *Modern Organizations*, Upper Saddle River, NJ: Prentice Hall.
Fairholm, G.W. (1996) 'Spiritual Leadership: Fulfilling Whole-self Needs at Work', *Leadership & Organization Development Journal* 17 (5): 11–17.
Franzen, J. (2010) *Freedom*, New York: Farrar, Straus and Giroux.
Fromm, E. (1985) [1942] *The Fear of Freedom*, London: Routledge.
Frost, P. J. and Egri, C. P. (1994) 'The Shamanic Perspective on Organizational Change and Development', *Journal of Organizational Change Management* 7 (1): 7–23.
Gajduschek, G. (2003) 'Bureaucracy: Is It Efficient? Is It Not? Is That the Question? Uncertainty Reduction: An Ignored Element of Bureaucratic Rationality', *Administration & Society* 34 (6): 700–723.
Gallagher, S. (1992) *Hermeneutics and Education*, New York: State University of New York Press.
Garcia-Zamor, J. (2003) 'Workplace Spirituality and Organizational Performance', *Public Administration Review* 63 (3): 355–363.
Garston, N. (ed.) (1993a) *Bureaucracy: Three Paradigms*, London: Kluwer.
Garston, N. (1993b) 'The Study of Bureaucracy', in Garston, N. (ed.) *Bureaucracy: Three Paradigms*, London: Kluwer.
Gehlen, A. (1980) *Man in the Age of Technology*, New York: Columbia University Press.
Giddens, A. (1972) *Politics and Sociology in the Thought of Max Weber*, London: Macmillan.
Giddens, A. (1991) *Modernity and Self-identity*, Cambridge: Polity Press.
Gompertz, W. (2019) 'Will Gompertz reviews John Lanchester's dystopian novel *The Wall*', https://www.bbc.co.uk/news/entertainment-arts-46919072.
Goodsell, C. (2004) *The Case for Bureaucracy: A Public Administration Polemic*, London: Sage.
Gouldner, A. (1954) *Patterns of Industrial Bureaucracy*, New York: The Free Press.
Graeber, D. (2015) *The Utopia of Rules: On Technology, Stupidity, and the Secret Joys of Bureaucracy*, London: Melville House.
Grey, C. (1994) 'Career as a Project of the Self and Labour Process Discipline', *Sociology* 28 (2): 479–497.
Grint, K. (1997) *Leadership: Classical, Contemporary, and Critical Approaches*, Oxford: Oxford University Press.
Hall, D. (1996) 'Protean Careers of the 21st Century', *Academy of Management Executive* 10: 8–16.
Handy, C. (1994) *The Empty Raincoat*, London: Hutchinson.
Hanegraaff, W. (1998) *New Age Religion and Western Culture: Esotericism in the Mirror of Secular Thought*, New York: State University of New York Press.

Harris, M. (2006) 'Technology, Innovation and Post-bureaucracy: The Case of the British Library', *Journal of Organizational Change Management* 19 (1): 80–92.

Harvey, J.B. (1988) *The Abilene Paradox and Other Meditations on Management*, Lexington, MA: Lexington Books.

Heckscher, C. (1993) 'Foreword', in Abrahamsson, B. *Why Organizations? How and Why People Organize?* London: Sage.

Heckscher, C. and Donnellon, A. (eds) (1994) *The Post-bureaucratic Organization: New Perspectives on Organizational Change*, Newbury Park, CA: Sage.

Heelas, P. (1996) *The New Age Movement: The Celebration of Self and the Sacralization of Modernity*, Oxford: Blackwell.

Hodgson, D. & Cicmil, S. (eds) (2006) *Making Projects Critical*, London: Palgrave Macmillan.

Hofstadter, D. (1980) *Gödel, Escher, Bach: An Eternal Golden Braid*, London: Penguin.

Holloway, J. (2000) 'Institutional Geographies of the New Age Movement', *Geoforum* 31 (4): 553–565.

Höpfl, H. (2000) 'Ordered Passions: Commitment and Hierarchy in the Organizational Ideas of the Jesuit Founders', *Management Learning* 31 (3): 313–329.

Houtman, D. & Aupers, S. (2007) 'The Spiritual Turn and the Decline of Tradition: The Spread of Post-Christian Spirituality in Fourteen Western Countries', *Journal for the Scientific Study of Religion* 46 (3): 305–320.

Huxley, A. (2004 [1959]) *Brave New World Revisited*, London: Vintage Classics.

Iedema, R. (2003) *Discourses of Post-bureaucratic Organization*, Amsterdam: John Benjamins.

Izak, M. (2010) *Exploring the Cogency of Organizational Spirituality: Functionalism, Boundlessness and Rationality*, PhD Thesis, University of Essex.

Jacques, E. (1976) *A General Theory of Bureaucracy*, New York: Halstead.

Jay, R. & Templar, R. (2004) *Fast Thinking Manager's Manual at the Speed of Life*, 2nd edn., London: Pearson.

Jensen, A. (2012) *The Project Society*, Denmark: Aarhus University Press.

Jones, E., Jones, R. & Gergen, K. (1963) 'Some Conditions Affecting the Evaluation of a Conformist', *Journal of Personality* 31: 270–288.

Jones, E., Stires, L., Shaver, K. & Harris, V. (1968) 'Evaluation of an Ingratiatory by Target Persons and Bystanders', *Journal of Personality* 36: 385.

Jones, J. (2010) 'Jonathan Franzen's Freedom: The Novel of the Century', *The Guardian*, 23 August, https://www.theguardian.com/artanddesign/jonathanjonesblog/2010/aug/23/jonathan-franzen-freedom.

Kallinikos, J. (2003). 'Work, Human Agency and Organizational Forms: An Anatomy of Fragmentation', *Organization Studies* 24 (4): 595–618.

Kallinikos, J. (2004) 'The Social Foundations of the Bureaucratic Order', *Organization* 11 (1): 13–36.

Kallinikos, J. (2006) 'The Institution of Bureaucracy: Administration, Pluralism, Democracy: A Review Article', *Economy and Society* 35 (4): 611–627.

Kapoor, R. (2007) 'Auroville: A Spiritual-social Experiment in Human Unity and Evolution', *Futures* 39 (5): 632–643.

Kets de Vries, M. (1980) *Organizational Paradoxes: Clinical Approaches to Management*, London: Routledge.

Kieser, A. (1989) 'Organizational, Institutional, and Societal Evolution: Medieval Craft Guilds and the Genesis of Formal Organizations', *Administrative Science Quarterly* 34: 540–564.

King, D. & Lawley, S. (2016) *Organizational Behaviour*, Oxford: Oxford University Press.

Knights, D. & Willmott, H. (2002) 'Autonomy as Utopia or Dystopia', in Parker, M. (ed.) *Utopia and Organization*, Oxford: Blackwell.

Kohli, M. (2007) 'The Institutionalization of the Life Course: Looking Back to Look Ahead', *Research in Human Development* 4 (3–4): 253–271.

Konnovs, H. & Vine, T. (2019) 'Enhancing the Employment Prospects of Young People with Autism Spectrum Disorder (ASD): A Pilot Study', *Journal of Social Science & Allied Health Professions* 2 (1): e7–e17, http://www.ssahp.com/vol-2—issue-1.html.

Korisettar, R. & Petraglia, M. (1998) *Early Human Behaviour in Global Context: The Rise and Diversity of the Lower Palaeolithic Record*, London: Routledge.

Kumar, K. (1991) *Utopianism*, Buckingham, UK: Open University Press.

Law, J. (1994) *Organizing Modernity*, Oxford: Blackwell.

Lévi-Strauss, C. (1966) *The Savage Mind*, Chicago, IL: University of Chicago Press.

Lichtenstein, H. (1977) *The Dilemma of Human Identity*. New York: J. Aronson.

Logan, G. & Adams, R. (1998) 'Introduction', in More, T. *Utopia* [1516], Cambridge: University of Cambridge Press.

Lopdrup-Hjorth, T. & du Gay, P. (2020) 'Speaking Truth to Power? Anti-bureaucratic Romanticism from Critical Organizational Theorizing to the White House', *Organization* 27 (3): 441–453.

Maffesoli, M. (1991) 'The Ethics of Aesthetics', *Theory, Culture & Society* 8: 7–20.

Magee, B. (2000) *Wagner and Philosophy*, London: Penguin.

Mannheim, K. (1955 [1936]) *Ideology and Utopia: An Introduction to the Sociology of Knowledge*, New York: Harvest.

March, J. & Simon, H. (1984) 'The Dysfunctions of Bureaucracy', in Pugh, D. (ed.) *Organization Theory: Selected Readings*, London: Penguin.

Marsden, J. (2002) *After Nietzsche: Notes Towards a Philosophy of Ecstasy*, London: Palgrave Macmillan.

McEvilley, T. (2002), *The Shape of Ancient Thought: Comparative Studies in Green and Indian Philosophies*, New York: Allworth Press.

McGrath, P. (2005) 'Thinking Differently about Knowledge-intensive Firms: Insights from Early Medieval Irish Monasticism', *Organization* 12 (4): 549–566.

McGrath, P. (2007) 'Knowledge Management in Monastic Communities of the Medieval Irish Celtic Church', *Journal of Management Inquiry* 13 (2): 211–223.

McLennan, G. (2010) 'The Postsecular Turn', *Theory, Culture & Society* 27 (4): 3–20.

McNeill, F. (2004) 'How to Deal with Jobsworths', *The Guardian*, https://www.theguardian.com/money/2004/jan/12/careers.jobsadvice4.

Meindl, J., Ehrlich, S. & Dukerich, J. (1985) 'The Romance of Leadership', *Administrative Science Quarterly* 30: 78–102.

Merton, R. (1940) 'Bureaucratic Structure and Personality', *Social Forces* 18 (4): 560–568.

Milgram, S. (1974) *Obedience to Authority: An Experimental View*, London: Tavistock.

Mill, C. W. (1959) *The Sociological Imagination*, Oxford: Oxford University Press.

Miller, N. (1993) 'Called to Account: The CV as an Autobiographical Practice', *Sociology* 27 (1): 133–143.

Mintzberg, H. (2010) *Mintzberg on Managing*, https://www.youtube.com/watch?v=_NRWtd_SiU8&t=209s (accessed 30 January 2020).

Minuchin, S. (1974) *Families and Family Therapy*, Cambridge, MA: Harvard University Press.

More, T. (1998 [1516]) *Utopia*, Cambridge: Cambridge University Press.

Morris, G. & Salamone, C. (2011) *Rescue America: Our Best America is Only One Generation Away*, Shipley: Greenlead.

Nietzsche, F. (2007 [1881]) *The Dawn of Day*, New York: Dover.

Nietzsche, F. (1968) *Twilight of the Idols (1889) and The Anti-Christ (1895)*, London: Penguin.

Office of Government Commerce (2005) *Managing Successful Projects with PRINCE2*, Stationery Office.

Orwell, G. (1999 [1949]) *Nineteen Eighty-Four*, London: Secker & Warburg.
Parkinson, C. N. (1958) *Parkinson's Law or The Pursuit of Progress*, London: John Murray.
Petriglieri, G. & Petriglieri, J. (2010) 'Identity Workspaces: The Case of Business Schools', *Academy of Management Learning & Education* 9 (1): 44–60.
Pfeffer, J. & Salancik, G. R. (1978) *The External Control of Organizations: A Resource Dependence Perspective*, New York: Harper & Row.
Phillips, N. & Hardy, C. (2002) *Discourse Analysis: Investigating Processes of Social Construction*, Thousand Oaks, CA: Sage.
Rego, A., Cunha, M. & Clegg, S. (2012) *The Virtues of Leadership*, Oxford: Oxford University Press.
Ridley, M. (2020). 'Britain's Coronavirus Testing is Bogged Down in Bureaucracy', *The Spectator*, 2 April. https://www.spectator.co.uk/article/britain-s-coronavirus-testing-programme-is-bogged-down-in-bureaucracy.
Rhodes, C. & Price, O. (2011). 'The Post-bureaucratic Parasite: Contrasting Narratives of Organizational Change in Local Government,' *Management Learning* 42 (3): 241–260.
Riggs, F. (1979) 'Introduction: Évolution sémantique du terme "bureaucratie",' *Revue Internationale des Sciences Sociales* (in French), Paris, XXXI (4).
Russell-Smith, H. (1914) *Harrington and His Oceana*, Cambridge: Cambridge University Press.
Schwartzman, H. (1993) *Ethnography in Organizations*, London: Sage.
Self, W. (1991) *The Quantity Theory of Insanity*, London: Bloomsbury.
Sennett, R. (1998) *The Corrosion of Character: The Personal Consequences of Work in the New Capitalism*, New York: W.W. Norton & Company.
Sennett, R. (2008) *The Craftsman*, London: Penguin.
Simon, H. (1962) 'The Architecture of Complexity', *Proceedings of the American Philosophical Society* 106 (6): 467–482.
Smith, W., Higgins, M., Parker, M. & Lightfoot, G. (2003) *Science Fiction and Organization*, London: Routledge.
Smith, W., Lewis, M., Jarzabkowski, P. & Langley, A. (2017) *The Oxford Handbook of Organizational Paradoxes*, Oxford: Oxford University Press.
Sofsky, W. (1997) *The Order of Terror: The Concentration Camp*, Princeton, NJ: Princeton University Press.
Standing, G. (2016) *The Precariat: The New Dangerous Class*, London: Bloomsbury.
Stark, R. & Bainbridge, W. (1985) *The Future of Religion: Secularization, Revival, and Cult Formation*, Berkeley: University of California Press.
Stopford, J. & Baden-Fuller, C. (1990) 'Corporate Rejuvenation', *Journal of Management Studies* 27 (4): 399–415.
Strati, A. (2000) *Theory and Method in Organization Studies: Paradigms and Choices*, London: Sage.
Strauß, A. (2017) *Dialogues Between Art and Business: Collaborations, Cooptations, and Autonomy in a Knowledge Society*, Newcastle-upon-Tyne: Cambridge Scholars.
Styhre, A. (2007) *The Innovative Bureaucracy: Bureaucracy in an Age of Fluidity*, London: Routledge.
Sutcliffe, S. (1995) 'The Authority of the Self in New Age Religiosity: The Example of the Findhorn Community', *Diskus* 3 (2): 23–42.
Sutcliffe, S. (2000) 'A Colony of Seekers: Findhorn in the 1990s', *Journal of Contemporary Religion* 15 (2): 215–231.
Sutcliffe, S. (2003) *Children of the New Age: A History of Spiritual Practices*, London: Routledge.
Symonds, M. & Pudsey, J. (2008) 'The Concept of "Paradox" in the work of Max Weber', *Sociology* 42 (2): 223–241.

Taylor, C. (1995) In Honderich, T. (ed.) *The Oxford Companion to Philosophy*, Oxford: Oxford University Press.

Thomas, R. & Linstead, A. (2002) 'Losing the Plot? Middle Managers and Identity', *Organization* 9 (1): 71–93.

Thompson, E. (1955) *William Morris: Romantic to Revolutionary*, London: Lawrence & Wishart.

Thompson, R. (1993) 'Bureaucracy and Society: An Institutionalist Perspective', in Garston, N. (ed.) *Bureaucracy: Three Paradigms*, London: Kluwer.

Tierney, J. (2020) 'The FDA Graveyard: Absurd Bureaucratic Strictures are Hindering Efforts to Fight Covid-19', *Eye on the News*, 8 April. https://www.city-journal.org/fda-bureaucracy-hindering-covid-19-fight.

Tönnies, F. (1887) *Gemeinschaft und Gesellschaft*, Leipzig: Fues's Verlag.

Tuckman, B. W. & Jensen, M. A. C. (1977) 'Stages of Small-group Development Revisited', *Group & Organization Studies* 2 (4): 419–427.

van Otterloo, A. (1999) 'Selfspirituality and the Body: New Age Centres in The Netherlands since the 1960s', *Social Compass* 46 (2): 191–202.

Vine, T. (2011) 'Book review: Ann Cunliffe – A Very Short, Fairly Interesting, and Reasonably Cheap Book About Management', *Management Learning* 42 (4): 459–466.

Vine, T. (2018a) 'Home-grown Exoticism? Familial and Organizational Identity Tales from a New Age Intentional Community', in Vine, T., Clark, J., Richards, S. and Weir, D. (eds) *Ethnographic Research and Analysis: Anxiety, Identity and Self*, London: Palgrave Macmillan.

Vine, T. (2018b) 'Methodology: From Paradigms to Paradox', in Vine, T., Clark, J., Richards, S. and Weir, D. (eds) *Ethnographic Research and Analysis: Anxiety, Identity and Self*, London: Palgrave Macmillan.

Vine, T. (2018c) 'The Sociology of Things: A Response to Peter Cochrane', https://www.uos.ac.uk/content/sociology-things-response-peter-cochrane (accessed 30 January 2020).

Vine, T. (2020a) 'Brexit, Trumpism and Paradox: Epistemological Lessons for the Critical Consensus', *Organization* 27 (3): 466–482.

Vine, T. (2020b) 'The Commodification of Re-sacralised Work in the Neoliberal Era', in Taylor, S., Bell, E., Gog, S. and Simionca, A. (eds) *Spirituality, Organization and Neoliberalism: Understanding Lived Experiences*, Cheltenham: Edward Elgar.

Vine, T. (forthcoming) 'Institution(alization), Bureaucracy and Well-being? An Organizational Ethnography of Perinatal Care Within the National Health Service', in Hackett, P. and Hayre, C. (eds) *Ethnography in Healthcare Research*, London: Routledge.

Violatti, C. (2018) 'Neolithic Period', *Ancient History Encyclopedia*, https://www.ancient.eu/Neolithic/ (accessed 18 February 2020).

von Mises, L. (1944) *Bureaucracy*, New Haven, CT: Yale University Press.

Vonnegut, K. (2006 [1952]) *Piano Player*, New York: Random House.

Walliss, J. (2006) 'Spiritualism and the (Re-)enchantment of Modernity', in Beckford, J. & Walliss, J. (eds) *Theorising Religion: Classical and Contemporary Debates*, Aldershot: Ashgate.

Wang, Q. & Leichtman, M. (2003) 'Same Beginnings, Different Stories: A Comparison of American and Chinese Children's Narratives', *Child Development*, 71 (5): 1329–1346.

Watson, T. (2002) *Organising and Managing Work*, London: Pearson.

Watson, T. (2006) *Organising and Managing Work: Organisational, Managerial and Strategic Behaviour in Theory and Practice*, London: Pearson.

Weber, M. (1947 [1915]) *The Theory of Social and Economic Organization*, edited and translated by Henderson, A. and Parsons, T., Oxford: Oxford University Press.

Weber, M. (1968 [1922]) *Economy and Society: An Outline of Interpretive Sociology*, New York: Bedminster Press.

Weber, M. (2001 [1948]) *From Max Weber: Essays in Sociology*, London: Routledge.

Weber, M. (1958) *The Religion of India: The Sociology of Hinduism and Buddhism*, Glencoe, IL: Free Press.

Weick, K. (1977) 'Enactment Processes in Organizations' in Staw, B. & Salancik, G. (eds) *New Directions in Organizational Behaviour*, Chicago, IL: St Clair Press.

Weigert, A. & Hastings, R. (1977) 'Identity Loss, Family, and Social Change', *American Journal of Sociology* 82 (6): 1171–1184.

Weir, D. (2018) 'An Autoethnographic Account of Gender and Workflow Patterns in a Commercial Laundry', in Vine, T., Clark, J., Richards, S. and Weir, D. (eds) *Ethnographic Research and Analysis: Anxiety, Identity and Self*, London: Palgrave Macmillan.

Willmott, H. (2011) 'Chapter 11: Back to the Future: What Does Studying Bureaucracy Tell Us?', in Clegg, S., Harris, M. and Höpfl, H. (eds) *Managing Modernity: Beyond Bureaucracy*, Oxford: Oxford University Press.

Wilson, J. (2000) *Bureaucracy: What Government Agencies Do and Why They Do It*, New York: Basic Books.

Wilson, W. (1887) *The Study of Administration, Political Science Quarterly* 2 (2): 197–222.

Wirth, L. (1955) 'Preface', in Mannheim, K. *Ideology and Utopia*, New York: Harvest Books.

Wood, L. (2008) 'Contact, Encounter, and Exchange at Esalen: A Window onto Late Twentieth Century American Spirituality', *Pacific Historical Review* 77 (3): 453–487.

Wood, Z. (2017) 'Paperback Fighter: Sales of Physical Books Now Outperform Digital Titles', *The Guardian*, 17 March, https://www.theguardian.com/books/2017/mar/17/paperback-books-sales-outperform-digital-titles-amazon-ebooks (accessed 16 September 2019).

Wortman, C. & Linsenmeier, J. (1977) 'Interpersonal Attraction and Techniques of Ingratiation in Organizational Settings', in Staw, B. and Salancik, G. (eds) *New Directions in Organizational Behaviour*, Chicago, IL: St Clair Press.

Zhang, Z., Spicer, A. & Hancock, P. (2008) 'Hyper-organizational Space in the Work of J. G. Ballard', *Organization* 15 (6): 889–910.

# INDEX

Ackoff, Russell 63
action, 'grammars' of 104
Adler, S. 79
*The Study of Administration* (Wilson, W.) 25
Aeschylus 99
*After Virtue* (MacIntyre, A.) 155
*Agamemnon* (Aeschylus) 99
Agre, P. 140
agriculture, emergence of 134
Albrow, M. 4, 119
Ancient Buddhism, hierarchy and 147
anthropological universals 134
anti-bureaucratic attitudes in context 20–21
anti-bureaucratic sentiment, pervasive nature of 25
*The Anti-Christ* (Nietzsche, F.) 153
*Arabian Nights* (Burton, R.F. and McCaughrean) 28
*The Architecture of Complexity* (Simon, H.) 141
Aristotle 19, 155
arts, representation of bureaucracy in 10
Association of Project Management 47
*The Atrocity Exhibition* (Ballard, J.G.) 91
attitudes towards bureaucracy, cyclical pattern of 26
authoritarianism, bureaucracy and 27–8
autoethnographic methods, deployment of 13
autoethnography *a posteriori* 100
automaton conformity, bureaucracy and 27, 28
autonomy as utopia and dystopia 95–6

*Bait and Switch* (Ehrenreich, B.) 51
balance: barometric tools, bureaucracy and antibureaucracy as 151–2; bureaucracy and 151–5; control, flexibility and 152; education and 154–5; importance of concept of 70; mindfulness and 155; Nietzsche's philosophy and balance in bureaucracy 153; objectivity and subjectivity, reconciliation of 152–3; paradox in organizations, Handy's perspective on 153–4; philosophy of balance, desire to establish 152; *phronesis,* concept of 155; 'salariat' and the 'precariat,' distinction between 154; security and 154; tenure in organizations 151
Ballard, J.G. 87, 91
Barley, S. and Kunda, G. 38–9, 43, 47
barometric tools, bureaucracy and antibureaucracy as 151–2
Bauer, Professor Rolf 157
Bauman, Z. 69, 95, 103, 150; Holocaust and bureaucracy 75–9, 80, 81
BBC (British Broadcasting Corporation) 156; BBC4 13; website 157
Beirne, M. and Knight, S. 84
Belbin, R.M. 70
belief systems, freedom and 27–8
Bell, E. and Taylor, S. 55
benefits of bureaucracy, Wilson's perspective on 27
Bennis, Warren 10
Berger, B. 84

Berger, P. 50, 54
Berger, P. and Luckmann, T. 67–8
Berger, P., Berger, B. and Kellner, H. 28–9, 30–31, 38, 41
Bezos, Jeff 124
*Big Brother* (Channel 4 TV UK) 14
Billing, Y. 21
binary debates about bureaucracy, move away from 9–10
biographical continuity 52–3
birth, bureaucracy of 115
Biswas, Soutik 157
*Of Blood and Bone* (Roberts, N.) 89, 90
Boje, D. 84
Boltanski, L. and Chiapello, É. 29, 30, 36–7, 38, 41, 57, 93
Boncori, I. and Vine, T. 100
*Brave New World* (Huxley, A.) 87, 88, 90
Braverman, H. 9, 122
British Standard 6079 (1:2) 48
Broughton, P.D. 93
Brouwer, M. 42
Bryman, A. and Bell, E. 12
Bullock, D.B. and Grimley-Evans, J. 73
bureaucratic biography 99–115; action, 'grammars' of 104; *Agamemnon* (Aeschylus) 99; autoethnography *a posteriori* 100; birth, bureaucracy of 115; bureaucracy, pervasive nature of 109–10; bureaucratic frustration 106; bureaucratic management, Holocaust and 103; centralisation and change 113–14; commercial bureaucracy, first experience of 105–6; commercial organization, early experience in 106; *Cooler* nightclub in Warwick University students' union 102; culture, bureaucracy and co-construction of 102–3; death, bureaucracy of probate and 114; Dinosaurs Playgroup 100–102; Electoral Reform Services 104–6; ethnographic work in study of bureaucracy, underrepresentation of 112; Findhorn Foundation 108–10; Her Majesty's Revenue and Customs (HMRC), dealing with 111; introduction to Findhorn community 108–9; London School of Management and Science (LSMS) 111–12; management pyramid inversion 110; marriage, bureaucracy of 114–15; MBA programme leadership 112–13; *Modern Organizations* (Etzioni, A.) 99–100; modularity and formality of involvement at Findhorn 109; officialdom, 'ridiculous' nature of 101; organizational identity-formation 101;

organizational society 99–100; organizational structure at Findhorn 110; organizational structure at LSMS, lack of 111–12; Our Lady of Muswell Roman Catholic Primary School 102–3; *pathei-mathos* 99; permanent work or contract work decision 106; personal experience, true learning and 99; PhD student 106–8; pro-formas 105–6; *Raiders of the Lost Ark* (Steven Spielberg film) 111; script ordering, bureaucracy of 107–8; secure bureaucratic environment, first experience of 101; St. Ignatius College 103; 'temping bliss' 104–5; University of Essex 106–8; University of Suffolk 112–14; University of Warwick 103–4; validation by bureaucracy 102; VineLogistics 111; *The Wicker Man* (Shaffer, A. and Hardy, R.) 109; 'Work as Dance,' Chandler on 104
bureaucratic flexibility, paradox of 148–9
bureaucratic frustration 106
bureaucratic fundamentals, distinct from bureau-pathology 116
'bureaucratic gaps,' coping with 130
bureaucratic management, Holocaust and 103
'bureaucratic personalities' 71
*Bureaucratic Structure and Personality* (Merton, R.) 71–2
bureaucratic themes: in bestselling dystopian fiction 89–90; beyond bestseller lists 90–93; in dystopian classics 87–9
bureaupathology, reflection on 81–2
Burke, Edmond 143, 155
Burrell, Professor Gibson 20–21, 103–4, 152–3
business and management discourses, focus of 118
business planning, enterprise bureaucracy in 126

Campbell, Dr David 101
Campbell, Jesse 101–2
capitalism, history of 37
career, bureaucracy, life and 44–5
*Career as a Project of the Self and Labour Process Discipline* (Grey, C.) 44–5
Carey, J. 88
Carrette, J. and King, R. 57–8, 109
Casey, C. 4, 10, 17, 18, 54; workplace spirituality, sociology of 55, 57–8, 59
cause-and-effect relationships 84
centralisation and change 113–14
'centralized decentralization,' forms of 146

Chandler, J. 104
change management, bureaucracy and 149
cinematographic talents 83–4
*City Journal* 6
Clegg, S. 4, 46, 49, 59, 63, 80, 95, 135–6
Clegg, S., Courpasson, D. and Phillips, N. 69, 71
Clegg, S., Harris, M. and Höpfl, H. 19
Clegg, S., Pina e Cunha, M., Munro, I., Rego, A. and de Sousa, M. O. 11, 18, 87, 133, 143–4
co-construction of bureaucracy 116
*Cocaine Nights* (Ballard, J.G.) 91
comedy and bureaucracy, relationship between 157
commercial bureaucracy, first experience of 105–6
commercial organization, early experience in 106
community and society, distinction between 31
computer software, bureaucratic office and 136
'The Concentration City' (Ballard, J.G.) 91
control, flexibility and balance 152
*Cooler* nightclub in Warwick University students' union 102
Cooper, Cary 73
Corbett, J.M. 85
*The Corrosion of Character* (Sennett, R.) 29, 33–6, 41
coworking, emergence of 49
crisis, rationale for terminology of 29–30
*Critical Analysis of Organizations* (Casey, C.) 55
Crozier, M. 28
cultural contingency and bureaucracy 129–30
cultural misrepresentation of bureaucracy 83
culture, bureaucracy and co-construction of 102–3
curriculum vitae 45
cyclical pattern of attitudes towards bureaucracy 26

*Daily Mail* 7
Davie, G. 53, 54
*The Dawn of Day* (Nietzsche, F.) 153
Dawson, L. 50, 54, 56
De Gournay, Jacques C.M.V. 3
death, bureaucracy of probate and 114
*The Death of the Guilds* (Krause, E.A.) 42–3
DeGregori, T. and Thompson, R. 9, 134–5
Dehler, G. and Welsh, M. 54

Deleuze, G. 60, 139; derivative transcendental 140; difference/repetition 140
Dent, E., Higgins, M. and Wharff, D. 55
Derrida, J. 122
desecularization 50–54, 61
*The Desecularization of the World* (Berger, P., ed.) 50
destructiveness, bureaucracy and 27, 28
Deutscher, I. 3
*Difference and Repetition* (Deleuze, G.) 60, 140
Dinosaurs Playgroup 100–102
discrimination, narratives and 84
*The Division of Labor in Society* (Durkheim, É.) 31
division of labour, organization and 135
Du Gay, P. 4, 7–8, 9, 11, 13, 16, 19, 20; paradox, importance of 150—51; pathological bureaucracy 75, 81; post-bureaucracy, new bureaucratic forms and 146; working with bureaucracy 116, 127, 132
Du Gay, P. with Morgan, G. 29
Durkheim, E. 44, 49
dynamic tension of being human, bureaucracy and 157–8
'The Dysfunctions of Bureaucracy' (March, J. and Simon, H.) 144
dystopia 84–5
dystopian bureaucracy 21, 83–96; academic literature and fiction, representation of bureaucracy in 92; *The Atrocity Exhibition* (Ballard, J.G.) 91; autonomy as utopia and dystopia 95–6; *Of Blood and Bone* (Roberts, N.) 89, 90; *Brave New World* (Huxley, A.) 87, 88, 90; bureaucracy, cultural misrepresentation of 83; bureaucratic themes beyond bestseller lists 90–93; bureaucratic themes in bestselling dystopian fiction 89–90; bureaucratic themes in dystopian classics 87–9; cause-and-effect relationships 84; *Cocaine Nights* (Ballard, J.G.) 91; 'The Concentration City' (Ballard, J.G.) 91; discrimination, narratives and 84; dystopia 84–5; dystopian fiction, bureaucracy and 86–7; dystopian fiction, influences of 85–6; dystopian fiction as agent for change 93; *Erin Brokovich* (Steven Spielberg film) 95; *Extracted Trilogy* (Haywood, R.R.) 90; *The Fever King* (Lee, V.) 89, 90; fictive defences of bureaucracy 95; *The Fifth Season* (Jemisin, N.K.) 90; *Freedom* (Franzen, J.) 92; future

of? 93–6; *The Handmaid's Tale* (Atwood, M.) 89, 90; 'hero-bureaucrats' 94–5; *High Rise* (Ballard, J.G.) 91; humanities, pedagogical importance and potential of 84; individualism, cultivation of sense of 84; Kafkaesque power and bureaucracy 86–7; literary and cinematographic talents 83–4; machine metaphor 94; *The Machine Stops* (Forster, E.M.) 89; mechanocomorphism 94; *Metropolis* (Fritz Lang film) 94; 'Minus One' (Ballard, J.G.) 91; *Nineteen Eighty-Four* (Orwell, G.) 88, 89, 90; nuclear family 'narrative' of 84; order in bureaucracy 94; *Organization Studies* (Sage journal) 91; *Player Piano* (Vonnegut, K.) 88–9; post-bureaucracy 93–6; preconceptions, reality and 83; prejudices, narratives and 84; *Ready Player One* (Steven Spielberg film) 89, 90; 'real-world' events, dystopian bureaucracies cast as 94; *Retrotopia* (Bauman, Z.) 95; *The Rise of Magicks* (Roberts, N.) 89.90; *The Rule of One* (Saunders, A.) 90; state socialism 94; storytelling 83–4; 'The Subliminal Man' (Ballard, J.G.) 91; *Super-Cannes* (Ballard, J.G.) 91; techno-bureaucratic dystopia 91; 'temping bliss' 94; *The Trial* (Kafka, F.) 86; *2001: A Space Odyssey* (Stanley Kubrick film) 90; unconscious biases, narratives and 84; *Utopia* (More, T.) 87–8; utopias 96; utopias, dystopias and 85–6

*Economy & Society* 18, 130, 142, 148
'Educating Managers for Post-bureaucracy' (Hendry, J.) 118
education and balance 154–5
educational innovation in respect of bureaucracy 118–21
efficiency, paradox of bureaucracy and 145–6
Ehrenreich, B. 51–3, 54, 61
Electoral Reform Services 72, 104–6, 119, 144, 147
emergent logic of bureaucracy 7–9
empirical materials, working through 11–12
employment, binding forces of bureaucracy and 128–9
engineered management methodologies 130–32
epistemological bias, bureaucracy and 120–21
epochal dialectic 139–40

*Erin Brokovich* (Steven Spielberg film) 95
Esalen Institute in California 58
esotericism 54
ethnographic methods: engagement with 12–13; explorations with 156–7; in study of bureaucracy, underrepresentation of 112
Etzioni, A. 99–100, 115
*Evening Standard* (London) 93
existential function of bureaucracy 13–14
existential security: bureau as broker of 157–8; post-bureaucracy, bureaucracy and 27
*Extracted Trilogy* (Haywood, R.R.) 90

Fairholm, G.W. 54
fate and agency, relationship between 142–3
*The Fear of Freedom* (Fromm, E.) 27, 92, 140
*The Feminist Case Against Bureaucracy* (Ferguson, K.) 20
feminist perspectives, anti-bureaucratic attitudes and 20–21
Ferguson, K. 20–21
fetishisation of Weberian bureaucracy 19
*The Fever King* (Lee, V.) 89, 90
fiction and academic literature, representation of bureaucracy in 92
fictive defences of bureaucracy 95
*The Fifth Season* (Jemisin, N.K.) 90
Findhorn Foundation 55, 57, 59, 133–4, 138, 140; bureaucratic biography 108–10; introduction to Findhorn community 108–9; modularity and formality of involvement at Findhorn 109; organizational geography 58; organizational structure at 110
Ford, Henry 88
Fordism 34–5
form-filling 124–5
Forster, E.M. 89
Foucault, M. 11, 45, 69, 122
Franzen, J. 92–3
'freedom' aspirations of 140
*Freedom* (Franzen, J.) 92
Fromm, E. 25, 27–8, 92, 139, 140
Frost, P.J. and Egri, C.P. 54
future enquiry on bureaucracy, areas for 156–8
future for dystopian fiction and bureaucracy 93–6

Gajduschek, G. 18, 148
Gallagher, S. 155
Garcia-Zamor, J. 54
Garston, N. 3, 5, 9, 136

Gehlen, A. 56
Giddens, A. 29, 30, 31–3, 38, 41, 79; desecularization 50–51, 54; self, spirituality and 56, 58, 59; self as reflexive project 43–4, 45
Glass, P. 60, 140
*Global Coworking Survey* 49
*Gödel, Escher, Bach: An Eternal Golden Braid* (Hofstadter, D.) 145
Goffman, E. 11, 69
*Golden Mean* (Aristotle) 155
Gompertz, Will 156
Goodall, Jane 18
Goodsell, C. 9
Gouldner, A. 12–13, 116, 139
Government Commerce, Office of 47
Graeber, A. 12, 13, 104, 112, 115, 146, 150; dystopian bureaucracy 86–7, 94–5; working with bureaucracy 124–5, 126, 127
Grey, C. 44–5, 46, 49, 52
Grint, K. 141
*The Guardian* 93
*Gurus, Hired Guns, and Warm Bodies* (Barley, S. and Kunda, G.) 38–9

*The Handmaid's Tale* (Atwood, M.) 89, 90
Handy, C. 137, 153–4
Hanegraaff, W. 54
Harris, M. 151
*Harvard Business Review* 6
Harvey, J.B. 118
Heckscher, C. 20
Heelas, P. 54, 56–8, 59, 61
Hendry, J. 118
Her Majesty's Revenue and Customs (HMRC), dealing with 111
Heraclitus 5
'hero-bureaucrats' 94–5
heterogeneity of New Age movement 55–6
hierarchy 140–41; natural world and 141; servant leadership model 140–41; structure, bureaucracy and 141; traditional pyramid of 140
*High Rise* (Ballard, J.G.) 91
historical-mnemonic function of bureaucracy 15–16
history of bureaucracy since Weber 19
Hitler, Adolf 79–80, 96
Hodgson, D. and Cicmil, S. 47, 48
Hofstadter, D. 145, 157
Holloway, J. 54
The Holocaust, pathological bureaucracy and 75–81

*The Homeless Mind* (Berger, P., Berger, B. and Kellner, H.) 28–9, 30–31, 41
Höpfl, H. 54
Houtman, D. and Aupers, S. 54
human action, paradox and 142
humanities, pedagogical importance and potential of 84
Husserl, E. 150
Huxley, A. 88

identity crisis, concepts of bureaucracy and 29–30
identity formation 38–9
ideological conviction, refusal to succumb to 143–4
*Ideology and Utopia* (Mannheim, K.) 12
Iedema, R. 148
immanent bureaucracy 131–2
'individual' as modern construct 44
individual involvement in organizations, new forms of 59–60
individualism, cultivation of sense of 84
instability, normalisation of 36
institutional certainty, bureau as broker of 157–8
institutional holding environments 36
institutional racism 68
Institutional Theory 135
institutionalisation: dysfunction associated with 69–70; Oxford Dictionaries definition of 69–70; pathological bureaucracy and 67–9; routine aspects of 68
institutions, bureaucratic organization forms and 57
instrumental rationality, Holocaust and excesses of 80
interactions with bureaucracy 116–32
intra-organizational relations 127–9
irreverence towards bureaucracy 16
isomorphic pressures 135
Izak, M. 55

Jacques, E. 118
Jay, R. and Templar, R. 73
Jensen, A. 46–7, 48–9, 61
jobsworthiness: experience of 72–3; fear of change and 73; origin of concept 71–2; understanding concept of 73
jobsworths 1; bureaucracy and, relationship between 73–5; pathological bureaucracy and 71–2; socialisation and creation of 74–5
Jones, E., Jones, R. and Gergen, K. 74

Jones, E., Stires, L., Shaver, K. and Harris, V. 74
Jones, Jonathan 93

Kafka, Franz (and Kafkaesque bureaucracy) 10, 11, 86–7, 133, 155–6
Kallinikos, J. 3, 8–9, 11, 105, 132, 135; bureaucratic flexibility, paradox of 148–9; technological and organizational change 59–60, 70
Kapoor, R. 58, 59
Kets de Vries, M. 137
Kieser, A. 42
King, D. and Lawley, S. 73
Knights, D. and Willmott, H. 95–6, 152
Kohli, M. 8
Konnovs, H. and Vine, T. 75
Krause, E.A. 42–3
Kumar, K. 85–6

Lanchester, J. 156
Lang, Fritz 94
Law, J. 13, 94, 125
learning from students 69–71
legitimacy, bureau as broker of 157–8
lessons in bureaucracy 121–32
Lévi-Strauss, C. 134
life experiences of bureaucracy 117–18
liminality and bureaucracy 157
linear logic: Holocaust and 74, 78; transcending allure of 142–3
Linsenmeier, J. and Wortman, C. 73–4
literary and cinematographic talents 83–4
*Little Britain* (BBC TV) 157
lived experiences of bureaucracy 11
London School of Management and Science (LSMS) 111–12, 117; organizational structure at, lack of 111–12
Lopdrup-Hjorth, T. and du Gay, P. 20
*Losing the Plot? Middle Managers and Identity* (Thomas, R. and Linstead, A.) 38
lucrotropism, Holocaust and concept of 78
Lynch, David 83

Maastricht School of Management 126
McEvilley, T. 155
McGrath, P. 54
machine metaphor, dystopian bureaucracy and 94
*The Machine Stops* (Forster, E.M.) 89
machismo perspectives, anti-bureaucratic attitudes and 20–21
MacIntyre, Alasdair 155
MacLaine, Shirley 56
McLennan, G. 50

McNeill, F. 71, 73
macrosociological responses to post-bureaucratic identity crisis 41, 42–59
macrosociological theorising about bureaucracy 21
Maffesoli, M. 49
Magee, B. 2, 19, 79–80, 152
*Management Learning* 118
management pyramid inversion 110
managerial initiative, Holocaust and 76
*Managing Modernity: Beyond Bureaucracy* (Clegg, S., Harris, M. & Höpfl, H.) 146
Mannheim, K. 12, 86, 139–40
March, J. and Simon, H. 144
market as social institution 39
marriage, bureaucracy of 114–15
Marsden, J. 140
Marx, K. 112, 122
Matterson, Matthew 72–3
MBA programme leadership 112–13
means constituting ends, recognition of existential importance of 150–51
'mechanisms of escape,' Fromm's notion of 27–8
mechanocomorphism 94
*Mein Kampf* (Hitler, A.) 80
Meindl, J., Ehrlich, S. and Dukerich, J. 131
Merton, R. 4, 19, 28, 145–6, 154–5; pathological bureaucracy 71–2, 73, 74–5
*Metamorphosis* (Glass, P.) 60
*Metropolis* (Fritz Lang film) 94
middle management, identity 'in flux' for 38
Milgram, S. 78–9
Mill, C.W. 12
Miller, N. 45
mindfulness and balance 155
Mintzberg, H. 128, 141
Minuchin, S. 118
'Minus One' *(Ballard, J.G.)* 91
modern organizations, threat to bureaucratic underpinnings of 42–3
*Modern Organizations* (Etzioni, A.) 99–100
modernity: bureaucracy and 29–30; problem of 30–31; self-defeating nature of agency in 143
*Modernity and Self-Identity* (Giddens, A.) 29, 31–3, 41
*Modernity and the Holocaust* (Bauman, Z.) 75–6
*Monty Python's Life of Brian* (Terry Jones film) 120
moral responsibility: bureaucracy and 150; towards Jews in Nazi Germany, neutralisation of 77
More, T. 87–8, 96

Morris, G. and Salamone, C. 151
MS Windows, bureaucracy and 136
multi-national organizations 134
multi-project organizations 60
Myatt, David 99

natural world and hierarchy 141
Naudi, Simon 73
navigating organizational life 117–18, 126–7, 156
negative accounts of bureaucracy 117
neoliberal era, class system in 39–40
Neolithic Revolution 134
networks, bureaucracies and 35–6
'New Age' spirituality 54–9, 61–2
*The New Spirit of Capitalism* (Boltanski, L. and Chiapello, É) 29, 36–7, 41
Nietzsche, F. 13, 15, 17, 128; philosophy and balance in bureaucracy 153
*Nineteen Eighty-Four* (Orwell, G.) 88, 89, 90
non-bureaucratic organization, possibility of 133–4
nuclear family 'narrative' of dystopian bureaucracy 84

objectivity and subjectivity, reconciliation of 152–3
*The Office* (BBC TV) 157
officialdom, 'ridiculous' nature of 101
ontology, anti-bureaucratic attitudes transcending 20
operational systems: problem-solving and expansion of 144–5; reliance on 145
order in bureaucracy 94
*Organising and Managing Work* (Watson, T.) 119
*Organization Studies* (Sage journal) 91
organizational craft 126
organizational geography 21, 41–63; Association of Project Management 47; *Bait and Switch* (Ehrenreich, B.) 51; biographical continuity 52–3; British Standard 6079–1:2 48; career, bureaucracy, life and 44–5; *Career as a Project of the Self and Labour Process Discipline* (Grey, C.) 44–5; coworking, emergence of 49; *Critical Analysis of Organizations* (Casey, C.) 55; curriculum vitae 45; *The Death of the Guilds* (Krause, E.A.) 42–3; desecularization 50–54, 61; *The Desecularization of the World* (Berger, P., ed.) 50; *Difference and Repetition* (Deleuze, G.) 60; Esalen Institute in California 58; esotericism 54; Findhorn Foundation 58; *Global Coworking Survey* 49; Government Commerce, Office of 47; heterogeneity of New Age movement 55–6; 'individual' as modern construct 44; individual involvement in organizations, new forms of 59–60; institutions, bureaucratic organization forms and 57; macrosociological responses to post-bureaucratic identity crisis 41, 42–59; modern organizations, threat to bureaucratic underpinnings of 42–3; multi-project organizations 60; 'New Age' spirituality 54–9, 61–2; organizations, archival function of 45; organized religious participation 53–4; post-bureaucratic flexible work patterns 53; post-bureaucratic identity crisis 46, 56–7, 62–3; post-bureaucratic identity crisis, responses to 41, 42–59, 62–3; 'Postsecular Turn' 50; Professional Association of Contract Employees (PACE) 43; Project Management Institute 47; projectification 46–9, 60; recruitor.com 48; religious participation 51–2; scientific reflexivity, internalisation of 44; self, spirituality and 56; self as reflexive project 43–6, 60; self-management, career and 45; self-surveillance 46–9; selfspirituality 58, 59; spiritual heterogeneity 54; 'Spiritual Management Development' 54–5; *Spirituality Sells* (Carrette, J. and King, R.) 57; trade guilds and professional associations 42–3, 60; workplace spirituality, sociology of 55, 57–8, 59
organizational identity-formation 101
organizational knowledge, bureaucracy and 15
organizational life skills, cultivation of 117–18
organizational order, bureaucracy and 135
organizational participation, quantity theory of 136–9; bureaucratic security, need for 138; coffee shops, telecommuting and 138; existential security 138; identity, sense of 137–8; institutional holding environments 137; pan-organizational association 137; post-industrial life narratives, transitional stages within 137; re-ordering our stuff, pleasure in 138–9; workplace identity 138
organizational society 99–100
organizational structure at LSMS, lack of 111–12
organizational universal, bureaucracy as? 134–6

organizations: archival function of 45; bureaucracy and 1–2; bureaucracy as organization 9; definitions of 122–3; institutions and 68
organized religious participation 53–4
Orwell, G. 88
Our Lady of Muswell Roman Catholic Primary School 102–3
Oxford Dictionaries 69–70, 71
*Oxford English Dictionary(OED)* 3, 68

pan-organizational association 17, 55, 60–61, 62–3, 134, 137, 140
paperwork: equity and 127; importance of 125; preponderance of 120
paradox: an integral aspect of human action 142; Ancient Buddhism, hierarchy and 147; bureaucracy and 14–15, 141–51; of bureaucratic flexibility 148–9; 'centralized decentralization,' forms of 146; change management, bureaucracy and 149; efficiency, paradox of bureaucracy and 145–6; fate and agency, relationship between 142–3; ideological conviction, refusal to succumb to 143–4; importance of 149–51; linear logic; transcending allure of 142–3; means constituting ends, recognition of existential importance of 150–51; modernity, self-defeating nature of agency in 143; moral responsibility, bureaucracy and 150; operational systems, problem-solving and expansion of 144–5; operational systems, reliance on 145; in organizations, Handy's perspective on 153–4; post-bureaucracy creates new forms of bureaucracy 146; routinization/charisma paradox 79–80, 147–8; sects, development of 147; social, economic, and technological change, bureaucracy and demands of 148–9; societal order, routinization of 147; Strange Loops, Hofstadter's notion of 145; trained incapacity, structure and 146; uncertainty, bureaucratic organization and reduction of 148; of unintended consequences 143–6; Weber and 141–2
Parkinson, C.N. (and Parkinson's Law) 14–15
Parsons, Talcott 19
*pathei-mathos* 99
pathological bureaucracy: balance, importance of concept of 70; bureaucracy 21, 67–82; 'bureaucratic personalities' 71; *Bureaucratic Structure and Personality* (Merton, R.) 71–2; bureaupathology, reflection on 81–2; The Holocaust and 75–81; institutional racism 68; institutionalisation 67–9; institutionalisation, dysfunction associated with 69–70; institutionalisation, Oxford Dictionaries definition of 69–70; institutionalisation, routine aspects of 68; instrumental rationality, Holocaust and excesses of 80; jobsworth and bureaucracy, relationship between 73–5; jobsworthiness, experience of 72–3; jobsworthiness, fear of change and 73; jobsworthiness, origin of concept 71–2; jobsworthiness, understanding concept of 73; jobsworths 71–2; jobsworths, socialisation and creation of 74–5; learning from students 69–71; linear logic, Holocaust and 74, 78; lucrotropism, Holocaust and concept of 78; managerial initiative, Holocaust and 76; *Mein Kampf* (Hitler, A.) 80; *Modernity and the Holocaust* (Bauman, Z.) 75–6; moral responsibility towards Jews in Nazi Germany, neutralisation of 77; organization, institution and 68; *Power and Organizations* (Clegg, S., Courpasson, D. and Phillips, N.) 69; routinization/charisma paradox, Holocaust and 79–80; rules, preoccupation with 72–3; scientific management techniques, Holocaust and 79; *The Social Construction of Reality* (Berger, P. and Luckmann, T.) 67–8; 'total institutions,' 'non-inclusive bureaucracy' and 70
Patriotta, G. 101
pattern and bureaucracy 139–41
Pentland, B.T. and Rueter, H.H. 104
permanent work or contract work decision 106
personal experience, true learning and 99
pervasive nature of bureaucracy 109–10
pervasiveness as life pattern of bureaucracy 14
Petriglieri, G. and Petriglieri, J. 137
Pfeffer, J. and Salancik, G.R. 141
PhD student 106–8
Phillips, N. and Hardy, C. 15
philosophy of balance, desire to establish 152
*phronesis*, concept of 155
Plato 96
*Player Piano* (Vonnegut, K.) 88–9
politics, anti-bureaucratic attitudes transcending 20
positive accounts of bureaucracy 117

post-bureaucracy, bureaucracy and 1, 4–5, 10, 19, 21, 25–40; anti-bureaucratic sentiment, pervasive nature of 25; *Arabian Nights* (Burton, R.F. and McCaughrean) 28; authoritarianism, bureaucracy and 27–8; automaton conformity, bureaucracy and 27, 28; belief systems, freedom and 27–8; benefits of bureaucracy, Wilson's perspective on 27; capitalism, history of 37; community and society, distinction between 31; contributions from early 21st century 38–40; *The Corrosion of Character* (Sennett, R.) 33–6; crisis, rationale for terminology of 29–30; cyclical pattern of attitudes towards bureaucracy 26; destructiveness, bureaucracy and 27, 28; *The Division of Labor in Society* (Durkheim, É.) 31; existential security, bureaucracy and 27; *The Fear of Freedom* (Fromm, E.) 27, 92, 140; Fordism 34–5; *Gurus, Hired Guns, and Warm Bodies* (Barley, S. and Kunda, G.) 38–9; *The Homeless Mind* (Berger, P., Berger, B. and Kellner, H.) 30–31; identity crisis, concepts of bureaucracy and 29–30; identity formation 38–9; instability, normalisation of 36; institutional holding environments 36; *Losing the Plot? Middle Managers and Identity* (Thomas, R. and Linstead, A.) 38; market as social institution 39; 'mechanisms of escape,' Fromm's notion of 27–8; middle management, identity 'in flux' for 38; modernity, bureaucracy and 29–30; modernity, problem of 30–31; *Modernity and Self-Identity* (Giddens, A.) 31–3; neoliberal era, class system 39–40; networks, bureaucracies and 35–6; *The New Spirit of Capitalism* (Boltanski, L. and Chiapello, E) 36–7; post-war period, identity crisis to post-bureaucratic identity crisis 28–9; power in post-bureaucratic epoch, obscuration of 34, 35; precariat, chronic insecurity of 40; *The Precariat: The New Dangerous Class* (Standing, G.) 38, 39–40; pro-bureaucracy in early 1900s to anti-bureaucracy 25–8; 'protective cocoon,' individuality and 32–3; *Protestant Ethic and the Spirit of Capitalism* (Weber, M.) 37; 'providential reason,' notion of 33; routine, abandonment of 34; 'science of administration' 26–7; scientific enquiry, existential doubt and 32–3; socio-cultural pluralism, bureaucracy and 30–31; sociology of critique, critical sociology and 37; stability, bureaucracy and 27; technologisation, bureaucracy and 30–31

post-bureaucracy, dystopian bureaucracy and 93–6

post-bureaucracy, new forms of bureaucracy and 146

post-bureaucratic flexible work patterns 53

post-bureaucratic identity crisis 140; organizational geography and 46, 56–7, 62–3; responses to 41, 42–59, 62–3

post-war period, identity crises and 28–9

'Postsecular Turn' 50

*Power and Organizations* (Clegg, S., Courpasson, D. and Phillips, N.) 69

power in post-bureaucratic epoch, obscuration of 34, 35

precariat, chronic insecurity of 40

*The Precariat: The New Dangerous Class* (Standing, G.) 38, 39–40

preconceptions, reality and 83

predisposition towards bureaucracy 134

prejudices, narratives and 84

pro- to anti-bureaucracy in early 1900s 25–8

pro formas: paperwork and 123–7

pro-formas 105–6

problem of bureaucracy 2

Professional Association of Contract Employees (PACE) 43

Project Management Institute 47

projectification 46–9, 60

'protective cocoon,' individuality and 32–3

*Protestant Ethic and the Spirit of Capitalism* (Weber, M.) 37

'providential reason,' notion of 33

punishment-centred bureaucracy 116

'Quantity Theory of Insanity' (Self, W.) 136
Quinlan, Sir Michael 150–51

*Raiders of the Lost Ark* (Steven Spielberg film) 111

Raisenen, C. and Linde, A. 61

re-emergence of bureaucracy, characterisation of 157

re-introduction to bureaucracy 7–16

*Ready Player One* (Steven Spielberg film) 89, 90

'real-world' events, dystopian bureaucracies cast as 94

recruitor.com 48

Rego, A., Cunha, M. and Clegg, S. 155

religious participation 51–2

representation of bureaucracy in arts 10

representative bureaucracy 116

*Rescue America* (Morris, G. and Salamone, C. M.) 151
*Retrotopia* (Bauman, Z.) 95
Rhodes, C. and Price, O. 10
Ridley, Matt 6
Riggs, F. 3
*The Rise of Magicks* (Roberts, N.) 89.90
Robertson, H. and Swan, J. 131
routine, abandonment of 34
routinization/charisma paradox 147–8; Holocaust and 79–80
'rubber time' in East, respect and 129–30
*The Rule of One* (Saunders, A.) 90
rules, preoccupation with 72–3
Russell-Smith, H. 85

Salaman, G. 63
'salariat' and the 'precariat,' distinction between 154
Schumacher, E.F. 134
Schwartzmann, H. 12
'science of administration' 26–7
scientific enquiry, existential doubt and 32–3
scientific management techniques, Holocaust and 79
scientific reflexivity, internalisation of 44
script ordering, bureaucracy of 107–8
secret joys of bureaucracy 150
sects, development of 147
security: balance and 154; secure bureaucratic environment, first experience of 101; *see also* existential security
self: as reflexive project 43–6, 60; spirituality and 56
Self, W. 136
self-management, career and 45
self-spirituality 58, 59
self-surveillance 46–9
selfsustaining replicative systems 135
Sennett, R. 29, 30, 33–6, 38, 41, 42, 43, 51, 54
sensemaking and bureaucracy 155–6
servant leadership model 140–41
Shakespeare, William 83
Simon, H. 141
Skinner, B.F. 96
*Small is Beautiful* (Schumacher, E.F.) 134
Smith, Adam 143
Smith, W., Higgins, M., Parker, M. and Lightfoot, G. 85
Smith, W., Lewis, M., Jarzabkowski, P. and Langley, A. 15

Smothermon, Ron 56
social, economic, and technological change, bureaucracy and demands of 148–9
social anthropology of organization and bureaucracy 122–3
*The Social Construction of Reality* (Berger, P. and Luckmann, T.) 67–8
societal order, routinization of 147
socio-cultural pluralism, bureaucracy and 30–31
sociology of critique, critical sociology and 37
Sofsky, W. 76
*The Spectator* 6
spiritual heterogeneity 54
'Spiritual Management Development' 54–5
*Spirituality Sells* (Carrette, J. and King, R.) 57
St. Ignatius College 103
stability, bureaucracy and 27
Standing, G. 15, 38, 39–40, 47, 153, 154
Stark, R. and Bainbridge, W. 50
state socialism 94
Stopford, J. and Baden-Fuller, C. 154
storytelling 83–4
Strange Loops, Hofstadter's notion of 145
Strauß, A. 84
structure, bureaucracy and 141
Styhre, A. 4, 10, 19, 20, 42, 61, 63, 101, 104, 148, 149; working with bureaucracy 119, 120–21, 131
'The Subliminal Man' (Ballard, J.G.) 91
*Super-Cannes* (Ballard, J.G.) 91
Sutcliffe, S. 54, 58, 59
Symonds, M. and Pudsey, J. 49–50, 142, 143, 147–8
systematic study of bureaucracy, need for 156–7

Taylor, C. 155
Taylorism 34, 79
techno-bureaucratic dystopia 91
technologisation, bureaucracy and 30–31
technology and bureaucracy 134–5, 135–6
'temping bliss': bureaucratic biography and 104–5; dystopian bureaucracy and 94
tenure in organizations, balance in 151
*That's Life!* (BBC TV) 72
Thomas, R. and Linstead, A. 38
Thompson, E. 86
Thompson, R. 12, 17, 135
Tierney, John 6
'total institutions,' 'non-inclusive bureaucracy' and 70
totalitarian governments 134

trade guilds and professional associations 42–3, 60
traditional pyramid of hierarchy 140
trained incapacity, structure and 146
*The Trial* (Kafka, F.) 86
Trump, D.A. 6, 20
Tuckman, B.W. and Jensen, M.A.C. 61
*Twilight of the Idols* (Nietzsche, F.) 153
*2001: A Space Odyssey* (Stanley Kubrick film) 90
typewriter, managerial bureaucracies and 136

uncertainty, bureaucratic organization and reduction of 148
unconscious biases, narratives and 84
undesirable nature of bureaucracy 1
unintended consequences, paradox of 143–6
University of Essex 106–8
University of Suffolk 112–14
University of Warwick 103–4
*Utopia* (More, T.) 87–8
utopias 96; dystopias and 85–6; 'freedom' of utopia of the ascendant bourgeoisie and 139–40

validation by bureaucracy 102
Van Otterloo, A. 58, 59, 61
Vine, Becky 114–15
Vine, Sophie 115
Vine, T. 2, 3, 13, 15, 16, 62, 69, 108, 144; working with bureaucracy 122, 130
VineLogistics 111
Violetti, C. 134
Von Mises, L. 28
Vonnegut, K. 88–9

*The Wall* (Lanchester, J.) 156
Walliss, J. 61–2

Wang, Q. and Leichtman, M. 84
Warner, M. 87
Watson, T. 71, 73, 119, 150, 152
Weber, M. 8, 9, 11–12, 25, 56, 94, 99, 110, 136, 146, 147–8; analysis of bureaucracy 16–18; bureaucracy 16–19; bureaucracy, post-bureaucracy and identity crisis 25, 27, 28; bureaucracy since 19; bureaucratization, direction of 156–7; commentary on bureaucracy 18; fetishisation of Weberian bureaucracy 19; fetishisation of Weberian bureaucracy, reversal of 18–19; history of bureaucracy since 19; organizational geography 43, 45; paradox 141–2; paradox, bureaucracy and 141–3; paradox, importance of 149–50; pathological bureaucracy 73, 79, 80; systematic examination of bureaucracy 18; working with bureaucracy 116, 117, 119, 130
Weick, K. 122
Weigert, A. and Hastings, R. 14, 45–6
*The Wicker Man* (Shaffer, A. and Hardy, R.) 109
Willmott, H. 3, 4–5, 8, 14, 17, 80–81, 121, 133, 148
Wilson, J. 4, 123
Wilson, W. 4, 25–7, 28, 139
Wirth, Louis 12
Wood, L. 58, 59, 61
Wood, Z. 124
'Work as Dance,' Chandler on 104
working definition of bureaucracy 2–5
workplace spirituality, sociology of 55, 57–8, 59
writing about bureaucracy, rationale for 5–7

Zhang, Z., Spicer, A. and Hancock, P. 91